Praise for Better to BEST

"Even Lincoln would have been impressed!"
—Steve Forbes
President & CEO
Forbes Inc.

"If you know your next public speech will be drop dead wonderful, this may not be the book for you. But should you belong to the remaining 95% of the world, David Dempsey's *Better to BEST* is full of easy to absorb, readily read ideas that will stay with you. Guaranteed applause at the end of your next talk."
—Gerald Grinstein
CEO
Delta Air Lines, Inc.

"From cover to cover, *Better to BEST* delivers on its promise to make anyone a more powerful and persuasive presenter. David Dempsey's real-world experiences and proven tips show you exactly how to get the bottom-line results you want from a business presentation. In my opinion, David is *the* Public Speaking Expert for no-nonsense executives."
—Peter Schwarzenbauer
President & CEO
Porsche Cars North America, Inc.

"With my busy schedule, I appreciate that David Dempsey has organized this book into quick, easy-to-read tactics for improving public speaking. I have found many informative and entertaining suggestions in *Better to BEST*."
—James C. Kennedy
Chairman & CEO
Cox Enterprises, Inc.

"*Better to BEST* is full of practical insights that will help anyone deliver presentations that connect with audiences. This is not a book of abstract theories. David Dempsey gives us guidelines that have been tested and proven. Pick it up. It's a great investment."
—Former United States Senator Bob Dole

"*Better to BEST* is a superb tool for any executive who wants to influence, persuade, and inspire every audience! It provides a precise blueprint for crafting and delivering an outstanding speech that will have your audience members sitting on the edge of their seats. The writing is engaging, the information is insightful, and the organization is excellent. The resources and Web sites listed are a great bonus. Any speaker would benefit enormously from reading and applying the advice in this book. It is an essential book for every leader."

> —Jack Guynn
> **President & CEO**
> **Federal Reserve Bank of Atlanta**

"David Dempsey's book, *Better to BEST,* written with wonderful humor, takes you on a journey of building a dynamic presentation. It is packed with invaluable lessons for all speakers and shouldn't be missed."

> —**Dr. Ken Blanchard**
> **Co-author of *The One Minute Manager*®**
> **and *The Secret***

"*Better to BEST* is a great resource! This excellent book shows you how to speak in a way that will cause audience members to sit up and listen. It demonstrates how to have a meaningful, heartfelt conversation that connects with your audience, how to stand out in today's cluttered, speaker-filled world. Every speaker would benefit tremendously from reading this book and applying its principles."

> —**John R. Alm**
> **Former CEO**
> **Coca-Cola Enterprises, Inc.**

"When Dempsey was a young trial lawyer, his knees once wobbled so violently during his summation to a jury that he overheard them dub him "Jell-O Boy." In *Better to BEST*, he describes the presentation wisdom he has learned since then that has helped him to become a professional communication skills trainer and coach. By detailing the minutiae involved in great presentations, including essential tips for conquering question-and-answer sessions, his professional advice can take the anxiety and uncertainty out of any presentation."

> — *Soundview Executive Book Summaries*

"Many people do not understand the importance of communicating clearly. David Dempsey's book, *Better to BEST*, is packed with numerous personal tales from the trenches and great ideas that he has learned through his lifelong experience in the speaking arena."

—**Garry Betty**
President & CEO
EarthLink, Inc.

"Clear, honest, precise and consistent communication is the ultimate tool for effective leaders and essential in captivating presentations. *Better to BEST* is a virtual toolbox of useful suggestions and guideposts to help you become the best, most effective communicator possible."

—**John Schuerholz**
Executive Vice President & General Manager
The Atlanta Braves

"*Better to BEST* shows you how to prepare and deliver better talks and presentations than you ever imagined. When you follow its advice, you will look and sound like a star."

—**Brian Tracy**
Author of *Maximum Achievement* and
The Psychology of Selling

"The last 30 years I have spent my life giving speeches before a wide variety of audiences. I am constantly on the lookout for books and articles that can help me give an extraordinary message each time I speak. There is no better resource than David Dempsey's *Better to BEST* when it comes to helping you experience extraordinary results when you stand to give your speech. I can honestly say that David is one of the best speakers in America today, and it's always wonderful to learn the secrets of the best!"

—**Dr. Dwight "Ike" Reighard**
Executive Vice President & Chief People Officer
HomeBanc

BETTER TO BEST

HOW TO SPEAK FOR
EXTRAORDINARY RESULTS
. . . EVERY TIME!

David J. Dempsey, JD

Miranda Publishing, LLC
Atlanta, GA

Miranda Publishing, LLC, Atlanta 30346
© 2006 by David J. Dempsey, JD
All rights reserved. Published 2006
First edition 2006
Printed in the United States of America.

Excerpts from *The Art of Public Speaking,* by Stephen E. Lucas, 7th ed. Copyright © 2001 by McGraw-Hill. Reprinted by permission of The McGraw-Hill Companies.

Excerpts from pp. 21, 23, and 72 of *The Elements of Style,* by William Strunk, Jr., and E.B. White, 4th ed. Copyright © 2000 by Allyn & Bacon. Reprinted by permission of Pearson Education, Inc.

Excerpts from Dr. Martin Luther King, Jr.'s "I Have a Dream" speech, reprinted by arrangement with the Estate of Martin Luther King, Jr., c/o Writers House as agent for the proprietor, New York, NY. Copyright © 1963 by Martin Luther King, Jr., copyright renewed 1991 by Coretta Scott King.

Excerpts from *On Writing Well,* by William K. Zinsser. Copyright © 2001. Reprinted by permission of the author.

Excerpts from *Secrets of Successful Speakers,* by Lilly Walters. Copyright © 1993 by McGraw-Hill. Reprinted by permission of The McGraw-Hill Companies.

Excerpts from *Success Secrets of the Motivational Superstars,* by Michael Jeffreys. Copyright © 1996. Reprinted by permission of Prima Publishing, a division of Random House, Inc.

Excerpts from *What to Say . . . When You're Dying on the Platform,* by Lilly Walters. Copyright © 1995 by McGraw-Hill. Reprinted by permission of The McGraw-Hill Companies.

Excerpts from *Words Fail Me,* by Patricia T. O'Conner. Copyright © 1999. Reprinted by permission of Harcourt, Inc.

Excerpts from *Writing with Style,* by John R. Trimble, 2nd ed. Copyright © 2000. Reprinted by permission of Pearson Education, Inc.

Library of Congress Control Number: 2005932800

Dempsey, David J.
Better to best: how to speak for extraordinary results . . . every time! / David J. Dempsey.—1st ed.
Includes bibliographical references and index.
  ISBN-13: 978-0-9715165-2-6
  ISBN-10: 0-9715165-2-9
  1. Public speaking.   2. Business communication.
  I. Title

Design and composition: Beverly Butterfield, Girl of the West Productions
Editorial Services: Allan Edmands, The Wordsman Editorial Services

This book is dedicated to Kathy, my best friend and the love of my life, and to Dee, a true inspiration, whose faith and courage will lift her over her challenges.

CONTENTS

ACKNOWLEDGMENTS

WHERE TO BEGIN? Many people contributed enormously to this book. Their insights and suggestions greatly enhanced the final product, and I am forever indebted to them for their contributions. Several deserve special recognition.

Michelle Collins, the Executive Editor of Miranda Publishing, LLC, patiently and painstakingly critiqued, revised, and polished the manuscript. She is a consummate professional who skillfully honed the language. She left an indelible imprint on the book. Her contributions were invaluable.

The editing of Allan Edmands made the language sing. His pleasant cajoling, diplomatic manner, remarkable eye for details, and artful buffing unquestionably improved the final product. I recommend him without reservation—except I fear that he will become too busy for our next project.

As the book evolved, Kathy Kuchta constantly added an objective perspective necessary when we were so deeply entrenched in the details that we lost sight of the big picture. She reviewed dozens of iterations of this book and was a perfect voice of reason when reason was called for.

Beverly Butterfield created an exceptional, reader-friendly layout for the book. She tolerated our quirky suggestions and cheerfully accommodated our perpetual tweaking. She is the best at her craft.

Bob Aulicino is an artist who blended a hodgepodge of ideas into a magnetic jacket design. He protected us from ourselves when our zany ideas strayed too far afield.

Finally, to the many businesspeople and university students across the country—far too many to list—whom I have trained and coached. I am constantly amazed by your courage, by your willingness to experiment, and most importantly, by your dramatic improvement. You inspire and reassure me constantly that the principles in this book work. You allow me to experiment and refine these ideas and theories in the most important laboratory of all—the real world.

I sincerely thank each of you.

INTRODUCTION

According to most studies, people's number-one fear is public
speaking. Number two is death. Death is number two.
Does that seem right? This means to the average person,
if you have to go to a funeral, you're better off
in the casket than doing the eulogy.

—JERRY SEINFELD

THE BEGINNING OF MY LEGAL CAREER was not merely inauspicious—it was disastrous. Ever since I was a small child, I had dreamed of becoming just like Perry Mason: a wizard in the courtroom, mesmerizing the jury with my eloquence and goring hostile witnesses with insightful questions. I was always the victor, never the vanquished. I would not simply be *a* trial attorney; I would be *the* trial attorney. Visions of grandeur played in my head. Alas, reality diverged so dramatically from those visions!

My first jury trial is indelibly seared in my memory. To this day, more than twenty-five years later, I can describe in minute detail the sights, the sounds, and the layout of that courtroom. I can picture the faces of the jurors and recall the name of the judge.

I remember being supremely confident before the trial—and why not? My argument was brilliant and my logic unassailable. When the judge instructed me to begin my opening statement, I slowly and dramatically swaggered toward the jury.

For the first five minutes of my opening statement, I waxed poetically about the enormous injustice that had befallen my client. I described his grievous injuries and exhorted the jury to do its grave and

1

solemn duty and right this wrong with a whopping award of damages. Just as I had envisioned, the jurors were nodding in agreement. They were putty in my hands, and my chest swelled with pride.

Then, I misspoke—twice—and as I tried to recover, I became hopelessly tongue-tied. Instantly, I began to unravel. My right knee began to twitch, gently at first, and then more violently. Within seconds the left knee joined in, bobbing in time with my right. As I struggled to regain my composure and recall my train of thought, my hips began to convulse, and I realized that I had become Attorney Elvis.

At this point, I longed for a dark cave to hide in. Unfortunately, however, I had the undivided attention of everyone in the courtroom. The jurors and the previously slumbering courtroom bystanders were now leaning forward, some of them amused, others wide-eyed with amazement at this startling spectacle. The bailiff was ready to pounce and administer cardiopulmonary resuscitation. The judge was scowling, noticeably annoyed at what he considered a transparent play for the jury's sympathy. My client was stunned, his mouth agape in disbelief. I suspected he was muttering a prayer that the previous settlement offer—at which I had scoffed in disdain—was still available.

Nonetheless, I pressed on. In order to avoid collapsing, I began wobbling back and forth in front of the jury box. My arms were flailing, my hands were shaking, and my voice was cracking as if I was reentering puberty. My brain turned to mush, and whatever I said over the next fifteen minutes remains a mystery. All I recall making were incoherent guttural sounds.

I hoped that my plight was not as bad as it seemed, and it wasn't—it was worse. And juror four confirmed that assessment when he leaned over to juror five and commented, in a voice that I imagined could be heard throughout several neighboring counties, "Hey, what's up with Jell-O Boy?"

I continued to stagger about for what seemed an eternity, and I lamely whimpered a conclusion. This humiliating fiasco was hardly the triumphant debut I had imagined, and for years I dodged the courtroom whenever possible. Instead, I devoured self-help books, struggling to restore a speck of my dignity. Joining a monastery seemed appealing. I have never forgotten that day, although I have desperately tried.

Over the years, I have come to realize that my experience was not unique. Most people have harrowing speaking tales of their own. If they were fortunate, they merely watched, from the comfort of their seats, a speaker unravel on the other side of the lectern. ("He just melted into a puddle; it was so sad.") If they were less fortunate, *they* were the pathetic souls withering under the sympathetic, puzzled, or perhaps annoyed gaze of the audience members. ("I blathered on like a nitwit and sweated like a plow horse.")

Everything is funny as long as it is
happening to somebody else.
WILL ROGERS

Either experience only reinforces the widely held perception that public speaking should be avoided at all costs. And so most people do avoid it. As a result, most people are mediocre speakers, but not all: Some are lousy, and some are perfectly dreadful. Few understand how to use their verbal and nonverbal tools to clarify their messages and to inspire or persuade their listeners. How could they? The incentive for many people when they speak is not to excel but merely to survive.

Since my courtroom calamity, I have learned that anyone can become a confident communicator, and some can become brilliant. "Not me," you think? Yes, even you. How do I know this? Because I have witnessed it thousands of times as a presentation skills trainer and coach.

Ironically, several years after my Jell-O Boy fiasco, I began working as an adjunct professor of communications at Oglethorpe University in Atlanta. (I somehow forgot to mention the Jell-O Boy episode to the faculty committee during the hiring interview.) I have taught beginning and advanced public speaking for over eighteen years, and whenever any of my students cower at the prospect of standing before an audience to speak, I see my reflection in their eyes. I remember that wobbly-kneed attorney who shook so uncontrollably that he could hardly squeak out a word. I understand their fear, and I empathize.

But with a bit of gentle nudging ("Speak or fail—your choice") and lavish encouragement ("I swear that not one of my students has ever died from acute stage fright when speaking"), I have seen these shy and fearful speakers undergo remarkable transformations. Students who, on the first night of class, could not string together two coherent sentences have, at the end of the semester, stepped onto the auditorium stage for their final speech and mesmerized hundreds of fellow students, faculty, and parents by speaking with passion and conviction. And I have witnessed similar transformations for many years coaching and training business executives throughout the United States.

There is nothing mysterious about learning to speak with confidence. It is a craft anyone—even you steely naysayers—can master with initiative, tenacity, and this blueprint for success.

I have also learned that the notion of someone being a "born speaker" is a myth. Gifted speakers make it look effortless, but it never is. Speaking is an art that you develop and constantly hone. Anyone who tells you otherwise is peddling snake oil. There is no magic wand that anyone can wave over your head, no elixir you can drink, no pill you can swallow to excel as a speaker. Reading about speaking will guide you, but you will learn to speak skillfully only by actually speaking.

Unfortunately, many people devote too little time to preparing and practicing their presentations. They should be clear and focused when they speak, but far too often they subject their audiences to gobbledygook and obscurity. Speakers sap their effectiveness in many ways: They ramble on without any apparent direction or purpose. They drone on hypnotically as the listeners doze. They listlessly read the insipid speeches they have lovingly written out word for word. They blur their points and frustrate the audience by packing their presentations with jargon, doublespeak, drivel, minutiae, pomposities, clichés, acronyms, and "eses" of all types (business-ese, academ-ese, official-ese, and legal-ese). And if they do not confound you with their words, they baffle you with muddled multimedia presentations. Their sterile messages are lost in a dark thicket of cluttered ideas and desultory anecdotes. Does any of this sound familiar?

These speakers have shown no mercy on the audience. When a speaker commits any of these sins, everyone (except, sadly, the speaker) can see that the listeners have lost interest and have wandered off toward the nearest mental exit. Communication has failed.

If all my possessions were taken from me with one exception,
I would choose to keep the power of speech,
for by it I would regain all the rest.
DANIEL WEBSTER

I hope to inspire you to do something that right now may seem unthinkable: *to embrace every speaking opportunity that comes your way.* I can hear you protesting, "Say what? I don't think so!" Just hear me out. You should do this for three reasons.

First, with your words, you have the power to leave a lasting imprint on people. I have seen trembling college students, self-conscious immigrants, and reticent executives alike engross listeners with their poignant messages. But that will not happen if the mere thought of speaking causes you to quiver like a frightened rabbit, or if your speeches are remarkably bad.

Second, when you connect with an audience—when you catch a spark in the eyes of your listeners, notice their heads nodding in agreement, or see them sitting spellbound, hanging on your next word—the feeling is empowering. Nothing else can duplicate that euphoria.

Finally, and perhaps most importantly, taking advantage of every speaking opportunity will benefit you—enormously. Speakers who can stand and deliver their messages with power, passion, and persuasion, regardless of their profession, are invariably more successful in attaining their objectives: to educate, to inspire, to close a deal, or to sell a product or service. Confident speakers produce *results*.

The purpose of this book is simple: to show you how to speak with utter confidence and conviction. This book contains the best lessons I have learned after twenty-five years working in the speaking arena as a professional speaker, university professor, and presentation skills trainer and coach. I learned many of these lessons the hard way—*painfully* hard—but, by using this book, you won't have to. It will dramatically accelerate your learning.

Some of the principles in this book may seem obvious, and some may surprise you, but all are battle-tested, and all will benefit you when you stand to speak. The book contains hundreds of secrets and insights that will enhance your communication skills regardless of where you begin this journey—as a neophyte speaker or as a seasoned platform veteran. It will show you how to become a much better speaker than you are now. Indeed, it will show you how to become your very BEST!

Study this book and practice these principles, and you absolutely will begin to communicate with unflappable confidence every time you speak. You will be far wiser about what it takes to speak persuasively, clearly, and concisely—to sweep away an audience with your words and attain the results you seek from your presentations. This transformation will not happen overnight, but it will happen. And I guarantee this: If you practice these principles, you will never hear an audience member say, "Hey, what's up with Jell-O Boy?"

PART I

MASTER THE MENTAL

S O, YOU WANT TO SPEAK with confidence? Let's start with your noggin (I promise, no psychological mumbo jumbo). First and foremost, you have to believe that you can, and envision yourself doing exactly that. You should visualize every detail of a successful presentation: a self-assured demeanor, a compelling message, a receptive audience, a forceful delivery, a rip-roaring round of applause, and of course, closing that huge deal after your amazing presentation.

Use your imagination not to scare yourself to death,
but to inspire yourself to life.
ADELE BROOKMAN

This type of visualization is often easier said than done, because insidious doubt and indecision can creep into your thoughts and erode your confidence. If unchecked, they can cause you to tremble, freeze, or mumble to yourself. Some of this speaking phobia stems from inexperience (your ducking every speaking opportunity will not help). Some of it might stem from a nightmarish speaking experience from your childhood (say, the time that your classmates mocked you as a "scaredy-cat" when you shook so wildly that your speech rattled in your hands as you solicited their votes to become the hall monitor). Or perhaps some of it stems from that wretched speech when your key client doodled and

7

yawned incessantly as you spoke. All such insecurities can combine, as if to plot your undoing. At best, they can severely handicap you as a speaker. At worst, they can virtually paralyze you.

Part I strips away the shroud of mystery surrounding stage fright and provides a blueprint for mentally preparing yourself to speak with conviction and confidence—without your needing to hypnotize or medicate yourself to calm your jitters.

CHANNEL YOUR STAGE FRIGHT

*The human brain is a wonderful thing. It operates
from the moment you're born until the moment
you get up to make a speech.*

—ANONYMOUS

People who profess that public speaking does not cause them anxiety cannot be trusted. Let's be honest: Speaking is scary. An audience of strangers—or even friends—can be daunting. You are alone up there, free to dazzle or to flop, free to convince your listeners that you are a genius or a buffoon. And your successes—or your failures—are as public as possible. Those are pretty high stakes.

Many people go to extraordinary lengths to diligently, creatively—even maniacally, in some cases—avoid every opportunity to speak, because it terrifies them. And here's the proof (sorry, this proof business is a lawyer's obsession). A 1999 study commissioned by the National Communication Association found that only 24 percent of Americans are very comfortable giving a speech or formal presentation.[1] In a survey that appeared in *The Book of Lists,* three thousand people were asked, "What are you most afraid of?" and the number-one response was "speaking before a group." It ranked higher than the fear of heights, insects, and even death.[2] In another study, twenty-five hundred people were asked to list their greatest fear, and the largest percentage of respondents listed public speaking.[3] A 1996 study revealed that we fear public speaking more than a job interview, a blind date, being the victim of a

9

practical joke, or being asked personal questions in public.[4] It seems that quite a few people belong to the Stage Fright Club.

Even those who appear to be very comfortable speaking admit to experiencing presentation phobia at times. Garrison Keillor, host of Minnesota Public Radio's *A Prairie Home Companion,* fought a fear of speaking as a youngster:

> I was terrified of everything [in high school], so afraid of being embarrassed in front of other people, afraid to speak up in class, afraid that I might have the wrong answer to a question that everybody else had the right answer to. . . . I was able to get up in speech class only because I could take off my glasses, and when I did, I could no longer see faces. It was just kind of an Impressionist tapestry.[5]

Actress Carol Burnett confessed,

> The idea of making a speech does more than make me a nervous wreck; it terrifies me. . . . I'd rather scrub floors—without kneepads.[6]

Oscar-winning actress Meryl Streep said,

> It is odd: I have a career that spans continents, but the pathetic thing is that I can't get up in front of people and speak. I get really nervous.[7]

Every speaker suffers some degree of stage fright, the mild-to-intense feeling of anxiety you experience when you are asked to make a presentation. You are nervous, and your body produces adrenaline in response. That process is what causes your mouth to feel as dry as the Sahara Desert and your heart to pound so wildly that it seems as if it will explode. In severe cases, you might become incapable of focusing on anything but your imminent demise. The paradox is that this stress, if you properly channel it, is enormously beneficial—Scout's honor. It infuses your speech with energy. The key is in learning how to harness the stress to your advantage rather than allowing it to cripple you.

SIX STAGE-FRIGHT SECRETS

Let's whittle this Stage Fright Bully down to size. When wrestling with speaking anxiety, keep the following six secrets in mind.

1. IT IS PERFECTLY NATURAL TO BE ANXIOUS

If speaking or the mere prospect of speaking scares you, you are in the majority. As you can see from the previous comments, speaking in public often intimidates even professional speakers and actors who make their living onstage. If the pros with thousands of hours of speaking experience, whose very livelihood depends on speaking confidently, become nervous, then it is certainly natural for someone who speaks infrequently to experience anxiety. You just do not want your anxiety to impair your speech or to become so severe that it drives you bonkers.

The best speakers know enough to be scared. Stage fright is the sweat of perfection. The only difference between the pros and the novices is that the pros have trained the butterflies to fly in formation.
EDWARD R. MURROW

---

2. YOUR WORST FEARS RARELY MATERIALIZE

Your imagination can be ludicrously turbulent when you are preparing to speak. You might visualize the worst occurring: Your knees knock, you hyperventilate, you babble incoherently, you faint, and you are publicly humiliated. Such fears are imaginary, and they rarely materialize, so stop cringing, breathe deeply, and get a grip on yourself. There are no known deaths attributed to stage fright, so the odds favor you.

3. IT ALWAYS SEEMS WORSE TO THE SPEAKER

Immediately after making a presentation, many of the speakers I coach swear that they had never been so nervous in their lives, that their hands had never before shaken and their knees had never before wobbled like that. But I videotape every speech, and together we immediately review it. Typically, they are surprised to discover that they appeared far more poised than they had felt.

When you are speaking, with hundreds of eyes focused on you, you often feel intimidated and your anxiety is naturally heightened. You can become your harshest critic. But rest assured: Though you may be scared stiff, your audience generally has no clue—unless you look wild-eyed, ghastly pale, or ramrod rigid.

Courage is resistance to fear, mastery of fear—not absence of fear.
MARK TWAIN

---

4. YOUR AUDIENCE EMPATHIZES WITH YOU

Every member of your audience has felt some level of anxiety when it has been his or her own turn to speak. And anyone who denies it is fibbing. As a result, many of them are looking at you with admiration and awe for having the courage to stand and speak; others are simply thinking, "There, but for the grace of God, go I!" They feel your pain.

5. YOUR AUDIENCE WANTS YOU TO SUCCEED

Audience members have come to hear you speak for a variety of reasons: to be informed, to be entertained, or perhaps to be inspired. They regard you as the expert, and they want their expectations fulfilled. Your audience wants you to succeed, for the simple reason that your success will benefit them. It is a collaborative effort: You want to give a good speech, and they want to hear one. Dispel the notion that your audience is lying in wait ready to pounce on any mistake.

6. YOUR AUDIENCE HAS NEVER HEARD YOUR PRESENTATION

Speakers often scowl and scold themselves (or even let a few invectives fly) when they forget a word, line, or point. But remember: Your audience has never before heard your speech. No one monitors what you say, line by line, word for word. No one will shout, "Hey, Bonehead, you forgot something!" In fact, listeners rarely know that you flubbed a line or dropped a thought. You can deliver an exceptional speech that only you realize is less than perfect—and you don't have to tell anyone.

Audience members do not know what you planned to say; they only know what you said. That knowledge should reduce your stress, because it affords you the freedom to omit something with very little risk. Of course, if you wince, curse, or mutter "Dadgumit—I blew it," you will highlight the gaffe for your audience. Fight the urge to be honest in these situations (your mother will understand).

No passion so effectually robs the mind of all its
powers of acting and reasoning as fear.
EDMUND BURKE

It is possible that my revealing the preceding six stage-fright secrets to you has not assuaged your presentation anxiety. If your anxiety is acute—if the mere thought of public speaking makes you nauseated, if you are wringing your hands and perspiring as you read this book, if you have changed jobs eighteen times to avoid speaking—then you should pore over the books and Web site included for this chapter in the list of recommended resources at the end of this book.

Learn to positively channel your anxiety, because the speaking game is often won or lost at this stage. If you want to speak with confidence, you have to believe you can. Rein in your fertile imagination. Learn to transform your anxiety into an asset, and you will take gigantic strides in the right direction. In the meantime, if you are frantic, try to relax for goodness' sake—and stay away from sharp objects.

PRINCIPLE 2

VISUALIZE SPEAKING SUCCESS

There is nothing either good or bad,
but thinking makes it so.

—WILLIAM SHAKESPEARE

THINK LIKE A CHAMPION! That message was painted above the door in my high school locker room. Over the years, the paint had chipped and faded, and thousands of players had smudged those words of inspiration, slapping them as they raced onto the field of battle. But the message permeated our thinking. Four powerful words that the coaches never let us forget, and we never did.

I can think of no better advice for speakers: *Think like a champion!* Before every presentation, visualize every speaking triumph you've ever had, in precise detail. Not just the presentation that was a monumental success. Visualize every victory, large and small: the day you weaned yourself off your script, the time you focused on the audience and really connected, or the time you first ventured away from the lectern, even if only a few steps.

I have participated in over one hundred public speaking contests throughout the United States. I won a few and lost plenty. Although many of these contests occurred years ago, I can recall everything about those that I won: the lavish applause, the stories I shared, even hoisting the heavy glass and marble trophies. Why? Because those vivid images enhance my confidence whenever I speak. I ingrain my successes into my mind. So should you.

Vision is the art of seeing things invisible.
JONATHAN SWIFT

Actors, athletes, musicians, politicians, business executives, and anyone else who appears in the public arena visualize success. This visualization bolsters their confidence and helps them mentally prepare to prevail. Former Olympic athlete Vicki Huber describes her visualization:

> Right before a big race, I'll picture myself running, and I will try to put all the other competitors in the race into my mind. Then I will try and imagine every possible situation I might find myself in . . . behind someone, being boxed in, pushed, shoved, or cajoled, different positions on the track, laps to go, and, of course, the final stretch. And I always picture myself winning the race, no matter what happens during the event.[1]

Notice that while Huber includes realistic, difficult elements in her vision, she always focuses on success. This type of mental preparation is enormously helpful for speakers as well. Imagine yourself confidently standing before an audience; envision the smiling faces and the nodding heads of your listeners; hear the hearty congratulations for a job well done. Rather than fretting, "This sure seems like a cranky audience" (and trust me, you will encounter audiences packed with sourpusses), substitute a positive thought: "This audience is gonna love me like my dog does! I will own the stage and close this deal!" Feel free to replace the "dog" image with one of your liking, but you understand the point: Visualize your successful presentation in detail.

---

*Obstacles are those frightful things you see when
you take your eyes off your goal.*
HENRY FORD

Dr. Wayne W. Dyer is the author of numerous best-selling books, including *Your Erroneous Zones, The Sky's the Limit,* and *You'll See It When You Believe It.* He is also a very successful speaker, and he often addresses audiences of several thousand people. His visualization ritual before speaking is precise and calming:

I create the speech in my mind before I go on stage. In other words, I meditate on it. I see the whole thing working. I see every little detail, from my arriving, to where I go in, what the room looks like, how the people are going to react to my speech, what I'm going to say when I walk out there, how I'm going to dress, how the lights are going to be. I play the whole thing out in my mind in the meditation, hours before I speak. I get very, very peaceful with that. It's a very comfortable, joyful, kind of blissful experience.[2]

Now, don't delude yourself that visualization will substitute for preparation and practice, because it won't. That is just wishful thinking. If you are unprepared, no amount of visualization—not about your speaking triumphs, not about your platform pizzazz, not even about your audience shouting hosannas—will help. And to make matters worse, if you are unprepared, your audience *really will* be cranky—and rightfully so. No matter how convincing your visualization, it is only one of many tools in your speaking arsenal. To transform your vision into reality, you must prepare for your moment in the limelight.

Eight Tips to Boost Your Confidence

You must aggressively battle the fear of speaking, because it is wickedly persistent. It will flourish if you give it room. Here are eight ways to begin developing unshakable confidence when you speak.

1. Seize Every Opportunity to Speak

"I don't think so!" I can hear you protesting at this utterly preposterous recommendation. Work with me here, because this is the truth: The more frequently you speak, the more confident you will become. As with any learned skill, you improve with practice. You would not wait until the senior prom to walk across the room and ask that little freckle-faced cutie-pie to dance if you had never danced before, would you? Okay, maybe you would, but for most of us klutzes, that is way too much pressure.

Don't wait to develop your speaking skills until that critical presentation (the one, for instance, that will determine if you will spend the balance of your career in the boardroom or in the mailroom). Practice speaking in such nonthreatening venues as church meetings, service organizations like Kiwanis or Rotary, or your child's grade school class. Refine your speaking skills in these forgiving environments, not when the stakes are colossal. This practice will produce a rich collection of successful speaking experiences from which you can draw confidence.

2. Prepare Early and Thoroughly

Unless you *know* you can devote ample time to prepare your speech, don't agree to speak. Even if you are asked to "just say a few words," decline if you cannot prepare. Those "few words" will haunt you if you misspeak, ramble, or fall to pieces. For many, just saying a few words causes the same intense anxiety as delivering a prepared presentation.

Does it really matter if you are prepared? Absolutely. Preparation can reduce your stage fright by as much as 75 percent.[3] That is a heap of worry and torment that you can avoid by preparing. Simply put, there is no better way to reduce your anxiety and bolster your confidence. So pass if you can't find the time to prepare.

3. USE POSITIVE SELF-TALK

Psychologists almost universally agree that positive self-talk enhances your confidence. You must believe that you will succeed and that the audience is on your side. Talk yourself into success, and disavow the possibility of failure. Tell yourself, "I am confident, because I know my topic better than anyone else. I am an expert, and the audience will see me that way." Just be careful to conduct your pep talk in private, or people may think you are slightly loony.

Bless your uneasiness as a sign that there is still life in you.
DAG HAMMARSKJÖLD

---

4. LOOSEN UP

The physical appearance alone of many speakers eliminates any doubt that they are nervous: They have taut, solemn expressions; their knuckles are white from clutching the lectern; their arms are tightly crossed; and their movements are robotic. Their body language sends a glaring nonverbal message that they are anxious, and everyone immediately senses it. They are downright scary to watch.

No audience will believe that you are confident as long as rigor mortis seems imminent. Instead, project a self-assured demeanor. Walk to the lectern confidently, not tentatively; act as though you are excited to be speaking, not as though you were marching to the gallows; pause before you begin; plant your feet firmly, and stand erect; look at your audience; and smile (principle 30). This will help you appear and feel more confident. The audience wants to see a relaxed speaker, not a somber starchy one.

5. REMEMBER THAT VERY FEW SPEAKERS ARE FLAWLESS

We often place unrealistic expectations upon ourselves ("I have to be flawless or my career is kaput and my life is ruined!"). We seldom live up to those intimidating standards, so don't yank your hair out trying. Professional speakers, who have devoted their lives to perfecting their craft, will tell you that they are constantly refining and honing their presentation skills, and that some of their earlier presentations were putrid.

Recognize that despite your best efforts, you will not excel in every presentation. Sometimes you will get rattled; sometimes your audience will not be receptive; and sometimes those blasted planets are misaligned. It happens. We do not have to be perfect, and we rarely are. Just remember: There will be another speech, another day. No speech is fatal (although if you bomb, you may spend a few years in the mailroom).

———

Progress has not followed a straight ascending line, but a spiral with rhythm of progress and regression, of evolution and dissolution.
JOHANN WOLFGANG VON GOETHE

———

6. MEDITATE, OR ENGAGE IN RELAXATION ACTIVITIES

If unchecked, your prespeech jitters can immobilize you. Whether you meditate, listen to music, or chant or sing (preferably in the shower) before you speak, engage in some activity that helps calm you. Try all of the following relaxation techniques:

- *Breathe:* Inhale deeply through your nose, drawing air into your diaphragm; hold it for several seconds, and then exhale slowly through your mouth.

- *Stretch:* Stretching will help relieve the tension in your head, shoulders, and back. Before your speech, retreat to another room to relax and stretch. To ease the tension, gently roll your head and shoulders clockwise and counterclockwise repeatedly. Finally, to loosen the muscles in your face, open your mouth as wide as possible and move your lower jaw around. Avoid doing this with small children present.

- *Move around:* Release nervous energy by taking a short walk to collect your thoughts and warm up your muscles before you speak. Just don't work yourself into a sweating lather or wander off—you still have to speak.

7. EAT SENSIBLY

Okay, so what does eating have to do with visualization? Well, you are not going to visualize *anything* positive if your body is rebelling. On the day you speak, avoid all dairy products (which create mucus), carbonated beverages (which can result in embarrassing belching), and caffeine (which can make you jittery). Eat only a light snack before you speak. Sip room-temperature water constantly throughout the day to hydrate your vocal cords, and always have a glass of water (no ice) available while you speak. Don't guzzle water like a camel, however, or you may need to bolt from the stage midway through your speech—never a confidence booster.

———

Before thou engagest, ask thyself,
What if my Design miscarr[ies]?
THOMAS FULLER

———

8. MENTALLY PREPARE FOR THE UNEXPECTED

Sometimes, the best of plans go awry. In *What to Say . . . When You're Dying on the Platform,* professional speaker Lilly Walters writes,

> Nothing is more terrifying than standing up in front of a group and finding that something is going VERY WRONG! Like, "I'm dying up here!" . . . How many times have you . . . [w]ished you'd "remained silent and been thought a fool" instead of opening your mouth and proving them right?[4]

You may encounter various problems while speaking, such as a bungled introduction, a microphone meltdown, a pesky questioner, a lost train of thought, and a few other snafus described in principle 40. Mentally preparing to address these challenges will reduce your anxiety.

---

*The greatest mistake you can make in life is to be
continually fearing you will make one.*
ELBERT HUBBARD

Enhance your confidence every time you speak by visualizing an ideal outcome and reliving previous successes. You must "*Think like a champion!*" to speak like one. Tape those words onto your computer, write them at the top of every speech, and most importantly—sear them into your mind. Make them your creed.

PRINCIPLE 3

PARK YOUR EGO AT THE DOOR

[O]ne who does less than he can is a thief.

—MOHANDAS K. GANDHI

There is no household repair or improvement project so simple that I cannot botch it. A hammer, a saw, a screwdriver, and heaven forbid, any power tool—they all haunt me.

After I purchased my first house more than two decades ago, a 1940s-era handyman special, I spent many weekends at Home Depot, eager to tackle dozens of challenges. I would wander the cavernous aisles with my list in hand, intrigued by the seemingly endless ways I could improve my house.

I would load my mammoth orange cart with a glut of supplies and tools for projects I had not even considered before entering the store. As I rolled along, I bonded and swapped how-to stories with other customers in the Home Depot fraternity. Although I was a bungler with tools, I rationalized, "Surely, with gritty determination, I can master any task that my fellow shoppers can. Bring it on!"

I was wrong. I accomplished only the simplest tasks, abandoning most of the projects out of sheer frustration. I had mistakenly assumed that because I had a law degree, home improvement would be a breeze. After repeatedly smashing my fingers, scraping my knuckles, and uttering more profane words than Sister Mary Margaret Rainey would ever have imagined were in her former pupil's vocabulary, I had to admit it: There was no correlation between being well educated and grasping the nuances of spackling a wall, mitering a joint, or caulking a bathtub (and don't even get me started on cutting tile). It was a humbling admission.

My frustration grew when I realized that my building brethren— even the ones who seemed to have the same intellectual capacity as the two-by-fours they were buying—were effortlessly completing projects far more difficult than mine. Embarrassed by my failures, I avoided Home Depot, fearing a chance encounter with someone who might ask how one of my many forsaken projects was progressing.

I have come to an equally startling realization about speaking: There is no correlation between your level of education and your ability to speak with power, passion, and persuasion. Some dunderheads are exceptional speakers, and some brilliant people are absolute bumblers when you place a microphone in their hand.

You can have brilliant ideas, but if you can't get them across, your brains won't get you anywhere.
LEE IACOCCA

It is no sign of weakness that your speaking skills are deficient, or even woefully inadequate, if you have never learned this skill. It would be an ugly spectacle if I strapped on a pair of skates, grabbed a hockey stick, slid onto the ice, and attempted to whack the puck around. I have never played hockey, so I would spend more time picking my fanny up off the ice than I would gliding effortlessly about dazzling everyone. I would have to learn and develop my skating skills. Speaking is no different.

The most difficult step on the path to becoming a more proficient, confident speaker may be the first: a willingness to park your ego at the door and recognize that there is always room for improvement. This is often an enormous challenge, especially for highly successful people. For many high achievers, acknowledging any shortcoming is tantamount to failure. They have risen to the pinnacle of their professions by resilience, focus, and determination; they resolve most problems through thinking and reasoning. But these virtues do not help with public speaking— a learned skill, one in which most professionals have had little or no training. If they develop any speaking skills, it is often done by hit-or-miss—and most miss. Typically, they either ramble aimlessly while their audience yearns deeply for some direction, or they drone on and on while their audience awaits vainly for some sign that it is a human being who is speaking.

Creativity is constantly in danger of being destroyed by success.
The more effectively the environment is mastered, the
greater is the temptation to rest on one's oars.
HENRY A. KISSINGER

ATTITUDE IS EVERYTHING

If you want to become a better speaker, pride must not stand in your way. No harm will be done and the sky will not fall if you admit that maybe, just maybe, you can and should improve. Here is the glaring truth: We can all become better speakers (yes, even you). But you must approach the challenge with a positive attitude.

Over the years, I have delivered over one thousand presentations and conducted hundreds of presentation skills workshops. It is only natural that, with so many opportunities, I have occasionally blundered and made some really dumb comments. When that happened in the early years of my speaking journey, my instinctive reaction was always the same: to avoid speaking. I concocted some amazingly creative excuses: "I would love to speak, but I have this darn recurring laryngitis." Or "I'm sorry, I have to attend *another* wedding at 9:00 a.m. on Tuesday." My rationale was simple. If I didn't speak, I couldn't fail.

But I soon realized that unless I was prepared to blaze a path as the mute trial attorney or be forever known as Jell-O Boy, I had to become a much better speaker. (Besides, the Tuesday morning wedding excuse was raising a few eyebrows.) I also realized that my attitude was critical to my success. I needed to glean whatever kernel of insight each speaking experience taught me and push myself to excel.

The only way to be absolutely safe is never
to try anything for the first time.
MAGNUS PYKE

You need to do that, too. You need to recognize that your speaking skills will only improve if you practice and approach every presentation with a willingness to learn. Don't let a false sense of pride restrain you. Honestly analyze each presentation, and ask yourself difficult questions: "Am I *really* always prepared to speak?" "Do I understand the issues facing my audience?" "Is my message muddled or my organization chaotic?" "Am I genuinely passionate about my topic?"

Videotape and critique every presentation (principle 21), and constantly challenge yourself. Seek blunt and honest feedback from people whose opinions you trust—and who have the qualifications and experience to evaluate your speeches constructively. Their input may be humbling, and sometimes dismaying, but it will invariably be revealing and helpful. Evaluate their suggestions objectively, not defensively (stop bristling). Your ego may be bruised, but your presentations will get better, and that should be your ultimate goal.

What I have learned bears no other fruit than
to make me realize how much I have to learn.
MICHEL DE MONTAIGNE

EVEN THE BEST GET BETTER

You will learn to speak with authority and confidence by consistently practicing and refining your craft. I have never worked with speakers, regardless of their skill level, who cannot improve if they are willing to constantly challenge themselves and set uncompromising standards.

Anthony Robbins, an electrifying professional speaker, built his career by demanding more from himself as a speaker than anyone else could possibly expect. How did he develop his speaking talent? In his words,

> I became an excellent public speaker, because, rather than once a week, I booked myself to speak three times a day to anyone who would listen. . . . My associates talked about how "lucky" I was to have been born with such an "innate" talent. . . . [But] mastery takes as long as you want it to take. . . . Were all my speeches great? Far from it! But I did make sure that I learned from every experience and that I somehow improved until very soon I could enter a room of any size and be able to reach people from virtually all walks of life.[1]

Les Brown is another prominent professional speaker who understands the importance of constantly improving. His simple philosophy:

> I know speakers who have given the same speech for thirty years and never changed and have no intention of changing. They have gone back to the same audiences and given the same speech several times. . . . [But speakers] interested in mastering the art of communication . . . [should] always [ask]: "What new things can I incorporate into my presentation that can take it to another level, that will have a greater impact on the audience?" . . .
>
> When you approach [speaking] from a growing perspective, as opposed to doing the same thing over and over again, the

possibilities are unlimited. . . . [N]ever be satisfied with your-self. Realize that you haven't given your best speech yet, and there's more within you. And learn from as many sources as you possibly can.[2]

Excellent speakers are always looking for techniques they can use to enhance their effectiveness. Their pride does not hinder their growth. They always strive to improve. What about you? Do you have the desire, the fire in your belly, to be your best every time you speak?

Some speakers, for a variety of reasons—fear, pride, denial—will never leave their speaking comfort zone. They delude themselves by thinking that their expertise is all that really matters.

If you refuse to honestly critique your presentations, or if you reside in the world of delusions and rationalizations, your prospects for truly effective communication will plummet. Ask yourself one simple question every time you speak: "Is this the very best I can do?" If yes, congratulations—to all three of you in the world. If no, park your ego at the door. Plunk yourself down, roll up your sleeves, and get to work.

PART II

PREPARE TO PRESENT

HERE IS A PROFUNDITY: Whatever your audience, whatever your topic, and whatever your purpose in speaking, if you fail to prepare, be prepared to fail. (All right, maybe not a profundity, but certainly a truism.) There is no substitute for preparation—not your knowledge, not your fearlessness, not even your lucky rabbit's foot. Exceptional speakers are fanatical about preparation. They leave nothing to chance. They understand their audience and, like skilled craftsmen, they meticulously build their presentations brick by brick.

I'm a great believer in luck, and I find that the harder I work, the more I have of it.
THOMAS JEFFERSON

If your speech begins to implode because you are unprepared, your confidence will evaporate. You may be able to blunder along and stagger to a conclusion, but little more. Even if the speech does not flop entirely, it will certainly disappoint your audience and fall short of the ideal mark. And if it really begins to crumble as you are babbling away, you will silently pray for the earth to open up and swallow you—and your audience may well join in that prayer. Part II addresses the preliminary steps you should take to avoid that fate.

PRINCIPLE 4

BUILD A SPEECH FOUNDATION

The unluckiest insolvent in the world is the man whose
expenditure of speech is too great for his income of ideas.

—CHRISTOPHER MORLEY

Polished delivery will never compensate for a speech that lacks substance. A frothy speech leaves the audience feeling empty and cheated. Your speech should be built on a solid foundation of facts, details, examples, and anecdotes. A presentation packed with substance enhances your credibility and clarifies your message so it is understandable, informative, and memorable for your audience.

Where can you find material for your presentations? Search anywhere and everywhere, and not just in the obvious places. Nose around in unusual crannies for your speech content: graffiti, cereal boxes, billboards, voice mail messages, idle musings, political babble—it is all useful grist. Collect any information that you find interesting or appealing. If it amuses or impresses you, chances are pretty good it will amuse or impress your listeners as well. Relentlessly clip or copy articles related to your topic. I hope it is not sacrilegious to say this, but rip articles out of the magazines in your doctor's waiting room if necessary—I am positive that is what they are there for. All that accumulated information will result in a richer, more colorful speech. Great material can make a dry topic sparkle.

But—and this is important—you must snatch the ideas immediately, because they will disappear in a flash. Poof! And those brilliant insights will be gone forever. Scribble them in a journal, store them on your computer, write them on your hand if necessary—just capture them. Hoard your ideas like a miser. Avoid wasting valuable time later, ransacking your porous memory for the pithy quote or provocative thought you were just sure you would remember.

My little [note]books were beginnings—they were the ground into which I dropped the seed. . . . I would work this way when I was out in the crowds, then put the stuff together at home.
WALT WHITMAN

Become a data pack rat. Better yet, if you feel especially industrious, become an organized pack rat and categorize those nuggets somehow as you gather them. If that seems too ambitious, just jam them in a shoebox, but secure the shoebox.

Don't wait to gather material until the evening before you plan to speak. At that point, it is too late. And don't expect the ideas to come cascading out of your head and leap onto your notepad. Fickle Mr. Inspiration seldom shows up on your schedule; he is pigheaded that way. That tick-tock sound will grow deafeningly loud as you stare at the blank computer screen and the fateful moment to speak draws near. You are not likely to produce your best work with your head in the deadline guillotine.

FIVE SPEECH RESOURCES

Here are a few suggestions for the types of materials you might incorporate into your presentation to make it more persuasive, entertaining, and informative, but don't limit yourself. Be creative. Stockpile anything that might give your talk a little zing even if right now you do not know exactly how you will use it. Principle 5 will share some ideas about where to search for your material.

1. PERSONAL STORIES

Everyone loves a juicy story—the juicier, the better (principle 13). The best speakers are typically masterful storytellers. They capitalize on this skill in their presentations. Why? Because a compelling story will rivet an audience and make any message unforgettable. Tell them a tale, and they will lend you their ears (or something like that).

A man would do well to carry a pencil in his pocket and write down the thoughts of the moment. Those that come unsought are commonly the most valuable and should be secured because they seldom return.

FRANCIS BACON

---

2. EXAMPLES

Let's face it: Some material is so darn complex or abstract that it baffles even the most intellectual audience. Examples can clarify the complex or abstract. They can make minute details understandable. For example (smooth segue, right?), instead of simply saying that the interest payments on the federal debt are a gazillion dollars a day (they are actually two gazillion, but let's not nitpick), describe your fact in a more understandable context: "How much does this deficit cost taxpayers every day? Imagine a football field, end zone to end zone, with every square inch tightly packed with ten-foot-high stacks of crisp one-hundred-dollar bills. That is what taxpayers shell out, every day, in interest on the federal debt." That example should make it easier to grasp than a "gazillion," I hope. The point: Use examples to make obscure, complex, or abstract points clear.

3. QUOTATIONS

Relevant quotations enliven your message and enhance your credibility, particularly if the source of the quotation is a well-known and respected figure, such as Mohandas Gandhi, Rosa Parks, or Theodore Roosevelt (principle 15). On the other hand, a quote from "Vinny the tollbooth operator" or from "Bart Simpson," though interesting and perhaps enter-taining, will have little persuasive impact (sorry, Bart). The quote must be relevant to your point and from a recognizable and credible figure.

4. COMPARISONS AND CONTRASTS

To clarify your points, compare and contrast situations and posi-tions. Apt comparisons make your topic more understandable and per-suasive. For example, President Ronald Reagan repeatedly asked voters to consider one simple question: "Are you better off now, or were you better off then?"

Contrasts can help listeners distinguish alternative positions. Politi-cians often draw a stark contrast between themselves and their opponents: "My opponent trusts big government. I trust you." Advertisers also fre-quently rely on contrasts: "Chuck says, 'Tastes great.' I say, 'Less filling.'" To be effective, however, contrasts must be clear and accurate. If they are confusing, exaggerated, or misleading, they are seldom helpful.

My task which I am trying to achieve is, by the power of the
written word to make you hear, to make you feel—
it is, above all, to make you see. *That—*
and no more, and it is everything.
JOSEPH CONRAD

------

5. STATISTICS

Statistics are a double-edged sword. The line between statistics that enlighten and those that confound is incredibly fine. Your statistics must be simple and understandable: "In a blind taste test given to one thou-sand New Yorkers, seventy-five percent preferred Death by Chocolate Brownies over Mama's Finest Brownies (notwithstanding Mama's protests of a fix)." If your statistics are complex and confusing, or if you overuse them, they quickly become a liability. You will bog your listeners down in the swampy wasteland of incomprehensible complexity: "Sixty-seven-point-four percent of the top three percent of the five hundred and ten ridiculously rich muckety-mucks who reside in the tony section of Manhattan prefer Mama's Finest Brownies." Many accountants and computer geeks live in that treacherous land of complex statistics and speak its occult language; you, however, should stay away from there when you speak.

A speech consisting solely of your impressions and opinions is seldom as valuable or persuasive as one grounded in concrete, clear facts—unless, of course, you are Bill Gates, Warren Buffet, or some other notable visionary (and then, why would you be reading this book, anyway?). The rest of us mere mortals must do our homework and build our speeches on a solid bedrock of substance.

PRINCIPLE 5

USE PRESENTATION BUILDING BLOCKS

He who resolves never to ransack any mind but his own will
soon be reduced from mere barrenness to the poorest of
all imitations; he will be obliged to imitate himself
and to repeat what he has before often repeated.

—SIR JOSHUA REYNOLDS

So, you are a little light on substance? (Don't get touchy—the speech, not you.) You have come to the right spot. Limitless resources are available for speakers to support, embellish, and enliven their presentations. The larger challenge may be in sifting through the mounds of information you will dredge up in order to discover the precious nuggets of substance. Within seconds, you can access the world's largest library, the World Wide Web, and conduct research that not long ago would have taken weeks or even months. Now, with the use of technology, you are able to tap into formerly unimaginable sources.

THIRTEEN SOURCES FOR SPEECH CONTENT

The following are just a few teasers on where to begin your search, but keep in mind that the possibilities are infinite. Follow your imagination (just don't go exploring places you would not be willing to take your mother).

Before you plunge in, my apologies. This section gets a bit bookish. Useful, I hope, but slightly tedious. Try digesting it in bite-size morsels. Plod through it one section at a time (pinch yourself periodically if that helps you to stay alert), and revisit it whenever the spirit moves you—or when you become absolutely desperate for ideas. I promise you, it's valuable, so steel yourself and forge ahead.

1. NEWSPAPERS

Newspapers are an excellent source for current facts, statistics, and anecdotes for your presentations. Newspapers such as the *Chicago Sun-Times, New York Times, Wall Street Journal,* and *Washington Post* offer current, in-depth coverage of events affecting the world. The writing is typically lively, the perspectives are diverse, and the range of topics addressed is very broad.

Many newspapers are available online; for example, the URLs for those mentioned in the preceding paragraph are, respectively, www.suntimes .com, www.nytimes.com, www.wsj.com, and www.washingtonpost.com. These publications will automatically e-mail you breaking news. This helps ensure that you have the most current information on your presentation topic.

Here are a couple of exceptional news-related Web sites:

- LexisNexis (www.lexis.com) is an online service composed of more than seven hundred full-text databases, including a significant number of U.S. and international newspapers and up-to-the-minute information from such news wire services as Reuters and the Associated Press. Heed the warnings that a fee is involved, however; with a minimum of puttering around, you can incur a thousand dollars in fees. That's a pretty hefty price for very little fun and no party favors.

- The Newsroom (www.auburn.edu/~vestmon/gif/news.html) links to most leading newspapers and broadcast news organizations and contains excellent business and financial information.

2. MAGAZINES

Magazines such as *Fortune, Harper's, The New Republic, Newsweek, The New Yorker,* and *TIME* explore diverse topics in great depth, making them rich resources of thought-provoking material that you can weave into your presentations. You can research many magazines on the Web. See, for example:

- *BusinessWeek* (www.businessweek.com)
- *Computerworld* (www.computerworld.com)
- *IngentaConnect* (www.ingenta.com), which indexes more than 26,000 scholarly journals and magazines
- *Newsweek* (www.newsweek.com)
- *Scientific American* (www.scientificamerican.com)
- *TIME* (www.time.com)

3. TELEVISION

Television can be a rich source of data, if you overlook such rubbish as inane reality shows and insipid sitcoms. Transcripts from investigative reports (for example, *Dateline NBC,* CBS's *60 Minutes,* and ABC's *20/20*) and other excellent television broadcasts (the Discovery Channel, the History Channel) are frequently available online, sometimes without charge. Morningside Partners (www.fdch.com), formerly the Federal Document Clearing House, has many transcripts, audiotapes, and videotapes available for free. Other useful television Web sites include:

- www.abcnews.go.com
- www.cbs.com
- www.cnn.com
- www.c-span.org
- www.foxnews.com
- www.msnbc.com
- www.pbs.org

4. BOOKS

Books are a valuable source of ideas and issues every audience confronts: personal responsibility, courage, dealing with change, life's passages, and—most importantly—the trendiest diets. Consider such a classic book as Napoleon Hill's *Think and Grow Rich;* such popular business books as *Built to Last,* by James C. Collins and Jerry I. Porras, and *The 7 Habits of Highly Effective People,* by Stephen R. Covey; or such favorites with simple but poignant messages as *The Prayer of Jabez,* by Bruce Wilkinson, *The Five People You Meet in Heaven,* by Mitch Albom, or *It's Not About the Bike: My Journey Back to Life,* by Lance Armstrong and Sally Jenkins. And for simple lessons that will spark the interest of every audience, peruse children's books, such as those by *Dr. Seuss, Sesame Street,* or *Mister Rogers.*

You can find hundreds of thousands of books at local bookstores or online at Amazon (www.amazon.com) or Barnes & Noble (www.bn.com).

What one knows best is . . . what one has learned not from
books but as a result of books, through the reflections
to which they have given rise.

SÉBASTIEN CHAMFORT

----

5. ENCYCLOPEDIAS

Encyclopedias offer a wealth of information to beef up any presentation. Many encyclopedias are readily available online, free or by subscription, including *Encyclopaedia Britannica Online* (www.eb.com) and Microsoft *Encarta* (www.encarta.com). In addition to such general encyclopedias, there are many on specialized subjects, including the following:

- *Asian American Encyclopedia*
- *Encyclopedia of Medical History*
- *Encyclopedia of Philosophy*
- *Encyclopedia of Religion*
- *Encyclopedia of World Art*
- *Encyclopedia of World Crime*
- *Food and Nutrition Encyclopedia*
- *Latino Encyclopedia*
- *McGraw-Hill Encyclopedia of Science and Technology*

6. DICTIONARIES

You should always have an excellent dictionary at your fingertips when you prepare any speech. *The American Heritage Dictionary, Merriam-Webster's Collegiate Dictionary,* and the *Oxford English Dictionary* are all respected general-purpose dictionaries. Many have downloadable software to expedite your search. Such specialized dictionaries as *Black's Law Dictionary,* the *Computer Dictionary,* and *Word and Phrase Origins* are also very helpful.

There are dictionaries about virtually every subject: dictionaries of slang, bad manners, dates, symbols, statistics, feminism, business, economics, biographical information, and foreign languages. The best Web site to begin your search is one with links to over 800 dictionaries in 160 languages, found at www.yourdictionary.com. OneLook Dictionary Search (www.onelook.com) allows you to type in a word and then search the Internet for dictionaries containing the word. This site indexes approximately six million words—that ought to be enough to get you started.

---

*Consider not so much who speaks
as what is spoken.*
THOMAS FULLER

---

7. ALMANACS

Almanacs are an excellent source for information on a diverse range of topics, including education, law, politics, sports, and dates and events in history. Many almanacs are found on the Internet. The Infoplease site (www.infoplease.com) contains about seventy almanacs grouped by categories, and Refdesk (www.refdesk.com) links to over twenty almanacs.

8. INTERNET SEARCH ENGINES

You can find a wealth of information on the Web to aid you in preparing any presentation. This is both a blessing and a curse, since your search for a particular topic may generate several hundred thousand entries.

To avoid getting smothered with information, master the rudimentary skills of Internet research. If you do not have those skills (or a child in grade school who can teach you), consider taking a class at a local college or university, or buy *How to Use the Internet,* by Rogers Cadenhead, *The Internet for Dummies,* by John R. Levine, or a similar how-to book. These books will save you countless hours of frustration.

————

Knowledge is the food of the soul.
PLATO

————

Learn how to refine your searches so an inquiry does not unearth thousands of marginally related sites. You can use a wide variety of search engines, such as the following, to find the information you need:

- AltaVista (www.altavista.com)
- Excite (www.excite.com)
- Google (www.google.com)
- Northern Light (www.northernlight.com)
- WebCrawler (www.webcrawler.com)
- Yahoo! (www.yahoo.com)

Also try several metasearch engines, such as Dogpile (www.dogpile .com) and Metacrawler (www.metacrawler.com). These Web sites send your information request to numerous search engines at one time. One particularly useful site, where you can simply type in a question rather than a keyword, is Ask Jeeves (www.ask.com). For example, if you were looking for information on bungee jumping, you would simply type in "Where do I find information on bungee jumping?" Click the Search button, and Presto! Hundreds if not thousands of Web sites would appear that address your question (including several that might suggest a saliva test to gauge your sanity—but I digress).

9. INTERNET REFERENCE SITES

The Internet has many excellent reference sites:

- NewsLink (http://newslink.org) is a great source for radio and television broadcast information.

- Refdesk (www.refdesk.com), already mentioned under the "Almanacs" source above, provides hundreds of links to other reference sources such as dictionaries, thesauruses, news media, and magazines.

- UCI Libraries Research (www.lib.uci.edu) contains useful references with links to encyclopedias, dictionaries, and historical documents.

10. THE PUBLIC LIBRARY

My younger readers are scratching their heads and asking: "What's a library?" Yes, libraries still exist, and they are excellent resources for information on virtually any subject. Rummage around, and you will discover a wealth of ideas.

Moreover, they usually have reference librarians (who are occasionally grumpy and sometimes scary, but harmless), who can help steer your research in the right direction. Endear yourself to them (calling them "grumpy" probably will not help your cause), because these experts can save you countless hours of digging for information, and they often come up with ideas and sources that you might not have considered.

In the library—and online in many cases—you will find all the sources already identified, as well as valuable research tools including:

- *Bartlett's Familiar Quotations*
- *Biography Index*
- *The Guinness Book of World Records*
- *Information Please Almanac*
- *The New York Times Index*
- *The Reader's Guide to Periodical Literature*

Some [people] regard the library as a sinner regards church—
as a place to be entered in the most desperate circumstances.
STEPHEN E. LUCAS

---

11. ORGANIZATIONS

The library and the Blue and Yellow Pages of the telephone book provide listings of many civic, historic, trade, and government organizations that are delighted to provide you with valuable background information and literature, and of course, a membership application. Start your investigation looking under key words, such as "associations," "organizations," "fraternities," "clubs," and "Chambers of Commerce," and you will discover many promising leads.

12. A SPEAKER'S LIBRARY

Build a personal library filled with research tools that you can use when drafting and revising your speech. While some of these reference tools are found on the Internet, sometimes the selection online is more limited. Recommended reference sources for your personal library include:

- *Bartlett's Familiar Quotations,* by John Bartlett
- *The Chicago Manual of Style,* 15th edition
- *The Elements of Style,* 4th edition, by William Strunk, Jr., and E. B. White
- *Garner's Modern American Usage,* by Bryan A. Garner
- *Merriam-Webster's Manual for Writers and Editors*
- *The New Dictionary of Cultural Literacy: What Every American Needs to Know,* edited by James Trefil, Joseph F. Kett, and E. D. Hirsch
- *The Oxford Dictionary of Quotations,* edited by Elizabeth Knowles
- *Random House Webster's Quotationary,* edited by Leonard Roy Frank
- *Roget's International Thesaurus,* 6th edition, edited by Barbara Ann Kipfer, PhD

You should also own several books of great speeches, which you can find in the business or speaking sections of any bookstore. All these books will generate ideas as well as illustrate how exceptional speeches are crafted.

13. GOVERNMENT RESOURCES

If you are searching for obscure or esoteric information from the government, such as studies, reports, bulletins, trivia, and miscellaneous gobbledygook, poke around on the following Web sites. Beware, however: Don't venture into these dreary sites without first gulping a triple jolt of java:

- The Federal Web Locator (www.infoctr.edu/fwl) links to all major U.S. government Web sites, including the sites for Congress, the FBI, the Department of Education, the FDA, the CDC, and the EPA.

- FedStats (www.fedstats.gov) provides statistics from over one hundred U.S. federal agencies.

- FedWorld (www.fedworld.gov) contains useful federal government information.

- State and Local Government on the Net (www.statelocalgov.net) links to all fifty state governments, as well as to selected cities and towns.

- *The Statistical Abstract of the United States* (www.census.gov/pub/statab/www) provides tables, statistics, and other information about life in the United States.

- *The World Factbook* (www.odci.gov/cia/publications/factbook), published annually by the U.S. Central Intelligence Agency, provides information about people, governments, economies, communication, and transportation from every country in the world.

Breathe! You made it through principle 5 without dozing off, although your eyes do look a little bleary. You might end up using only a fraction of what you discover while ransacking for information, but the range and depth of knowledge that you will gain during your quest will broaden your perspective, prepare you to answer questions, and enhance your confidence and credibility. Start sleuthing.

ANALYZE YOUR AUDIENCE
BEFORE YOU SPEAK

A speech is a solemn responsibility. The man who makes a bad thirty-
minute speech to 200 people wastes only a half hour of his own time.
But he wastes 100 hours of the audience's time—more than
four days—which should be a hanging offense.

—JENKIN LLOYD JONES

Why is it important to research your audience before you speak? (It had better be important, to warrant devoting an entire principle to it, right?) Here's why: Your typical audience member today has a microscopic attention span, about thirty seconds—forty-five on a really good day. I hate to burst your bubble if you are fancying the romantic notion that your listeners are riveted to your every word. Sorry, they are not.

But you can't blame them, because the competition for their attention is stiff. The lives of most of your audience members are stretched paper thin; they are juggling tight schedules, with crushing personal and professional demands on their time. While listening to you, each of them is simultaneously thinking about a variety of issues unrelated to your speech: "Will wispy Joey *finally* make the peewee football team (the sixth time is the charm, after all), or will his dreams be dashed once again?" "Will I have to spend hours trapped in horrendous rush-hour traffic, listening to sappy elevator music?" "Will the tyrants at Weight Watchers somehow bless the triple-butter biscuit I just gobbled down?" And if the idea of all that chatter and hubbub competing for their attention is not enough, the following assertion will really dismay you: Many people in your audience could probably point out numerous places they would rather be, and a dozen things they would rather be doing, than sitting in their uncomfortable seats listening to you.

So what does all that mean for you as the speaker? You had better know your audience and what they want to hear. And you had better give them exactly that—and give it to them quickly, too. Otherwise, they may hang around for a while during your talk, but not for long; by the forty-sixth second, they will be off and away, thinking about far more pressing personal matters.

This principle examines *why* you need to know your audience and *what* you need to know about them; principle 7 will give you some techniques on *how* to know your audience.

WHY YOU NEED TO KNOW YOUR AUDIENCE

Look at it from your audience's perspective: As they sit there, they are giving you their most precious commodity—their time. Waste that time at your peril. An audience resents a speaker who knows nothing about them, who is unprepared, who rambles aimlessly, who doesn't appreciate the gift of time he or she has been given, and who brazenly squanders that gift. A speaker who commits these transgressions sends a clear message to everyone listening: "I'm important, but you and your time are not. Deal with it." Do that too often, and your speaking prospects will shrivel up—fast.

Suppose you are advocating a zoning variance at a neighborhood planning meeting. You are the big enchilada of Boffo Builders, and you need the variance so you can begin construction of your dream project: a sewage treatment facility (some people have peculiar dreams). Your crack attorney has pondered and churned this issue for weeks and finally advised you, for a legal fee that would purchase a small yacht, that, by golly, you are legally entitled to the variance.

Still, you have no desire for a nasty, costly dispute with the proactive neighborhood group, who—Surprise!—prefers that you build the sewage plant anywhere else (for instance, in your lawyer's neighborhood). You prefer to resolve this amicably, by engendering goodwill with the neighbors (well, as much goodwill as anyone plunking down a sewage plant in the neighbors' backyard can expect).

There are some who speak one moment before they think.
JEAN DE LA BRUYÈRE

Unfortunately, rather than studying and understanding your audience's perspective, you, being the wily advocate that you are, decide to rely solely on the strength of your legal arguments when addressing the neighborhood zoning board. You spout legal mumbo jumbo: "The legal precedent for unfettered construction of sewage plants on every street corner was first set in 1876 in the case . . . *blah, blah, yammer, yammer.*" But something promptly goes amiss, and your listeners become surly. They shake their heads in disagreement, lock their jaws, and glare menacingly. You begin to fear for your safety. Round one in the titanic sewage plant struggle goes to the homeowners. Why?

You did not know your audience. If you had bothered to nose around before you spoke, you would have discovered that the planners were wary because a previous builder had lied to them. You might also have learned that it was just one or two instigators from the neighborhood who were fueling the flames of discontent (and they own a port-a-potty company). Perhaps you could have earned the confidence of the planners if you had addressed their concerns, defused or neutralized some of their hostility, or focused your talk on the advantages of a sewage facility (increased tax revenue, more jobs, surplus yard fertilizer—okay, I'm grasping here).

A presentation based on law and logic might have been entirely appropriate for a different, more receptive, less emotional group. But your legal and technical arguments were doomed to fail with these planners, because of their peculiar circumstances: the previous lying builder and the couple of instigators with their own hidden agenda. Unfortunately, you needed to uncover those critical details *before* the presentation, not after you finished. Once you are in the midst of the maelstrom, with your agitated listeners spewing invectives and hurling books and drinks at you, it's too late. At that point, you can only duck and pray.

In a conversation, keep in mind that you're more interested in what you have to say than anyone else is.
ANDREW S. ROONEY

The bottom line is simple: Know your audience. Before you can tailor your presentation to your audience's interests, you must get to know them by answering the questions below. No one can *make* them listen to you, and if you don't lure them in, they won't. It is up to you to make them *want* to listen. If you are only guessing about their backgrounds, experiences, interests, and concerns, you are simply rolling the dice. And the chances are excellent that you will guess wrong.

WHAT YOU NEED TO KNOW
ABOUT YOUR AUDIENCE

All right, you think that maybe you ought to get to know your audience a little better. What do you want to know about them? Everything—but since knowing "everything" might be somewhat overwhelming (not to mention intrusive), let's use the tips in principle 7 to focus on finding answers to a few demographic, philosophical, and psychological questions, such as the following:

- What is the size of your audience? The dynamics of speaking at an intimate gathering in a conference room are far different from those of speaking in a civic center jammed to the rafters with bodies.

- What is the ethnicity of your listeners? Do they share a collective heritage and a sense of ethnic pride? Do they share customs, culture, language, or history?

- What is the economic status of your listeners? Are they living in poverty, comfort, or luxury? Listeners will be more receptive to a message that demonstrates an understanding of and sensitivity to their economic conditions. For example, college students sustaining themselves on canned Spam and KooKoo cupcakes will not relate to some filthy-rich windbag huffing and puffing about his stock portfolio and his "cottage" in the Hamptons.

- Are your listeners there voluntarily, because they are genuinely interested in your topic, or are they required to attend your presentation by the bigwigs? That makes a huge difference.

- What group affiliations do your listeners have, such as social, golf, or tennis clubs, university alumni clubs, political parties, sororities or fraternities, civic organizations, professional associations, or religious affiliations? Members of the Sierra Club would react far differently than would a group of petroleum executives to a presentation on increasing oil exploration in wilderness regions.

- Do your listeners share common values and beliefs that are consistent with your message, or will your speech challenge or threaten their values and beliefs?

- What is your audience's attitude toward you and your topic: receptive or hostile, interested or indifferent? Do they have inflexible opinions that will prevent them from really listening to you?

- Do members of your audience have a hidden agenda?

- Will your message rankle anyone in your audience because of its controversial, religious, or political content? The mere mention of such words as "abortion" or "gun control" (or maybe "sewage plants") will cause some people to bristle.

- Have previous speakers addressed your topic? If so, does your slant support or contradict the position of those speakers? Does your presentation offer a new perspective?

- What do your listeners *expect* to hear? What do they *want* to hear? What do they *need* to hear?

- What is the average age of your listeners? Why is that important? Because if your message is centered on a historical event that occurred before your listeners were born (the Cuban Missile Crisis or Captain Kangaroo's exploits, for instance), you will need to explain that event in more detail. Conversely, your message involving the latest rage in body piercing and tattooing might be lost on your audience of senior citizens unless you give them some background. If you don't consider your listeners' average age, expect looks of bewilderment.

- Are your listeners familiar with the issues you will be addressing? Don't waste time belaboring what they already know, and, conversely, don't talk about some esoteric issue that will whiz right over their heads.

- What is the general education level of your listeners? Will they understand the industry-specific, scientific, or technical terminology you may be using? Don't try to impress them with pretentious terms, because that is just as likely to baffle them. And ask yourself, for the sake of simple clarity, do you *really* need to use jargon, euphemisms, or pompous language even if they do understand it?

- Finally, to summarize, what are the real-life experiences and concerns of your listeners?

Once you have all this information—and principle 7 will provide tools to help you find it—you can decide what is important to your listeners, what motivates them, and how you might persuade them. Then you can tailor your talk in the most productive way. Does this mean that you should skirt controversial issues, or kowtow to your listeners? No, but it does mean that you had better be well prepared. Anticipate their reactions, and craft your presentation with all the potential risks and benefits in mind.

I once heard an abominable speech by a pasty civil servant in which he droned on for an hour (though it seemed like an eternity plus a day to every unfortunate soul in his audience) about the proper way to complete a twenty-five-page procurement proposal for a government contract. Beyond being dreadfully boring, the speech was crammed with dense terminology and obscure acronyms that few in his audience understood, and few were up for the challenge of trying to understand. His audience was composed of predominantly ambitious Internet entrepreneurs who had zero interest in listening to his irrelevant topic.

It was apparent that his listeners were detached and stupefied. I am sure I heard someone from the back of the room plead, "Please, please make him stop!" Many were talking on cell phones, others were reading *Fast Company* or the *Wall Street Journal,* and still others were toying with their BlackBerrys. Meanwhile, up at the podium, the hack trudged along, but no one was listening. His mistake? He had failed to assess his audience before speaking, and it seemed clear that he knew nothing—or cared nothing—about them. He was probably still humming along when they shut off the lights; I didn't stick around to find out.

Every fact depends for its value on how much we already know.
RALPH WALDO EMERSON

I know what you're thinking: "Gosh, this sounds like a lot of work!" It is, but it makes a bloody big difference. When you tailor your presentation to your audience, you are far more likely to be persuasive and achieve the results you desire, and your audience is far less likely to vote with their feet and bolt for the exits during your talk. Invest the time necessary to get to know your audience and reap the enormous benefits.

PRINCIPLE 7

USE THESE TOOLS TO KNOW YOUR AUDIENCE

I keep six honest serving-men
(They taught me all I knew);
Their names are What and Why and When
And How and Where and Who.

—RUDYARD KIPLING

As a speaker, you want your listeners to go where you want them to go, to see what you want them to see, and ultimately to agree with or, at the very least, thoughtfully consider your conclusions. But that is not always easily accomplished. Why? Because your listeners may not be hearing or processing the information the way you would like them to. They may not get it the way you intended. And bludgeoning them with your message, grousing that they are buffoons, or even holding your breath until you turn blue will not help.

You are dealing with human beings with preconceptions; they hear your message through the filters of their experiences and expectations. This means that they typically hear only what they want to hear, and they disregard the rest. So they are very likely to veer off the course you have charted for them:

> [People] usually want to hear about things that are meaningful to them. People are *egocentric.* They pay closest attention to messages that affect their own values, their own beliefs, their own well being. Listeners typically approach speeches with one question uppermost in mind. "Why is this important to *me?*" [1]

52

It can be daunting to determine what is important to an audience, because each audience is different. But determining what is important is your task, so keep it in mind at all times. If you talk about only what matters to *you* and focus on only *your* perspective, you cannot expect your audience to concur with your conclusions or even tag along as you make your points. To be an effective speaker, you need to anticipate your listeners' interests, likes, dislikes, ambitions—the whole shebang. Let them know that you understand their perspective and their concerns. Sharpen your focus, and tailor every presentation to your listeners. It will make a huge difference.

EIGHT TIPS ON RESEARCHING YOUR AUDIENCE

Instead of wailing and gnashing your teeth about this challenge ("Gee, more work?"), or blindly throwing darts and hoping that something you say might pertain, act like a private investigator (all right, strap on a cap gun and pin on a badge if you must), and start researching. Before you begin crafting your speech, you need to find answers to the questions posed in principle 6. The following profitable tips will help you find those answers:

1. SEND A PREPRESENTATION QUESTIONNAIRE

Here is a novel concept: If you want to know what is important to your listeners, ask them. Insightful, right? Months before the event, send a prepresentation questionnaire to the organization or association where you will be speaking. Tailor your questions to the purpose of your talk. Ask prospective audience members to complete the questionnaire and return it to you. Make it easy for them by allowing them to complete and submit the information by e-mail. Assure them that their responses will be kept anonymous if you want to enhance participation.

Not everyone will respond, so don't get your feelings hurt. But any kernel of insight can help you gauge their knowledge, interests, and expectations regarding the presentation. That is a huge step on the road to understanding your listeners.

2. Explore the Organization's Web Site

Most organizations and associations have a Web site that is a gold mine of information. It typically contains a flowery letter from the CEO or president, a mission statement, the company's vision, current company news, press releases, and other valuable tidbits that you can blend into your speech. Just as important, you might discover the political quagmires you should skirt in your speech—company downsizing, pending federal investigations, or setbacks for the company's golf team.

3. Search the Internet

Thanks to the World Wide Web, precious information is at your fingertips, including many recent newspaper and magazine articles and press reports (principle 5). Explore away on Google, Yahoo!, or your Internet search engine of choice. Hoover's Online (www.hoovers.com) has current and historical information on thousands of companies. The Internet Public Library's Census Data and Demographics Reference (www.ipl.org/div/subject/browse/ref24.00.00/) gives demographic profiles of people based on country, state, county, city, and zip code. The U.S. Census Bureau *Gazetteer* (www.census.gov/cgi-bin/gazetteer) makes it easy for you to customize a search for demographic information based on zip codes. Finally, the Better Business Bureau Web site (www.bbb.org) contains profitable historical information on more than two million businesses and charities.

Every great work is the fruit of patience,
perseverance, and concentration.
Santiago Ramón y Cajal

---

4. Review Company Literature

Obtain copies of programs or handouts from any recent meetings if available (brochures from an annual meeting are a great starting point), as well as a preliminary draft of the agenda for the event where you will speak. If the organization has a newsletter or an e-zine, request copies of the past few issues. Some of these materials may be available at the company's Web site. These sources will provide current, relevant information you can use fruitfully in your presentation.

5. ANALYZE SHAREHOLDER REPORTS

Quarterly and annual shareholder reports contain the lowdown about a company's philosophy and culture. You may doze off as you pore over portions of this mind-numbing information, but try to stay alert, because it can be valuable digging. And a word of caution: These reports are often written euphemistically, to paint a rosy picture. There is probably an untold story between the lines, so review this information with a skeptical eye.

6. INSPECT PUBLIC RECORDS

There is a prodigious—some might even say frightening—amount of information in the public records on many individuals and most organizations: news articles; reports filed with governmental agencies, including filings with the Securities and Exchange Commission; pending litigation; or outstanding judgments. Root around to identify current developments, the influential representatives of the organization (CEO, president, chief financial officer), and the company's position on various issues. You can find much of this information online, in the county courthouse records, in the public library, and in the Library of Congress.

7. INTERVIEW YOUR HOST

Buy your host, or some knowledgeable insider with the organization or association where you will speak, a bagel, a cup of coffee, or a scoop of Cookie Dough ice cream, and interview him. Many corporations and associations have a public relations coordinator, who can provide you with a wealth of information. Start there.

Be focused and precise in your inquiries. Don't start racking your brain for questions while your interviewee is fidgeting before you, drumming his fingers, rolling his eyes, and anxiously anticipating the end of the meeting. Be prepared, with a tight agenda and specific questions.

Emphasize how important this information is to the success of your presentation. Typically, the person you interview has a vested interest in providing you with this information, since your presentation will also be a reflection on him or her. Subtly mention: "If I flop, we both flop" (or something perhaps a tad more diplomatic, but you get the point).

He is considered the most graceful speaker who
can say nothing in [the] most words.
SAMUEL BUTLER

---

8. INTERVIEW AUDIENCE MEMBERS

If possible, talk to some of the influential audience members (the CEO, a director, the president, or the true oracle of most organizations: the receptionist). Interview them using the questions in principle 6. Ask them about the most important issues facing the company, such as what the company could do to improve employee loyalty or morale, what the employees like most about working for the company, and how the company differs from its competitors. This information will not only help you customize your speech; it will also bestow upon you the added cachet of being an insider and a member of the team.

Be careful not to use information that might embarrass or offend anyone. When in doubt, take it out. If you use it sensibly, however, the information you gather in this interviewing process will add interest, credibility, and perhaps a splash of humor to your speech.

So, there is the task and the starting point. Completing the task will require some plain old hard work and a dollop of gumption, but rest assured that your listeners will be flattered that you have customized your comments for them. Get into their heads and answer their critical question: "What is in this for me?" Listeners are remarkably perceptive, and they will quickly spot, and appreciate, a prepared speaker. Make sure that is the conclusion they form about you.

PRINCIPLE 8

ADOPT FROM THE BEST SPEAKERS

Example, the surest measure of instruction.

—PLINY THE YOUNGER

Here is a bit of advice that may sound like pure heresy: Disregard what you learned as a child, and become a relentless copycat. Steal (okay, stop squirming, "imitate" if that eases your conscience) techniques from the best speakers, and make them yours. Don't just do this occasionally; do it constantly, shamelessly, and proudly. Look for anything you can use to sharpen your speaking skills, from minor tweaks to sweeping changes. It is perfectly acceptable to do this. Alarms will not sound, and even your clergy would approve.

Why copy? To dramatically accelerate your progress. Emulate, and you will not only enhance your skills as a speaker, but just as important, you will avoid many speaking snafus, those painful goofs that can bruise your fragile speaking psyche. If you are resisting the idea of copying because you are intoxicated with your speaking prowess, sober up (and review principle 3). Even exceptional speakers can get better; they constantly work to improve their presentations, and you should, too.

Brian Tracy, a prominent professional speaker, credits much of his speaking success to studying others:

The key to success is to learn from the experts. Study and copy the very best people in your field. Do what they do, day after day, until it becomes second nature. And then, Surprise! Surprise! You will begin to get the same results.[1]

Your ultimate goal is to develop a speaking style that fits you now and that will evolve with you over the years, a style that makes you the most effective, authentic, and compelling speaker you can be.

Don't wring your hands about borrowing from others, because no two speakers are alike, and there is no one perfect speaking template that applies to every speaker. Even if you adopt *every* technique a certain speaker uses, you will never be able to exactly replicate that speaker's style. Virtually every aspect of your delivery—the cadence, timing, pausing, intonation, vocal energy, movement, body language—will be different. Not only that, certain techniques that work for others may fail miserably for you.

Better be wise by the misfortunes of others than by your own.
AESOP

For example, consider two exceptional professional speakers, Paul Harvey and Anthony Robbins. It would be hard to find two more diverse speaking styles. Mr. Harvey cajoles and soothes, while Mr. Robbins thunders and rants. Mr. Harvey would hardly seem genuine, and would probably look absurd, bounding around the stage like a whirling dervish, thumping his chest, exhorting the audience to jump about wildly, and slapping hands with perfect strangers. In fact, he might hurt himself if he tried. But that is Mr. Robbins's unique style. At the same time, Mr. Robbins would not seem authentic planted in one spot, relying on Mr. Harvey's easy, folksy manner, replete with dramatic pauses, titillating stories, and frequent surprises. His audiences would suspect that he had been sedated. Each speaker, however, excels with what works for him. Experiment using some of their techniques—just be careful not to bruise yourself.

Study other speakers, and ask probing questions about them and their speeches:

- Does the speaker seem to be authentic, or does she seem phony?
- Does he project confidence, or does he exude fear?
- Does she talk *to* you, or does she simply talk *at* you?
- Does he move fluidly, or does he seem as stiff as one of NASA's robots?
- Is her delivery natural, or is it disjointed and choppy?
- Is his pacing so fast that he jabbers, or so slow that he drags?
- Are her words precise and vivid, or is the speech riddled with jargon and pretentious language?
- Are his descriptions and stories fresh and engaging, or are they hackneyed and lackluster?
- Are the theme and points concise, or is the speech just a big blob of words?
- Is her organization tight, or does it veer around like a yo-yo?
- Does he smoothly segue from point to point, or does he lurch along?
- Does she seem passionate, or does she seem apathetic?
- Does he sound pleasing, or does he sound strident, shrill, and unnatural?
- Does she engage you, or does she bore you?

EIGHT POWERFUL SPEAKING TECHNIQUES

If you want to emulate the best, begin by studying the speech that many experts consider to be one of the finest of all time: "I Have a Dream"[2] by Dr. Martin Luther King, Jr. He delivered it from the steps of the Lincoln Memorial in Washington, DC, on August 28, 1963, to more than two hundred thousand people. The speech is packed with outstanding lessons.

It is a masterpiece, both because of the way it was crafted and because of the manner in which Dr. King delivered it. To fully appreciate the artistry of this speech, you should study a tape of it. Simply reading the words, though instructive, does injustice to Dr. King's eloquent delivery. His speech illustrates at least eight exceptional speaking techniques:

1. IMAGERY

Dr. King used descriptive phrases, such as "a great beacon light of hope," "flames of withering injustice," and "crippled by the manacles of segregation and the chains of discrimination." He created vivid pictures that each audience member could clearly visualize, and precise images make any speech more memorable.

Genius . . . is the child of imitation.
SIR JOSHUA REYNOLDS

---

2. METAPHOR

Dr. King relied on metaphors throughout his speech. Expressions such as "down in Alabama, with its vicious racists, with its governor having his lips dripping with the words of interposition and nullification" and a "lonely island of poverty in the midst of a vast ocean of material prosperity" breathed heart and soul into the speech. These graphic metaphors intensified his message by providing physical examples of the raw emotions he was expressing.

3. ALLITERATION

Through the adroit use of repeated consonant sounds, such phrases as "the bank of justice is bankrupt," "marvelous new militancy," and "they will not be judged by the color of their skin, but by the content of their character" made the message rhythmic and poetic.

4. VOCAL ENERGY

Listen to a recording of the speech, and study how Dr. King used his voice—the inflection, the vitality, the variation in his highs and lows—to convey his emotions and engage the listeners. He used his voice masterfully to express his passion and conviction about his topic. Unquestionably, this heightened the impact of his words.

5. REPETITION

To further heighten the impact, Dr. King repeated such phrases as "now is the time," "let freedom ring," and, of course, "I have a dream." These phrases forcefully emphasized the theme of his speech, especially as the intensity of his delivery built with each repetition.

All great speakers were bad speakers at first.

RALPH WALDO EMERSON

---

6. RHYTHM

The carefully selected language in the speech created a rhythm of expression. The following selections are prime examples of this: "We cannot be satisfied as long as a Negro in Mississippi cannot vote and a Negro in New York believes he has nothing for which to vote" and "we will be able to work together, to pray together, to struggle together, to go to jail together, to stand up for freedom together. . . ."

7. PAUSES

Dr. King paused repeatedly throughout the speech—when he delivered key passages, when he made transitions from point to point, and when the crowd was applauding. This focused the attention of his listeners on the point he was about to make or had just made. It also allowed the listeners time to process the message.

8. AUDIENCE CONNECTION

To forge a strong connection with his audience, Dr. King used the word "we" throughout the speech. Such phrases as "we have come to this hallowed spot," "we can never be satisfied," and "when we let freedom ring" created a sense of inclusiveness between Dr. King and his audience.

––––––––

We are, in truth, more than half what we are by imitation.
The great point is, to choose good models and
to study them with care.
LORD CHESTERFIELD

––––––––

To find great speeches, rummage around the Internet as well as in your local library, bookstore, or video store. Analyze videos, ranging from the basics on how to make a persuasive speech, to the greatest speeches of all time.

Surf the Web, and you will also discover a variety of exceptional speeches on an array of topics, both historic and current. To watch these videos, you need software such as RealPlayer or Apple's Quicktime, which you can download free. Go to the Web site Rhapsody & RealPlayer (www.real.com) or Apple-Quicktime-Download (www.apple.com/quicktime/download/win.html), and follow the prompts for downloading. The History Channel speech archive (www.historychannel.com/speeches) has the speeches of such prominent figures as Amelia Earhart, Winston Churchill, John F. Kennedy, and Malcolm X. FedNet (www.fednet.net) provides real-time as well as archived presentations.

Watch the television evangelists on Sunday morning. Analyze their body language, gesturing, storytelling, vocal variety, pacing, and dramatic pausing (but be careful not to get seduced into a tithing frenzy). Study the man standing on the park bench, raging about our decadent lifestyles, as well as the candidate, wheedling voters with grandiose promises. The world is your speaking laboratory, and you just never know where you will find inspiration.

Keep company with those who make you better.
ENGLISH PROVERB

Be a shameless copycat. You will not turn into a pillar of stone if you "emulate," "copy," "borrow from," or "mimic" exceptional speakers. Become a critic and a sponge, absorbing techniques from every speaker you hear; be constantly vigilant for anything that will help you improve. Cultivate role models. There are all kinds of speakers and all kinds of techniques. Fiddle endlessly until you find the paragon that works for you. Do you want to become your best? Then adopt from the best.

PART III

BUILD WITH A BLUEPRINT

I F YOU ARE A PROCRASTINATOR stimulated by a deadline—that is, if you budget about eight minutes to draft your speech in the car on the way to your speaking engagement—this truism may jolt you: Exceptional speeches are *never* created in a single draft—ever. Sorry, but even the finest speakers wrestle with their texts. More likely than not, your initial stab at the speech will be plagued with faults: tortured logic, circular construction, cluttered language, and obscure jargon . . . and that is on a good day.

---

*You've got to be very careful if you don't know where
you are going, because you might not get there.*
YOGI BERRA

Exceptional speeches don't just tumble out of your head or come up and bite you on the bottom. They are carefully planned, meticulously drafted, and repeatedly refined. They share one common characteristic: uncompromising attention to detail. Excellent speeches are constructed with solid building blocks, which include a clear theme, logical organization, a captivating opening, precise sentences, vivid imagery, colorful language, engaging stories, and a dynamic closing.

As you craft and edit your speech, decide whether you are saying what you want to say in the most compelling manner. Ask yourself one simple question at every stage: "Will my listeners *want* to listen to this?" Be brutally honest. If the answer is no, grab your editing pen, because you will not get a second chance to make a favorable impression. Part III provides the blueprint for building a memorable presentation.

STATE YOUR PURPOSE

He is one of those orators of whom it is well said,
"Before they get up, they do not know what they are going to say;
when they are speaking, they do not know what they are saying;
when they sit down, they do not know what they have said."

—WINSTON CHURCHILL

The caffeine is flowing through your veins, and you are ready to write your speech. You have read Part II (you didn't skip ahead, did you?) and carefully followed the guidelines. Your shoebox of speech material is brimming with clippings, notes, random thoughts, and insightful snippets that you have squirreled away for this speech, and you are sure you know the audience like you do a good friend. Even better, the ideas are floating around in your noodle, and you are raring to go. But, before you draft your first word, answer this one pressing question:

What's your point?

You muse: "To write a speech?" "To make a report?" "To please my boss, who actually expects me to say something meaningful?" All true, perhaps, but dig deeper. Never lose sight of the reason why you are speaking—a simple rule that mediocre speakers regularly flout. You should always be able to state in one concise sentence: "My purpose in speaking is _____" (this is the part where you fill in the blank). If you cannot state your purpose so succinctly that you could write it on the back of a business card, then maybe, just maybe, you don't know the point of your talk. And, rest assured, your evident failure to know it *will not* please your boss or your audience.

If you don't know your point, watch out, because you are sliding down the slippery slope of Murky Thinking, plunging head first toward Utter Confusion. You will barrage your listeners with minute details, or you will ramble aimlessly from topic to topic, creating a hodgepodge of random thoughts. The befuddled audience members will impatiently mutter, "Sheesh, where in the world is this going?" At best, your message will be severely diluted; at worst, utterly ineffective.

What's the point of coming to the point when you don't have *a point?*
JOHN R. TRIMBLE

Cavett Robert, an exceptional speaker and the founder of the National Speakers Association, used a wonderful expression that precisely summarizes the importance of making your purpose clear: "If it's foggy in the pulpit, it's foggy in the pews." If the message is not clear to you, it will not be clear to your audience. Sometimes the fogginess is so maddening you just want to leap from your seat and shout, "My kingdom for a point . . . any point!" When that happens—and, with many speakers, it happens far too frequently—the audience will straggle off in search of another speaker, one who can be clear. And they will not easily be lured back.

Why are so many speakers unfocused? There are several plausible— but unacceptable—explanations.

Perhaps the speaker is attempting to establish his expertise by smothering his listeners with information. Such a strategy is never productive, because his listeners cannot and will not process an avalanche of words. They will just shut down. Too many details are just as confusing as too few; an effective, focused speaker provides the pertinent facts but not every tiny factoid.

Perhaps the speaker is unprepared, and she has deluded herself into thinking that she can dazzle her listeners by speaking "off the cuff." Doubtful. She would have to be amazingly good to do that, and most of us are not amazingly good when speaking "off the cuff." You seldom hit your target with this haphazard approach. You typically lose your bearings early in the speech, and then you soon notice—if you are looking, that is—the puzzled looks of your listeners.

Sometimes a speaker is unclear because he has failed to clarify his purpose in his own mind; he just doesn't know what he wants to say. He hopes that if he yammers long enough, his listeners may grope around until *they* somehow understand the purpose. As a result, what should be clear, informative, and persuasive is often jumbled, obscure, and disappointing.

Finally, there is the speaker who is intentionally vague, to diffuse opposition or to mask her position. If she could honestly explain it to you, she might say, "Being vague is the only refuge I have—my smoke screen. . . . Vagueness lets me get by with sort-of-understanding, and it disarms you a bit, since you'll have difficulty knowing where you disagree with me."[1]

---

*I love talking about nothing, Father. It is
the only thing I know anything about.*
OSCAR WILDE

One of the senior partners at my first law firm used to listen to each of the neophyte attorneys advocate a position. I can still remember the pensive pause at the end of one of my dismal, meandering presentations. Finally, after clearing his throat, he began his critique. His scathing words wilted me and to this day still send shivers down my spine: "I've just heard a lot of fuzzy-headed thinking in this room." This is an apt litmus test for any speaker. Ask yourself: "Am I fuzzy-headed about my reason for speaking?"

How can you enhance the prospect that your audience will grasp your message? Simple: Be clear. Not to be flippant, but it really is not much more complicated than that. Make your theme clear from the outset. Give your audience direction. In the first minute of your presentation, tell them what you intend to accomplish. Help them understand;

don't make them guess (because usually they guess wrong) or work too hard to decipher your meaning (because usually they won't work at all).

Say you lived in Orlando, and you wanted to drive to Des Moines, but you had never driven there before. (All right, choose a different destination if Des Moines doesn't get your juices flowing.) Would you embark by simply packing the car, crossing your fingers, and heading off into the great unknown ("Maybe I will drive due west for a bit, then I will head north for a while . . . ")? Would you stubbornly press forward even if your path were leading you directly to the middle of nowhere? I hope not. And most of the passengers in your traveling party would be worried about your adventuresome approach; they would prefer to know that you had a precise plan, or maybe even a map guiding you.

Audiences are no different from your passengers (in fact, they *are* your passengers): They want to know where you are headed, and they want to know it quickly. You need to provide your listeners direction.

Men of few words are the best men.
WILLIAM SHAKESPEARE

LIMIT YOUR POINTS

After you have clarified your purpose, distill your message to just those points that are essential for supporting your theme.

One aspiring politician began a campaign speech with this startling pronouncement: "There are *twenty* reasons why I deserve your vote." The audience laughed awkwardly, no doubt hoping that he was simply engaging in hyperbole. He was not. Thirty minutes into the presentation, after he had covered the fifth reason, it was obvious that he intended to discuss all twenty reasons in excruciating detail. He lost the audience that day, and he ultimately lost the election—probably because the voters feared they would have to listen to another one of his rambling speeches.

There are no categorical rules on how many points you should include to support your primary theme. That depends on such factors as the amount of time you have to speak, the relative importance of each point, and your audience's interest level and knowledge of your topic. Clearly, twenty points are far too many; no audience will stay focused for the time it would take to develop so many ideas. Keep this thought in mind: In the entire history of speaking, only a handful of audiences have ever complained that a presentation was too short. Let that be your ultimate guide.

Don't drown yourself in details.
FERDINAND FOCH

Just because you know everything about your topic does not mean that you should bore your listeners with every detail. Tell them only what they need to know, that which affects them, and eliminate the rest. And don't try to squeeze in more information by simply talking faster. That strategy undermines your professional image and credibility.

Never lose sight of your purpose in speaking as you draft and revise your speech. Weed out any cluttered thinking or random thoughts— even the witty ones if they sidetrack you. Know exactly what you want to accomplish with your speech. Eliminate all "fuzzy-headed thinking," so that when you step up to the lectern, you will be clear.

ORGANIZE FOR COHERENCE

Order and simplification are the first steps
toward mastery of a subject.

—THOMAS MANN

The rules of speaking are constantly evolving; what was forbidden yesterday is acceptable today. There are simply very few immutable maxims. Nevertheless, here is one: *Be organized.* Your stories might be interesting, your delivery might be energetic, and you might just be an unbelievably charming person (stop puffing out your chest)—but if your speech is disorganized, you will not be effective.

This rule may cause a hissy fit among some speakers and an outright conniption among others, those who just like to "wing it," confident that they are "at their best when they just talk." Sorry, they are not. With *rare* exceptions, a disorganized presentation is typically mediocre and sometimes appallingly bad. As the speaker staggers around in a mental fog, the audience is more often baffled than enlightened. It is not enough just to be an expert on your topic; you must be able to convey your expertise in an understandable fashion. Allow me to illustrate.

During a jury trial, one of the lawyers was woefully disorganized; every one of his presentations was a labyrinthine tangle of random thoughts. Ironically, he knew the facts and the law better than anyone else in the courtroom, but his inability to convey that information in a coherent fashion to both the judge and the jury undercut his case.

As he shuffled documents and fitfully zigzagged from point to point, he repeatedly apologized for his lack of organization. Where the goal should have been clarity, confusion reigned. For a while, the jurors struggled mightily to comprehend his points (his floundering aroused their sympathy if nothing else), but their struggle was all in vain. They remained bewildered. Frustrated, they eventually stopped listening; they began doodling on their pads, counting ceiling tiles, and inspecting their fingernails to pass the time. The results were awful for his client (though excellent for mine).

Half the world is composed of people who have something
to say and can't, and the other half who have
nothing to say and keep on saying it.
ROBERT FROST

All right, we might as well get it out in the open: You must be organized, *and* it is a difficult task for many of us. It requires plain hard work:

> [Organization is not] the part where you roll right along, humming a merry tune as the words tumble over one another in their eagerness to get on the page. Writers seldom shout, "Boy, this outline is really cookin'!" . . . What's more, the effort that goes into organization is largely invisible. You'll never hear a reader say, "My, this (essay/letter/novel/report) is beautifully organized." The job may be a pain in the butt but it's thankless too.[1]

I know, I know: The "wing it" school of thought is looking better every second. Don't despair. Becoming organized is much easier if you have a plan, and—Look!—there are a few plans below. Mush on.

EIGHT WAYS TO ORGANIZE YOUR SPEECH

So, how do you go about structuring your speech? There are many options, and you do not need to be ridiculously rigid about your organization

("I have five major points, each containing three subpoints, and four sub-subpoints . . ."). The touchstone is always the same: "Is my message clear?" Here are a few excellent plans for organizing a speech:

1. TELL 'EM, TELL 'EM, TELL 'EM

Sister Teresa's words still ring in my ears: "Tell 'em, tell 'em, tell 'em!" (Perhaps my ears are also still ringing from her perpetually tugging on them as she dragged me to the time-out corner.) Anyway, she was right, as usual. Her rule is an excellent way to organize any speech. The opening of the speech is an introduction that tells the audience what you will be telling them, the body actually tells them, and the closing is a summary that tells them what you have just told them—a simple, concise, and clear format. This is a proven method for structuring your thoughts.

[A person] who forms a judgment on any point but
cannot explain it might do well never to have
thought at all on the subject.
PERICLES

---

2. TOPICAL ORGANIZATION

With topical organization, you address issues in a logical fashion based solely on—Surprise!—the topic. For example, if you were describing a camping adventure to Jellystone Park, you might break your talk into three topics: packing ordeals, the costs, and your exploits wrestling bears (go ahead and embellish). Lump all the relevant details into each appropriate major topic, discuss that topic, and then proceed to the next. Be careful not to bounce back and forth between and among topics (from packing your sleeping bag, to your fearless encounter with the bears, and then back to the chagrin you felt when you realized you forgot to pack your deodorant), or you will confuse your listeners.

3. PROBLEM AND SOLUTION

As you might have guessed (and if you haven't, I am worried about you), you first explain the problem and then propose a solution. For example, if you were addressing the traffic congestion in your city, you would first denounce the problems (clogged roadways, accidents, loss of productivity, pollution, rampant hand signals being flashed among drivers) and then propose the solutions (carpooling, telecommuting, mass transportation, bicycle paths, prayers).

4. CAUSE AND EFFECT

Illustrate how an effect was caused by the cause (or how the cause caused the effect, for you active-voice purists). For instance, in explaining the decrease in Girl Scout cookie sales over the past few years, you could list all the contributing factors (stiff competition from the Cub Scouts, an appalling shortage of Thin Mints, less aggressive sales tactics) before ultimately explaining the effect (canceling the Girl Scout Jamboree, firing the Girl Scout troop leader).

Any man may speak truly; but to speak with order, wisely and competently, of that, few men are capable.
MICHEL DE MONTAIGNE

---

5. ADVANTAGE VERSUS DISADVANTAGE

This is a simple way to clarify your message. In essence, you draw a line down the middle of the paper and list the pros and cons of a particular decision. Either you list all the advantages first, followed by all the disadvantages, or you alternate back and forth, pairing each advantage with its corresponding disadvantage. Objectivity helps with this method: If you skew the facts excessively to favor your position, or if you ignore obvious alternatives, you undercut your credibility. (Shameless fact spinning usually backfires, unless you are a politician.)

6. ACRONYM

Constructing an easy-to-remember acronym from the initial letters of a group of words in your speech is an effective way both for you to organize your points and for your listeners to recall them. For example, Mr. Big Honcho, the CEO of a behemoth company, was addressing more than ten thousand company troops assembled at an annual meeting. Attempting to inspire them (in lieu of cash bonuses, apparently), he challenged them to exceed their accomplishments of the previous year by making *"BHAG"* their mantra for the upcoming year: "**Big Hairy Audacious Goals**." (This is the PG version of the letter *A*, but you get the point.) Using this road map, he proceeded to outline what he meant by **Big** (20 percent increase in sales); **Hairy** (thinking creatively); **Audacious** (securing dozens of new clients); and **Goals** (implementing personal, departmental, and company goals). While his message was clear, it was obvious that the employees would have preferred a *"BHAB"*: "Big Hairy Audacious *Bonus.*"

7. CHRONOLOGICAL ORGANIZATION

With this method of organization you convey details in the sequence in which the events occurred. Storytellers frequently use sequential order to tell a story from start to finish (principle 13). This is also the way we generally communicate, so it is easy for the audience to follow along as the speaker moves from point to point.

The following story illustrates chronological organization: "Little Davey Joe was determined to finally see Santa that year, and so he devised a plan. At 6:00 p.m. on Christmas Eve, he set the sugar cookies and chocolate milk at the base of the Christmas tree, slid behind the sofa, and began the stakeout. 7:00 p.m., no sign. 8:00 p.m., nothing—no reindeer, no Santa, no elves. He was sleepy but determined. At 8:30 p.m., he waged a fierce battle with his mother and fought off her attempts to coax him to bed. 9:00 p.m. It was just a matter of time, he thought, as he nodded off." I still believe in Santa.

8. Numbering and Grouping Points

Keep your listeners focused by telling them how many points you will be making. You might say, for example, "There are four reasons this proposition should be rejected: first, the cost; second, the safety issues; third, the inherent unreliability of the proposition; and finally, the better alternative—mine. Let's begin with reason one, the cost." Numbering also provides your listeners with signposts ("The *third* issue, inherent unreliability, is illustrated by . . ."), so that they know which point you are addressing.

I take the view . . . that if you cannot say what you have
to say in twenty minutes, you should go away
and write a book about it.
Lord Brabazon of Tara

Don't expect your audience to struggle to understand your message. Organize every speech so that your message flows logically and coherently. Guide your listeners with painstaking precision from point to point. A disorganized speech is built on a flimsy foundation. You can adorn such a speech with colorful words and lively stories, and even deliver it with heartfelt conviction, but your adornment and delivery will never remedy the speech's fundamental flaws. Get organized—it's the law.

PRINCIPLE 11

OPEN WITH A HOOK

*Unless a speaker can interest his audience
at once, his effort will be a failure.*

—CLARENCE DARROW

I ran track in high school. Our team was bad, and I was the worst. I have forgotten most of what I learned from this unpleasant period, but I do recall one nugget of wisdom. Crusty Coach Heengin would bellow and growl incessantly: "Explode out of the starting blocks, you sissies!" Sometimes we were "weenies," "wimps," or "weaklings" (and a few choice descriptions unfit for print), but his dictate never changed: "Explode!"

That is also your challenge as a speaker: to draft an opening that will cause you to *explode* out of the starting blocks and instantly create a thrilling buzz in your audience. Your opening is the most important part of the speech. A feeble one can contaminate your presentation, and a rotten one can ruin it. How about that for a little pressure? You have mere seconds to persuade your audience that you have an excellent message that warrants their fickle attention, so don't futz around.

With your first words, say something that snaps your listeners to attention and compels them to literally perch on the edge of their seats and think: "WOW! This is going to be exceptional!" Let your opening surprise, delight, and intrigue your listeners—occasionally even make them gasp—and they will stay with you for the rest of the journey. An exceptional opening will enhance the likelihood that they will not only *listen* to your message, but also—and this is critical—*hear* it.

I can hear you musing, "*Surely*, the listeners will tag along until I make a few points, right?" *Surely, they won't.* Your opening determines whether your audience will stampede toward the mental exits (or, worse, the real exits). If your opening does not entice them, they will be off and away. And an audience is a terrible thing to waste.

If the opening is crucial, why are so many openings as bland as oatmeal? They feel like a moist, limp handshake to the audience (no one enjoys that, do they?). Some are tired. Some are pure rubbish. And sometimes there is no opening at all: The speaker just starts droning or jabbering, plunking his listeners down somewhere on the winding speech trail, never giving them a clue about where they are going and how they will get there. Everyone, including the speaker, is discombobulated.

Immediately give your audience a compelling reason to listen—period.

I think the end is implicit in the beginning. It must be. If that isn't there in the beginning, you don't know what you're working toward. You should have a sense of a story's shape and form and its destination.

EUDORA WELTY

EIGHT OPENINGS TO AVOID

Before I identify some top-notch openings, I have to caution you about a few openings that are just real yawners—unimaginative, stale, and counterproductive. Here is a list of the usual suspects. If you feel an urge to begin your speech in any of the following ways, fight it.

1. AN ADMISSION

Never admit that you are unprepared, because it alerts the audience that your talk may be a waste of their time. Few things gut a speech more quickly. Save the confessions for the confessional. If you are not prepared to speak, do the best you can under the circumstances—then go to your room without supper.

2. An Apology

Bite your lip if you have the urge to apologize for your lack of speaking experience ("Who knows why they asked me to speak"); your anxiety ("Sorry, but speaking gives me the heebie-jeebies"); or the length of your speech ("Better get comfortable, folks, because this bombast is going to drag on for a while"). Your apology will seldom generate sympathy, understanding, or goodwill, so don't handicap yourself.

3. A Prolonged Opening

Some speakers spend a maddening amount of time *preparing* to speak *after* they are introduced (were they surprised that they would be speaking?). They adjust the lectern light; bang on the microphone and ask, "Is this on?"; methodically arrange and rearrange their notes; guzzle water; groom themselves; smooth their clothing; and check the time. Finally, they begin. Those moaning and hissing sounds are coming from the audience.

Your audience is evaluating you from the moment they first see you, so be ready to speak within seconds after you are introduced. Adjust, test, arrange, gulp, preen, smooth, and check long before you stand to speak.

4. Insincere Flattery

I once attended a black-tie banquet that was a disaster. For no apparent reason, the event began one hour late. The room was too hot, and the lights were too dim. The microphone regularly emitted shrill feedback, and the food was greasy, cold, and inedible. Nonetheless, the keynote speaker began, just as he had planned, fawning over the host: "Hasn't Jill done a marvelous job planning this special event?" His audience, of course, was prepared to bury Jill (alive), not praise her.

Jill might have appreciated the speaker's comments, but the miserable audience members concluded that the speaker was disingenuous.

Insincere flattery erodes your credibility and alienates your audience. Don't go there.

Once a word has been allowed to escape, it cannot be recalled.
HORACE

---

5. A CLICHÉ

Clichés tell the audience that your talk will be dreary and that you are not too finicky about how you express your ideas. Clichés are nothing more than convenient crutches for speakers. Such vapid, trite phrases as "comparing apples and oranges," "crystal clear," "fast and loose," "to make a long story short," and "pulled no punches" make hackneyed openings, and for that matter, they gum up any part of the speech. There is nothing creative or captivating about them, so prune them from your presentations. They are the "kiss of death," "if you catch my drift."

6. A JOKE

Unless your joke is *very* brief, *utterly* hilarious, and *directly* related to your topic (and most jokes pass none of those tests), save it for the next dinner party. The opening of your speech is not the time to hone your clunky skills as a stand-up comedian.

Why? A joke is way too risky. Maybe it's funny, but maybe it's not. Many jokes bomb and are greeted with throat-clearing silence or perplexed looks (the type of painfully awkward moments that will make you question your sanity for ever having agreed to speak). And it may confuse a few of the dullards ("Huh? I don't get it!"); you definitely don't want to have to explain it. Worst of all, your joke may offend someone (and audiences today have the thinnest of skins). Avoid these pitfalls.

Humor can add a little zing to most speeches, however, and there are better ways to be humorous than to stick a risky joke into the opening of your speech. To learn about injecting humor into your speech as a whole, see principle 14.

---

*There is all the difference in the world between having
something to say, and having to say something.*
JOHN DEWEY

---

7. AN EMBARRASSING STATEMENT OR ACT

Some speakers have intentionally stumbled as they approached the lectern, and then opened with a ridiculous comment: "I sure had a nice trip up here!" Some engage in pure nonsense, such as shooting a squirt gun or hurling confetti or foam balls into the crowd. These are excellent openings—in the circus. Leave them there.

8. A SHOCKING ACT

Here is the booby prize for the worst opening ever in the history of speaking. I would not have believed this, except that I was actually there (and no, I was not the speaker). The speaker's talk was to be about his experience running the Boston Marathon. Apparently he wondered: "What can I do to re-create the feel and excitement of the race?" Then he stumbled upon what he believed was an ingenius idea.

After being introduced, he walked to the front of the room, reached into the lectern, and abruptly hoisted above his head a starter's pistol— which looks and sounds like a real gun—and fired a blank. (If you've learned from this principle the importance of starting your presentation with a bang, please understand that this lamebrained opening is *not* what I meant.) The audience was at first stunned and frightened, and then they were furious. This dimwit had nearly re-created the feel and excitement of an angry lynch mob. If you choose to shock the audience in the opening, use a smidgen of common sense.

A good beginning hath a good ending.
JAMES HOWELL

FOUR PROVEN OPENINGS

So, now that we have examined and spurned several disastrous openings—
from wimpy apologies to bombing jokes to circus pratfalls and idiotic
stunts—let's explore some openings more likely to captivate an audience.
You need to hunt for one that is fresh, lively, and intriguing. Remember,
you have only seconds to prove yourself worthy of your listeners' attention. To open your speech, use the same formula that exceptional writers employ:

> If, at the very outset, a writer seems bored, unwilling to use his
> imagination, indifferent to his reader, and unclear in his think-
> ing, he's apt to remain that way. But if his opener reveals pas-
> sion, a clear perceptive mind, and a flair for drawing in the
> reader, the odds are he will stay true to form. . . . It's like a good
> comedy situation: it ignites.[1]

Where can you find an opening like that? Well, don't expect trumpets to magically blare, with the town crier heralding the arrival of the
perfect opening for you: "The opening is here, the opening is here—long
live the opening!" Like most inspirations, these brainstorms will typically come moseying along when you least expect it—when you are jog-
ging, driving, or even showering. Reflect on your topic, and be ever
vigilant. Ask yourself one question when drafting the opening of your
speech: "Will this intrigue my audience?" Here are four proven openings.

1. OPEN WITH A QUOTE

Why open with a quote? Because a pertinent, succinct quote will
seize the attention of your audience and add sparkle to your talk.

One savvy speaker opened a poignant presentation about risk taking by quoting that inimitable *Sesame Street* sage, Big Bird: "The tragedy
in life, Oscar, is not that it ends; it's that we wait too long to begin it."
Big Bird's discerning wisdom charmed this speaker's audience; they began
recalling times in their lives when they had procrastinated and missed

opportunities. The speaker had hooked the audience. Read more about the power of quotations in principle 15.

2. OPEN WITH AN INTRIGUING STATEMENT

Entice your listeners by saying something interesting or fascinating. Try something that will make them smile. I am easily amused, so a pithy opening like the following works for me:

> I've often wondered what goes into a hot dog. Now I know and I wish I didn't.[2]

Peruse literary classics for ideas, because exceptional writers are adept at snagging their readers' attention immediately. For example, consider what George Orwell wrote in the opening line from *1984:*

> It was a bright cold day in April, and the clocks were striking thirteen.

One of my law school professors (a humorless woman and an alumna of the World Wrestling Federation, I am pretty sure) opened her first lecture of the semester in this memorable way: "My name is Helga [name changed for author protection]. Look at the person sitting on your right. Now look at the person sitting on your left. One of them is going to fail my class." By opening with these terrorizing words, she had our undivided attention for the entire semester.

Begin with something interesting in your first sentence. Not the second. Not the third. The First! F–I–R–S–T! *First!*
DALE CARNEGIE

---

3. OPEN WITH AN ANECDOTE

Narrative works because we love stories (principle 13). Here is an example: "When I was three, my father died suddenly. We lived with my

Grandmother Valasek for several years while my mother found her way in life. Grandma was a stern woman, who kept a thick leather belt hanging behind the refrigerator to enforce the peace. She wasn't bashful about using it either. This iron-willed lady taught me three valuable lessons."

Crisp, concise, and relevant anecdotes will engage your audience and set the tone for your presentation. But, be brief. Avoid long or convoluted stories, because by the time you get to the point, your audience won't know, and won't care, what your point is.

4. OPEN WITH A QUESTION

Opening with a thoughtful question is a great way to captivate your listeners immediately as well as establish the theme of your speech. "If you could do it all over again, what would you change?" "How many of you would rather swallow worms than give a speech?" "Where do you stand on the great cookie debate: Snickerdoodle or oatmeal?" Your listeners will begin to contemplate the question and formulate their answers.

But when you ask your question, remember to pause and allow your audience to process it. I repeat: *Be sure to pause.* If you ask a question and then dash ahead without pausing, your listeners will necessarily conclude that you really don't care what they think, and they will ignore the question.

Create an opening that will propel you forward. Be selective. Never settle for something that just "works"—*explode* at the outset. Capture the hearts and minds of your audience with creativity, surprise, and suspense, and you will set the tone for a successful speech. But leave the starter's pistol at home.

REVISE, REVISE, REVISE

*Modern English, especially written English, is full of bad habits
which spread by imitation and which can be avoided
if one is willing to take the necessary trouble.*

—GEORGE ORWELL

I can hear you grousing (or are you whining?): "Ugh, this is going to be grimy, grunt work. Maybe I will just skip ahead to the next principle, and peek at this later." Hold on.

Okay, I will be honest: Revising is hard work. It can actually drive you loony. At times, as words and ideas fail you, you will wince, tug your hair, and grind your teeth. Your lucid moments may be rare. And during the darkest hours, when you see no glimmer of light at the end of the tunnel, you will want to capitulate and just settle for a serviceable but mediocre speech.

Why should you bother revising? Because it will make a colossal difference in your speech. Because it will distinguish your speech from the thousands and thousands of pedestrian to remarkably bad speeches thrust upon us every day by indifferent speakers who don't bother. And because it will send an unmistakable message to your audience: This is a speaker who cares—this is a speaker who deserves my attention.

Unfortunately, exceptional speeches *never* just leap out of your head on the initial draft. The first draft of your speech will probably be a messy blob of tangled words and thoughts. It may be mired in the muck of tortured logic, convoluted organization, hazy ideas, and anemic language. Your elusive gem may not even begin to surface until the sixth or seventh draft. And you'd better sit down for the following distressing bit of news: Sometimes your first stab at a speech may be so bad that you will not be able to resuscitate it; a swift burial may serve you best. It is okay, you are not sinning by doing that.

I am an obsessive rewriter, doing one draft and then another and another, usually five. In a way, I have nothing to say but a great deal to add.

GORE VIDAL

Don't dismay. Even the best writers (a very select club, which most of us don't belong to) struggle at this stage, but they understand the importance of revising and honing their work:

> Revising is part of writing. Few writers are so expert that they can produce what they are after on the first try. Quite often you will discover, on examining the completed work, that there are serious flaws in the arrangement of the material. . . . [D]o not be afraid to experiment with what you have written. . . . Remember, it is no sign of weakness or defeat that your manuscript ends up in need of major surgery. This is a common occurrence in all writing, and among the best writers.[1]

TWELVE RULES FOR REVISING YOUR SPEECH

Good, you are still with me, and hopefully you are no longer whimpering. I suggest that you pour yourself a cup of coffee (extra strong), and with a red pen in your hand or with your fingers poised on the keyboard, begin to revise. Here is how:

Set your initial draft aside for a few days, and then revisit it with a fresh perspective. Obviously, you need to budget some time for this (more bad news for you procrastinators). What seemed so logical and persuasive initially may now seem verbose and muddled. Ask yourself some tough questions (no fudging here—no one will see your answers):

- "Is my speech logically organized, or is it hopelessly disjointed?"
- "Does it make sense, or am even *I* scratching my head?"
- "Are my points clear and concise, or are there even *any* points?"
- "Is my opening captivating, or does it meander?"
- "Is my theme precise, or is it jumbled?"
- "Is my language crisp and colorful, or is it stale and tepid?"
- "Do my descriptions launch word pictures floating, or do they lull listeners into dozing?"
- "Does my closing solidify my message, or does my speech end with a resounding thud?"

So, you have a little work to do? Begin ruthlessly revising every point, sentence, and paragraph. Slash away, without compunction or hesitation. Cut, paste, juggle, and tinker with everything. Lop off entire sections if necessary.

Here are several useful revising guidelines. (You didn't think I would send you into battle ill prepared, did you?)

1. USE THE FIRST PERSON

Build rapport with your listeners by using the first person ("I," "we," "us"). The first person is inclusive; it involves your listeners in the presentation and makes you one of them. Constantly referring to "you" or "they" creates a buffer between you and the audience. It seems as if you are lecturing to them or pointing an accusatory finger at them (and it is never polite to point, remember?).

2. USE THE ACTIVE VOICE

Wimps hide behind the passive voice ("mistakes were made," "the doughnuts were eaten"), so they do not have to take a position. This kind of obscure evasion of responsibility begs the question about who did what (*Who* made the mistakes? *Who* ate the doughnuts?). Nike's slogan "Just Do It!" is precise and motivating; "It Should Just Be Done by You!" only inspires us to reach for another doughnut. Whenever possible, eliminate the passive voice from your speech. Instead, be clear and forthright with the active voice: "I made mistakes" (be bold and accountable); "I devoured the doughnuts" (or better yet, blame someone else).

Simple speech is the best and truest eloquence.
MARTIN LUTHER

---

3. ELIMINATE QUALIFIERS

Stop hedging points and qualifying your words: "assuming this occurs," "perhaps this might explain," "it might be said that, all things considered, some scholars feel that in certain circumstances there might be occasional instances of similar behavior on the part of likely participants— possibly." One speaker vacillates out of fear that she will alienate her listeners; another speaker has no idea how he really feels about what he is saying, so he flops around, groping for clarity in his confused mind.

Embarrassed, obscure, and feeble sentences are generally, if not always, the result of embarrassed, obscure, or feeble thought.
HUGH BLAIR

If you equivocate, your listeners will conclude that you are unconvinced of your own position, that you are a milquetoast, or that you are untrustworthy. Such conclusions will obviously sap your credibility and persuasiveness. Say what you think, even if your listeners disagree (just abandon any dreams of becoming a lawyer).

4. Avoid Hyperbole

In an effort to be more persuasive, a speaker might exaggerate ("clearly," "undoubtedly," "unquestionably," and "indisputably"). She might be embellishing out of an attempt to prop up her flimsy arguments, or maybe she is really intoxicated with her own passionate conviction. Some hyperboles just sound downright silly: "The pancakes were stacked a mile high on my plate," or "This is the most despicable act any person has ever committed in the history of mankind!" Unlikely.

Overstatements actually weaken your point and undermine your credibility. Listeners will become suspicious of everything else you say (or waste time imagining a mile-high stack of pancakes). Weed hyperbole out of your speech.

You mustn't exaggerate, young man. That's always
a sign that your argument is weak.
BERTRAND RUSSELL

---

5. Eliminate Offensive Language

Eliminate all potentially sexist, biased, or offensive language ("you guys"; "lady boss"; "those people"). Audiences today are attuned and sensitive to these gaffes. Be aware of what you say. If you are unsure whether your choice of words or ideas might offend someone in the audience, purge them.

In the 2004 presidential campaign, Democratic candidate Howard Dean constantly handicapped himself with flippant comments. For example, he tried to win Southern votes by blustering that he wanted to be the candidate for "guys with Confederate flags on their pickup trucks." He later backpedaled from that comment for weeks with implausible explanations, all to no avail. Several similar speaking blunders helped to doom his campaign. Choose your words carefully.

6. ELIMINATE NEEDLESS WORDS

Always choose a single word if it can do the work of two or three. Ruthlessly prune the verbal clutter that creeps into your presentations: "at the present time" (now); "he is the man that" (he); "owing to the fact that" (since); "during such time as" (while); "notwithstanding the fact that" (although). Verbal clutter only begets presentations that are mystifying and lifeless. They are mystifying, because it is hard for a listener to parse through all the clutter. They are lifeless, because there is no net gain from the clutter: The effort to parse produces exhaustion. And eliminate redundant words ("free gift"; "mix together"; "new recruit"; "actual fact"; "regress back"; "mutual agreement"; "learned, educated person"; "future plans"; "a hot, steamy, torrid day").

Let thy speech be short, comprehending much in a few words;
be as one that knoweth and yet holdeth his tongue.
ECCLESIASTICUS

Also, a speaker may draft a speech chock-full of clauses, riddled with prepositional diversions, and garnished with parenthetical thoughts. Such flowery prose might work well in a book (I certainly hope so, since I've practiced it in this book), but it has no place in speeches. Have mercy on your listeners. By the time you finish delivering your convoluted utterance, even you cannot decipher who did what to whom, or when or where it was done. Rest assured, your audience has already started searching for another speaker, one who can be clear.

Verbosity smothers the message. Lean, succinct sentences have the most impact. Strip every sentence down to the bare essentials:

A sentence should contain no unnecessary words, a paragraph no unnecessary sentences, for the same reason that a drawing should have no unnecessary lines and a machine no unnecessary parts. This requires not that the writer make all sentences short, or avoid all detail and treat subjects only in outline, but that every word tell.[2]

7. AVOID JARGON

Resist any temptation to camouflage your points with authoritative-sounding twaddle or obscure, pretentious language: "b2b" (business to business); "portfolio optimization" (profit); "suffering from the hyper-ingestation of ethanol" (drunk).

Avoid journalese, euphemisms, legalese, technical gobbledygook, clotted language, doublespeak, verbal sludge, pompous acronyms, and other mumbo jumbo (that ought to cover the gamut), which merely conceal your message and cause listeners' eyeballs to roll. Most listeners are confused rather than impressed by obscure expressions. Let it rain, not precipitate.

The chief virtue that language can have is clearness, and nothing detracts from it so much as the use of unfamiliar words.
HIPPOCRATES

---

8. BE CLEAR

Your audience is not clairvoyant (thank goodness for us speakers!), so be brave enough to be clear. That advice can be simply gut-wrenching to the legions of speakers who hide behind ambiguity. If you are vague, your listeners will get stuck attempting to understand what you said or what you meant. They may also conclude that you are sneaky, so don't pussyfoot around. If you express yourself obscurely ("If we do not see a precipitous increase in performance and return on expenditures, the pointed expressions of concern from the Board of Directors may escalate"), your audience will most likely think, "Huh?" Be clear: "If we don't do a better job, the Board of Directors will fire us."

9. BE SPECIFIC

Drab, toothless descriptions such as "car" or "fruit" dilute your message. Select descriptive words, such as: "canary-yellow Volkswagen Beetle" and "shiny Red Delicious apple." Give your speech zing; make it glitter with precise and vivid words:

> Prefer the specific to the general, the definite to the vague, the concrete to the abstract. . . . The greatest writers—Homer, Dante, Shakespeare—are effective largely because they deal in particulars and report the details that matter. Their words call up pictures.[3]

Dull and dreary words result in a dull and dreary presentation. Rather than simply stating that it was a "beautiful morning at the beach," describe the "dazzling sun and powder-white sand, the waves gently folding over themselves and the sea oats swaying in the mild breeze." Transport your audience with lively details.

---

*Words have weight, sound, and appearance; it is only by
considering these that you can write a sentence that
is good to look at and good to listen to.*
W. SOMERSET MAUGHAM

---

10. CREATE IMAGERY

Make your text breathe and spring to life, so that your listeners will experience your message, not just hear your words. Set images floating in their minds with your words.

An excellent example of a speech that effectively painted vivid word pictures was the moving eulogy that President Ronald Reagan delivered after the space shuttle *Challenger* tragically exploded on liftoff from Cape Canaveral, Florida, in 1986. All seven astronauts, including the first civilian on a space flight, were killed. Millions of Americans witnessed this horrifying space disaster. His nationally televised eulogy included the following poignant language:

> There's a coincidence today. On this day 390 years ago, the great explorer Sir Francis Drake died aboard a ship off the coast of Panama. In his lifetime the great frontiers were the oceans, and a historian later said: "He lived by the sea, died on it, was buried in it." Well, today we can say of the *Challenger* crew: Their dedication was, like Drake's, complete.
>
> The crew of the space shuttle *Challenger* honored us by the manner in which they lived their lives. We will never forget them, nor the last time we saw them, this morning, as they prepared for their journey and waved good-bye and "slipped the surly bonds of earth" to "touch the face of God."[4]

11. MAKE YOUR MESSAGE CONVERSATIONAL

Choose plain English and conversational language over rigid and pedantic prose. Make your speech friendly and inviting. You don't want to sound like a pompous windbag. Talk *to* the audience, not *at* the audience. Draft your presentation as if you were speaking to a friend rather than to hundreds of strangers. Imagine that you are talking to them in your living room (all right, imagine you have a humongous living room if that helps).

Words are, of course, the most powerful drug used by mankind.
RUDYARD KIPLING

---

12. WRITE YOUR SPEECH TO BE SPOKEN

"Write my speech to be spoken? Duh!" you think? Well, this is a little trickier than it sounds, unless you keep in mind the differences between that which we read and that which we hear. (And there are some differences other than our ability simply to toss aside a boring book, something that is often tempting, but much more difficult to do, with a boring speaker.) Let's review three of the distinctions.

First, your listeners can absorb only a limited amount of information. At some point, they will think, "Enough already!" and shut down. Although a writer can cover ten or more points, and readers can review and process those points at their own leisurely pace, listeners cannot do that. They may hear each of your points only once or twice, and—if you are really lucky—they might recall a few of the more memorable ones: "Read my lips: No new taxes!" "If it doesn't fit, you must acquit!"

Second, written material often has headings set in italic or boldface type (as in this book), which makes it much easier for readers to see the transitions from point to point. They know where they are all the time, and they can reread passages to clarify questions. In contrast, your listeners are relying on you, the speaker, to be their guide, so you need to point out the critical facts on the sightseeing tour: "The *first* of three distinctions, that old impediment, the price. . . ."

Put the argument into a concrete shape, into an image—some hard phrase, round and solid as a ball, which they can see and handle and carry home with them—and the cause is half won.
RALPH WALDO EMERSON

Finally, we typically read in the solitude of our office, bedroom, or secret hideaway in a cranny of our home, but when we listen to speeches, we are surrounded by many distractions (inconsiderate yakkers, a baby wailing, the sick-as-a-dog person at the next table hacking, industrious waiters banging dishes). Your listeners can be easily sidetracked.

You need to keep in mind these inherent differences between writing and speaking. If you want to hold your listeners' attention, write your speech using crisp, concise sentences; limit your points; and signal when you are moving to the next topic.

Review some of the classic works on the basics of cogent, precise writing listed in the recommended resources at the end of this book. Most of the books listed there are relatively short and easy to read. They are excellent refreshers on the rules of grammar, diction, punctuation, and style—the hallmarks of effective writing.

In addition, several useful Web sites can help you determine if your sentences or words are redundant or hackneyed. Deadwood Phrases (www.pnl.gov/ag/usage/deadwood.html) is a compilation of abused and overused expressions frequently included in speeches; each expression is accompanied by a suggested alternative. Common Errors in English (www .wsu.edu/~brians/errors) identifies frequently misused words and phrases. Finally, Merriam-Webster Online (www.m-w.com) provides a dictionary, thesaurus, and valuable links to other language-related sites.

Author Truman Capote summarized in four words what it has taken me multiple pages to say:

Good writing is rewriting.

Yes, it is time-consuming, and at times frustrating, but it makes an unmistakable difference. It will make your speech distinctive. Diligently revise your speech, and you will take a gigantic step to separate yourself from the bloated ranks of average speakers.

PRINCIPLE 13

HARNESS THE
POWER OF STORIES

The best orator is one who can make men see with their ears.

—ARAB SAYING

We all love a roaring good yarn. As kids, we pleaded: "Tell me a 'nuther story, Grandpa!" "Daddy, read me 'bout the lil' enjun' train that could!" We couldn't wait for story time in preschool, and as adults we are captivated by stories on television and in the newspaper.

Excellent speakers are invariably excellent storytellers. Tell your listeners a story—merely mention the word *story*—and you will grab their attention. Perfect this skill, and you can enthrall them. A story packed with vivid images and told with passion will infuse life into any speech and make your message reverberate with your listeners. Look at each story not merely as a vehicle to clarify your points but as a means to connect with your listeners intellectually and emotionally.

Imagination is more important than knowledge.
ALBERT EINSTEIN

A courtroom drama often involves all the key elements of a gripping story: a whodunit, seeking to unravel who, what, when, where, and why.

To illustrate the power of storytelling, let's dissect a story describing an automobile accident.

Consider several ways a lawyer might describe the event. For example, she could simply convey the facts to the jury: "Mr. Gleason was severely injured in a terrible automobile accident when the defendant's SUV crashed broadside into his car. He was paralyzed, and his life has been dramatically altered."

Accurate, yes, but pretty feeble. This might engage the jurors intellectually (they understand the facts) but not emotionally (they feel no connection with Mr. Gleason). Moreover, this description uses such vague words as "severely" and "dramatically," which have different meanings to listeners, depending on their life experiences and a host of other factors that skew their perceptions.

But what if the attorney shared the events using the techniques of a gifted storyteller, painting vivid pictures with details?

At 8:45 a.m., Sunday, September 25, Albert Gleason, the manager of the Ace Hardware store in midtown, was enjoying a morning drive with his seven-year-old son, Justin. They both cherished these Sunday mornings, because Albert's job required long hours, and this was their precious time together.

They were traveling south on Peachtree Street near the Brookhaven train station, enjoying the beautiful, sunny day, when Justin suddenly screamed: "Dad, look out!" Albert reacted instinctively and immediately jammed on the brakes. And out of the corner of his eye he caught a glimpse of a gigantic black Hummer barreling through the red light.

Albert swerved, but he was too late. He recalls the horrific sounds of metal ripping and glass shattering as that mountain of steel slammed broadside into the Gleasons' tiny green Toyota Corolla. The violent impact whipped him about like a rag doll. The air bag exploded with so much force, Albert's head snapped back and his glasses cracked. He soon felt warm blood trickling down his forehead and into his eyes, but when he tried to wipe it away, he couldn't . . . because he had no feeling in his arms. He was paralyzed, his neck shattered. And he was terrified, because he was unable to help his only son, who was screaming. He cried out to him, "Justin! . . . Justin! . . . Justin!" This is the last image Albert remembers before he blacked out.

The facts remain the same, but the second story resonates with the jurors. Why? It is gripping. It humanizes the characters and conveys the details in a personal way (a father and son bonding). We relive the accident with the Gleasons, and we feel as if we are in their car, because the story is so vivid. This version precisely describes the vehicles, and uses descriptive words: "barreling," "slammed," "metal ripping," and "glass shattering." We empathize with Mr. Gleason, because we understand the fear a parent experiences when his child is in danger, and we can visualize the horror of a huge sport utility vehicle smashing into a much smaller passenger car. We can imagine the terror of being trapped in crumpled wreckage, helpless and paralyzed.

Let thy speech be better than silence, or be silent.
DIONYSIUS THE ELDER

SEVEN KEYS TO POWERFUL STORYTELLING

All right, let's shuttle the lawyer off the stage (*It's about time!*) and get back to the business at hand. What are the secrets of the master storytellers? Here are several techniques used by the best.

1. CONSTANTLY GATHER STORIES

Exceptional speakers are always searching for ideas they can weave into a story. You should, too (principles 4 and 5). Save ideas and articles that amuse you (the lowbrow *Redneck Olympics,* involving such events as toilet lid tossing, bobbing for pigs' feet, or the mud-pit belly flop—I am easily tickled); infuriate you (the egomaniacal athlete making $15 million for playing baseball six months a year, who complains about his "stressful job"); or inspire you (Lance Armstrong surviving cancer and winning his seventh consecutive Tour de France). Stockpile these stories, because you just never know how or when you might be able to knit them into a speech. You have to capture these stories immediately, however, because those fickle thoughts will evaporate in a flash if you don't.

2. STRIVE FOR UNIVERSAL APPEAL

Search for stories that have universal appeal. What lesson did you learn about perseverance by continuing to try out for the swim team or cheerleading squad despite repeatedly being cut? What lessons about optimism does your disabled child teach you? What lessons of loyalty can you learn from Jethro, your golden retriever? What lesson did you learn about commitment as you watched your grandparents renew their wedding vows after being married for seventy years? Everyone has real-life experiences that can become the vehicle for a universal message that will move and teach any audience.

What comes from the heart, goes to the heart.
SAMUEL TAYLOR COLERIDGE

---

3. MAKE YOUR STORIES RELEVANT

Select stories that are relevant to your talk, stories that clarify, not cloud, your purpose. For example, imagine that you are making a sales presentation, unveiling a revolutionary new product, "Chicken Paste." Rather than plunging, as you should, right into your talk by highlighting all the benefits of congealed chicken parts in a handy tube ("My children love this more than they do Pop Tarts and Coco Puffs, the Chicken Paste package fits in your purse, Chicken Paste has a shelf life of two hundred years"), you instead begin with your hilarious but irrelevant airline story ("It was a nine-hour flight from London, I was shoehorned in the middle seat between two sumo wrestlers adjacent to the latrine . . . *blather, blather*").

Your flight debacle might amuse the listeners, but you will have diverted their attention from Chicken Paste. They will be contemplating your airline predicament rather than focusing on the advantages of a meal in a tube. Make your stories relevant, or you will only confuse your audience and dilute your message. Ask yourself, "Does this story support my point?" If the answer is no, discard it.

4. Describe People, Not Concepts

People are always fascinated with human-interest stories. *People* magazine, *Entertainment Tonight,* and *The Oprah Winfrey Show* succeed because they involve people. Tell your audience about the courageous athlete who repeatedly failed but refused to quit or the teacher who sacrificed lucrative business opportunities because of his love for teaching. Your audience will not relate to abstract concepts, such as "courage" and "heroism." They care about real people and real events.

Rattling good stories . . . contain characters so filled with the breath of life that [you] can no more forget them than [you] could forget [your] most intimate friend.
WILLIAM LYON PHELPS

---

5. Deliver the Details

Provide precise, meaty descriptions. If you rely on bland, commonplace words rather than fresh, colorful ideas, you will dull the senses of your listeners. For example, if you merely mention a "car" and leave it at that, your listeners will filter that word through their individual perceptions. To some, the word signifies a Ford minivan; to others, a compact Honda sedan; to still others a Porsche 911 Turbo (well, maybe for you, but not for me). But if you instead describe a "fire-engine-red Corvette," you will conjure up an exact picture.

To help your listeners visualize exactly what you want them to see, provide details. Choose words that are whimsical, offbeat, arresting, or vivid—for good reason:

> Words can reveal thoughts, conceal pain, paint dreams, correct errors, and pass along dearly bought lessons to the latest generation. . . . Words can build walls between people, or bridges. Words can tear down or build up, wound or heal, tarnish or cleanse.[1]

We think in generalities, we live in detail.
ALFRED NORTH WHITEHEAD

---

6. DISPLAY EMOTIONS

You need to share your story in a way that is congruent with the message. If you tell a tale indifferently, then indifference is exactly the response you will get from your audience. The very best stories crackle with feeling: the powerful emotions of love, passion, fear, antipathy, and anger.

Let's say you are disgusted with your cellular phone service provider (all seven of you in the world who are not disgusted may skip ahead). If you were merely to share, meekly and dispassionately, the relevant facts concerning the company's abysmal service ("Gosh, Simple Cellular disappointed me again"), you would evoke little more than a so-what-else-is-new response from your listeners.

On the other hand, imagine if you were to select concrete words and deliver your story with fire and passion: "Let me be blunt: Simple Cellular stinks! The service is atrocious, the charges excessive, and the billing nightmarish. And I defy you to ever get a human being rather than a recording maze when you call. Simple Cellular epitomizes all that is wrong with businesses that focus only on the bottom line and that could care less about customer service!"

Pound your fist, wag your finger, rumble and thunder—heck, toss in some salty language if it's appropriate. Your voice, body language, and facial expressions must depict the emotion and convey the anger you feel. Don't blow a gasket, but you get the point. To really engage your audience in your stories, create drama.

[The passions] are the winds that fill the ship's sails. Sometimes they submerge the ship, but without them the ship could not sail.

VOLTAIRE

---

7. TITILLATE THE SENSES

A mesmerizing story engages the senses, emotions, and intellect of your listeners. Infuse life into your stories by delivering them using vocal energy, diverse pacing, timely pauses, expansive gestures, and wide-eyed excitement.

In the same way that your dad might have eerily described the slimy, green monster lurking under the bed (and why was there always one under every child's bed?), ready to snatch your ankles if you dared to get up, you need to share vivid, lifelike details with excitement and passion. Make your listeners experience your story by taking them on a journey and describing the events in a way that will touch their senses. If you can get beyond your listeners' minds and into their hearts, you will elevate your message from the merely interesting to the unforgettable.

Enhance your storytelling skills by poring over the list of recommended resources at the end of this book.

We always hope that our listeners will cling to our words and recall them forever, but typically, they don't. Most audiences forget most of what speakers say—quickly. Disheartening, but true. If listeners remember what you said even a week after your speech, you are ahead of most speakers. But your listeners seldom forget a story that moves, surprises, or enchants them. Do you want your messages to be remembered? Then forget what you learned in grade school—go ahead and tell stories.

PRINCIPLE 14

MAKE 'EM LAUGH

Why doesn't the fellow who says, "I'm no speechmaker,"
let it go at that instead of giving a demonstration?

—KIN HUBBARD

Do you wring your hands at the very thought of using humor in your speeches because—Horrors!—it might flop? Do you always stick to the facts, the facts, and nothing but the facts? Does the title of this principle make you cringe or break out in a cold sweat? If so, don't even think about skipping ahead.

If your presentations are a tad boring—or, worse, real snoozers—humor will add some pizzazz. Do I hear howls of protest? "I'm not funny!" "That's not my style!" "I'm a corporate bigwig, who must be taken seriously!" Take a breath. You don't have to morph into a stand-up comedian, be sidesplitting hilarious, or engage in shenanigans (slinging food, banging gongs, or rattling off jokes incessantly). Acting foolish would undermine your professional image and destroy your credibility. Just consider adding a few zany twists or snappy tidbits to punch up your talk and evoke a smile from the audience.

There are several excellent reasons to try incorporating humor into your speeches. First, you engage your audience. Audiences today are bombarded with a seemingly endless parade of tiresome speakers. If it is drudgery to listen, your listeners will mentally check out. They will hear a humming sound as you drone on ("So our quarterly projections for the eastern region . . . *yammer, yammer*"), but they are not listening; you might as well be speaking Hungarian.

Many times what cannot be refuted by
arguments can be parried by laughter.
DESIDERIUS ERASMUS

Second, audiences need to relax periodically, to smile and breathe, especially when you are addressing a serious, complex, or statistic-laden topic. Some of the greatest speakers in history—Winston Churchill, John F. Kennedy, and Ronald Reagan—dealt with topics of enormous importance, yet they often made their points with humor. Even if your talk has gargantuan implications for your audience (unlikely in most cases), loosen up.

Finally, humor humanizes you, and that will make your listeners far more receptive to your ideas. It also alerts them that you are confident and willing to take a risk. Your humor may not always work, but the potential rewards more than justify the risks.

Humor can turn the serious into the bearable, the humiliating
into the humbling, the mundane into the unique.
LIAN DOLAN

TEN TIPS FOR ADDING HUMOR TO YOUR TALKS

All right, so you want to make your talks more entertaining. How can you do that without undermining your professional image and without taking inordinate risks?

Well, don't just start lobbing out one-liners willy-nilly and hoping for the best. That haphazard approach is likely to come crashing down around you. Use the following plan to add a little mirth to your talks.

1. STUDY OTHERS

Study and emulate entertainers who successfully incorporate humor into their performances. Comedians such as Jim Carrey, Eddie Murphy, and Jerry Seinfeld each use humor differently, but they are all very entertaining. In the same manner, there is no humor template that applies to every speaker, so experiment and develop your own style.

Analyze entertaining speakers, and ask what makes them funny: Is it the topics they discuss, their animated delivery, or perhaps the unexpected twists they intersperse in their presentations? Watch their body language, gestures, and facial expressions as they speak. Listen to their timing and their use of pauses. Study how they recover when something bombs. (At some point in your speaking life, that will come in really handy—trust me.) Learn from the best, but be selective. Resist the urge to smash watermelons, hurl confetti, blare air horns, or jump around like a raving loony (see tip 7, "Don't Go Bonkers")—there are limits.

———

All the wit in the world is lost upon him who has none.
JEAN DE LA BRUYÈRE

———

2. REMAIN VIGILANT

Entertaining material for your speeches is floating around everywhere: current events, personal exploits, the lessons of eternal optimism that your mutt, Shep, has taught you. Everything has potential if you are attuned and creative. Study how such comedians as Jay Leno, David Letterman, Dennis Miller, and Conan O'Brien twist ordinary events into extraordinarily funny observations. Often the best ideas come from our own embarrassing experiences (see tip 5, "Take Aim at Yourself").

If it amuses you, it will probably delight your audience, so try it. And if it bombs, it will not be fatal (I have a rich bombing history, yet I live to bomb another day). If no one laughs, it may be because your audience is riddled with killjoys. Some sourpusses in your audiences have never laughed, have seldom smiled, and basically have no sense of humor. Although it is difficult, you just have to endure them.

3. CAPTURE YOUR THOUGHTS

When you see or hear something that amuses you, snatch it immediately, because those pearls of wit and wisdom will vanish in an instant, and our memories are notoriously unreliable. I don't know about you, but inspiration seldom shows up on my schedule.

Write down your mirthful observations or that zany story, or create a repository of humor on your computer, entitled: "Really Funny Stuff." (Or, "*Potentially* Really Funny Stuff.") Stockpile this material; you can never have too much, and you can never anticipate how it might come in handy.

4. MAKE IT CREATIVE AND RELEVANT

Do not aim for a laugh at any price. Avoid irrelevant, inane, or predictable humor that reeks from the outset: "You meet ol' Saint Peter at the Pearly Gates, and he seems a little annoyed as he reviews your life's records . . ." or "Two fat ducks waddle into a bar in Boston. . . ."

Please spare everyone. That type of humor wears the Hackneyed Brand. You may get a laugh, but it is just as likely to bomb and be greeted with rolling eyes and rampant groans—a reaction that will erode your confidence.

But the real downside of stale humor is that it diverts your audience's attention if it does not relate to your talk (and Pearly Gates and fat-duck humor seldom relate to any talk). Once the fickle attention of your audience has vanished, it may never return. That is a very steep price to pay for a chance at a laugh.

5. TAKE AIM AT YOURSELF

Does anyone enjoy listening to a somber windbag? You are giving a speech, not resolving world hunger. Ease up, and add a dollop of self-deprecating humor to your talk. Disarm your listeners by showing them that you do not take yourself too seriously.

Describe a thorny predicament you experienced, or perhaps recount a humbling speaking gaffe (I know—so many to choose from). Let them

know that underneath that sober patina, a likable human being resides.
Do that, and you are far more likely to connect with your listeners.

————

To make other people laugh is no great feat so long as one does not
mind whether they are laughing at our wit or at ourselves.
GEORG CHRISTOPH LICHTENBERG

————

6. CONSIDER USING VISUAL AIDS

Visual aids can have a greater impact on the audience than anything
entertaining you might say during your speech, so consider using such
visual aids as photographs or drawings to add to your speech a little snap,
crackle, and pop. Principles 36, 37, and 38 delve into all the ways that
you can weave visual aids into your presentations, but be careful: You
need to be comfortable incorporating this added layer of complexity, and
the timing and use of the visual aid must be strategically planned.

7. DON'T GO BONKERS

Don't go wild injecting snappy banter every other line. Aim for well-
timed humor rather than an endless succession of bon mots or anecdotes.
Incorporate humorous material sparingly until you get a better sense of
what works for you.

Your purpose in speaking will dictate the amount of humor you mix
into a presentation. For example, if you are making a toast, talking at a
roast, or speaking after dinner, liberally sprinkle entertaining stories, par-
odies, or satire into your talk. But if the mood is more serious, and you
are simply attempting to ease the tension or provide a brief interlude
from a weighty or complex message, just add an occasional quip or
a brief entertaining story. During the memorial service for President
Reagan, former President George Herbert Walker Bush spoke of his
memories of President Reagan's quick wit by sharing a conversation he
once had with him: "Mr. President, how did your meeting go with

Desmond Tu Tu?" he asked. "So so," President Reagan responded. The congregation laughed, and that eased the tension.

8. USE DISCRETION

Use only humor that is appropriate for your listeners. Research your audience, and tailor the humor to the group (principle 6). What works when you speak at the Real Manly Men's Club may flop when you speak at the Southern Baptist Ladies' Auxiliary. When in doubt, err on the cautious side, and leave it out.

It sometimes works to direct your pithy comments toward someone well known in the audience. This approach can make your presentation seem more customized to that audience. Just be careful not to aim your jest at a humorless target—your boss, for example—unless you enjoy scouring the help-wanted ads.

Laughter is wine for the soul.
SEAN O'CASEY

---

9. CRITICALLY ANALYZE YOUR HUMOR

Ruthlessly slash any humor that has even the slightest sexist, ethnic, or racial connotation. Never use offensive humor or language in a speech. Even if some people laugh, others may become defensive and resentful toward you. It is unlikely that audience members who are seething with resentment will be receptive to whatever else you might say. Your talk could be doomed, and you may not even know it.

10. PRACTICE

Here is the big fat secret about humor: two words, timing and delivery. They count as much if not more than your material itself. Such factors as pausing, pacing, body language, facial expressions, and tone of voice are all critical. If your timing is off, if your body language or facial expressions are incongruent with your words, or if the tone of your voice is lifeless, the humor will fizzle.

So, before you deliver your ripsnorting funny speech to your intended audience, you had better test it out. Gather family members, friends—even strangers at the bus stop if you are really desperate for an audience—and deliver your speech. Then perform an objective assessment: "Did they laugh, or at least smile, or did they react with icy silence?" "Did they understand my humor, or did they stare at me with inane grins and puzzled looks?"

Don't despair if your humor didn't work as well as you had expected. You may only need to tweak the wording or hone your comedic timing. Often slight adjustments will make a dramatic difference. Even speakers who regularly use humor in their presentations constantly refine their material and rehearse their delivery. Don't expect perfection immediately. If it was easy, everyone would be doing it successfully.

I'd like to begin today by quoting Homer from The Odyssey. . . .
In the Eleventh Book of The Odyssey, *he writes, "There is a time for many words, and there's also a time for sleep." That's true. I just hope my remarks won't be a time for both.*
OLYMPIA SNOWE

If you need to add zing to your speeches—and most of us do—review the recommended resources at the end of the book, and sleuth around on the Web (just avoid risqué humor sites that your grandmother would disapprove of). Here are a couple of places to start mining for funny material:

- Comedy Zone (www.comedy-zone.net), which offers a broad range of humorous ideas
- Murphy's Laws and Corollaries (http://dmawww.epfl.ch/roso .mosaic/dm/murphy), which contains a wide variety of clean humor

If you really want to connect with today's audiences, make your presentations distinctive and entertaining. You don't need a walloping stand-up comedy routine, and you don't need to repeatedly blow up paper bags and pop them to engage the audience. Just add a surprising tweak or a juicy quip that will add a little sparkle. If you flub, you'll survive. And if it works, it will be magical, and your chest will swell with confidence. Be brave—try it.

PRINCIPLE 15

QUOTE FOR CREDIBILITY

I often quote myself; it adds spice to my conversation.

—GEORGE BERNARD SHAW

L et's start with an embarrassingly easy pop quiz (I said, *easy* quiz, so no carping): Would you like to add a smattering of wit to your speech, perhaps a poignant observation that causes your audience to reflect or that stirs their imagination? If you answered yes, step forward to accept your gold star (all right, two gold stars), and begin hunting for the perfect quote.

Speakers can embellish their presentations by sprinkling in quotations from a variety of sources: Scripture, poetry, literature, politics, and writings of virtually any type. An apt quotation will add pizzazz to a tepid presentation, charm or surprise your audience, enhance your credibility, and perhaps persuade skeptics where your words alone may fail. To make your speech distinctive (and who among us would not like to deliver a more distinctive speech?), intersperse a few quotations.

SEVEN QUESTIONS TO ASK YOUR QUOTATIONS

Excited by the possibility of making your speech distinctive, with a wild glint in your eyes, you dash out lickety-split searching for quotations. You are not too particular in your hunt, because any handy quotation will work, right? No. And you will miss the mark if you simply begin cramming quotes into your speech, hoping that somehow one might resonate with your audience.

Let's adopt a few rules before you go bananas quoting. Become judicious and selective (bordering on obsessive) about whom you quote and where you plug them into your speech. Don't just settle for any motley quote that comes sauntering to your doorstep. Inspect all potential quote candidates, and choose carefully among them (because, as we know, "Many are called, but few are chosen").

Turn the hot spotlight onto each quotation, and subject it to the following seven-question inquisition. (Don't be testy, now; the questions are addressed to your potential quotations, not to you personally.) For your quotation to pass muster, you want the first four answers to be yes, the last three to be no.

1. ARE YOU SHORT?

Limit the length of your quotations. Most audiences will not be able to—or want to—focus on and process lengthy quotations. Shorter, punchy quotes are typically more compelling and memorable. You also appear to be well prepared when you recite a quotation from memory, a task much easier to accomplish with a short quote.

Every quotation contributes something to the stability or enlargement of the language.
SAMUEL JOHNSON

---

2. ARE YOU THE RIGHT FIT?

Regardless of how pithy or inspirational the quotation, it must be appropriate for the speech. Does it intrigue your listeners? Does it cause the speech to ripple with emotional energy? Does it add a smidgen of comic relief? Sometimes a wonderful quotation just may not fit the mood or tone of your speech. For instance, a playful quotation at the wrong moment in a serious message may perplex your audience. They will not know whether to laugh or to remain stoic.

You may be loath to say good-bye to a snappy quotation, but if it does not enhance your speech or support your point, reject it. Don't let it lurk around, because you can become emotionally attached ("But I just *love* that saying") and tempted to sneak it into your speech. Root around until you find the right candidate for the job. Be fastidious.

3. ARE YOU CLEAR?

Will your audience immediately understand why you interjected the quotation? Will they readily grasp the point of the quote, or will the quotation shroud your message in obscurity? You do not want it to create a mental logjam, leaving your audience wondering, "Where on earth is she going with that point?"

If you do that, your audience will be left behind, pondering the meaning of the quotation while you proceed with your presentation. Most audiences will not work hard, and they will shut you off in a flash. Avoid that by carefully selecting quotations that support and clarify your point.

That is always the grand challenge of good writing, isn't it: to bring
people around—*to teach them, amuse them, inspire them,
goad them, charm them, awaken them, convince them.*
JOHN R. TRIMBLE

---

4. DO YOU PACK A PUNCH?

Quotations from well-recognized sources have impact; obscure sources do not. Such respected and highly acclaimed people as Mother Teresa or the Reverend Billy Graham enhance your credibility. On the other hand, however much Ralph, the towel boy in the locker room, is a recognized authority on gym politics, he is still unknown to the general public. Citing Ralph is likely to cause your listeners to puzzle

"Who?" rather than to concur "Absolutely!" Unless you are addressing your locker room buddies, dig deeper for your quotations.

5. ARE YOU HIGHBROW?

Try this quote: "'Now lat us ryde, and herkneth what I seye.' And with that word we ryden forth oure weye." This quote from Chaucer sounds so stuffy that, unless you are speaking to a group of Middle English scholars, it does not entice your listeners to "rydeth" any further on the journey with you or to "herkneth" to anything else you have to say.

Don't try to dazzle your audience with esoteric or pretentious quotations, because if the import of the quote zips right over their heads, they will neither be impressed nor persuaded. Instead, they are likely to conclude that you are pompous. Highbrow quotations label you as someone intent on impressing, rather than reaching, your audience.

6. ARE YOU TAINTED?

Does the person you are quoting dogmatically advocate only one view? For example, political talk show hosts typically see the world and its many issues in black and white, never in subtle shades of gray, and they frequently manipulate facts to suit their purposes. Some cavalierly disparage opposing viewpoints without any factual or logical basis for doing so, thus undermining their own credibility. Listeners are rightly suspicious of such sources, so avoid quoting someone whose credibility is tarnished by a narrow-minded agenda.

7. ARE YOU A LIGHTNING ROD?

Will the quotation inflame the audience for the wrong reason? Some quotes may be right on point but all wrong for your speech. For instance, quotes from such celebrities as President George Walker Bush, Senator Hillary Rodham Clinton, defrocked diva Martha Stewart, and heavyweight boxer Mike Tyson, are likely to be counterproductive. These sources are so controversial that merely mentioning their names evokes strong negative reactions (bulging veins, flaring nostrils, hyperventilation) from many people.

By citing such provocative sources, you risk polarizing some of your listeners: They will react emotionally rather than logically, and they will discount anything you say regardless of its merit. Always know your audience (principles 6 and 7), and weigh the potential ramifications when quoting controversial figures. If you are unsure, opt for the safe choices (Big Bird, Winnie the Pooh, and Elmo spring to mind).

Almost every wise saying has an opposite one, no less wise, to balance it.
GEORGE SANTAYANA

To trigger ideas for your presentation, leaf through a book of quotations. There are hundreds available, but the best is *Bartlett's Familiar Quotations,* which contains more than twenty thousand gems of wisdom from historical and contemporary figures. For example, if you are looking for an insightful saying on "truth," you will find nearly three hundred entries under that topic. You can easily draw from such sources as William Shakespeare, Blaise Pascal, Victor Hugo, and John Lennon (and it does not get much more eclectic than that).

Bartlett's is an invaluable friend when you are drafting a speech and hunting for the ideal quote. It belongs in every speaker's library, so splurge for your own copy, or put it on your birthday wish list. Additional sources for quotations can be found in principle 5 and in the recommended resources at the end of this book.

Decorate your talks with quotations. Use them to create frivolity, profundity, and drama. They can make your presentation shine. Don't settle for merely an adequate quote—find an exceptional one. You may have to interrogate hundreds of candidates before you settle on the right ones, and yes (ugh), the interrogation will require an investment of time. But those little pearls of sagacity and inspiration can help to dramatically differentiate your speech from the mundane. Most importantly, you will earn a few extra gold stars with the audience—guaranteed.

PRINCIPLE 16

CLOSE WITH A BANG

I love a finished speaker,
I really, truly do.
I don't mean one who's polished,
I just mean one who's through.

—RICHARD ARMOUR

Assume that the closing of every speech is critical. (It is, so work with me, all you Doubting Thomases.) How should you close your speech?

Which of the following should you be?

- A *packer*, who mumbles her final words while staring at the lectern and simultaneously gathering up her notes and accessories

- A *randomizer*, who has no prepared closing, someone who is never quite sure what the closing will bring and who simply goes where the fickle spirit of the moment moves him

- A *rigid reader*, who reads her closing, because she fears ever varying from the exact words on her script

- A *skedaddler*, who is anxious to dart away, just darn thankful he survived the speech with a speck of dignity

The answer? None of the above. (Yes, I know that was not a choice.) If you ever learned that any of those methods is the right way to close your speech, unlearn it now. From all indications in the speaking world, quite a few speakers should start unlearning.

How important is the closing, you ask? Crucial, because most audiences will remember what you said first in the speech, followed by what you said last, and, if you are really lucky, they might recall something that you sandwiched in the middle. This conclusion may dismay you, but numerous studies support it. Your closing is your final opportunity to make a lasting impression with your audience, so capitalize on it.

The closing is not the time to pack, shuffle, organize, mutter, ramble, waffle, ponder, read, or skedaddle (that ought to cover the spectrum of closing sins). End on a high note, with your audience wishing that you would continue, not celebrating your exit.

FIVE CLOSINGS TO SHUN

If the closing is so blasted important, why are so many baffling or anemic? Often the audience is stupefied, dozing during the grand finale, or left scratching their heads, wondering: "What'd he say?"— hardly a monumental ending. Let's banish the worst villains from your closing repertoire. With apologies to David Letterman: "From the home office in Wahoo, Nebraska, The Top Five Dreadful Closings:"

1. THE ABRUPT CLOSING

If the audience is not sure that you have closed until you start walking away from the lectern ("What, it's over? That's it?"), you have left them dangling. Your audience should never be surprised that you have closed. Plan your closing precisely. Ease into the closing, and alert the audience that the journey is concluding: "In closing, . . ." or "My final words to you today are these. . . ." Never close abruptly, in the middle of a thought. Close your speech emphatically.

2. THE WHIMPERING CLOSING

Don't cower in the closing like the Cowardly Lion from *The Wizard of Oz*. If your position is controversial, even if you risk alienating some in your audience, stick your neck out: Look them in the eye, and have the courage to speak with clarity and conviction. Your audience may not like what you have to say, they may even glare, hiss, and flat reject your conclusion, but they will certainly remember it, so don't be a wussy.

———

Better never to begin than never to make an end.
JOHN CLARKE

———

3. THE ENDLESS CLOSING

You have rounded the closing corner, and you are barreling toward the finish line. Never tease an audience by promising to close ("In closing, let me just say . . .") and then drone on . . . and on . . . *and on.*

Audiences become grouchy, and their grouchiness quickly morphs into hostility, if speakers continue to yak after signaling that they are closing. This invariably seems to happen with the most excruciating presentations (those that are too long, too boring, too disorganized, or—Horrors!—all of these). When the speaker finally stops yapping, the audience applauds not in appreciation of the speech, but in relief that it's over. Adhere to the advice of President Franklin D. Roosevelt: "Be brief, be sincere, be seated."

You delude yourself if you think your listeners are enraptured with the sound of your voice and are always eager to hear more from you. They are not. Listeners *rarely* complain that a speech was too short, but when a speaker exceeds the time allotted, the restless listeners are not just looking at their watches—they are tapping them to see if they are still working. Wrap it up and get out while the gettin' is good.

4. THE "AND ANOTHER THING . . ." CLOSING

Sometimes during the closing, a light bulb will go off above a speaker's head, and she will recall something she had planned to discuss earlier in the speech but forgot ("Oh yes, now I remember what I wanted to say . . ."). Or she might spontaneously interject new ideas in the closing ("And another issue that deserves mentioning . . ."). Too late. Those thoughts might have deserved mentioning in the body of the speech, but they are unwelcome intruders in any closing.

Do not introduce new topics when closing. You will not have time to develop these points, and they may obscure the points you have already addressed. Know your purpose and remain focused and organized; this is not the time to improvise. Save your unexpressed ideas for the next presentation.

Good to begin well, better to end well.
JOHN RAY

---

5. THE READ CLOSING

Among the vast multitude of wretched closings, there may be one that is worse than a closing that is read—but I doubt it. You might as well pass out a script of the closing to your audience, exit stage left, and just let them read it at their leisure.

Barbara Bush delivered a commencement address at Wellesley College that was drafted with a wonderful mix of personal stories, humorous anecdotes, and fitting quotations, and, miraculously, it was a true rarity for a commencement address—it was short. But it was apparent that Mrs. Bush had spent no time reviewing or practicing the speech, so she awkwardly read the closing. She concluded with a resounding thud (I don't think it caused her husband to lose the 1992 presidential election, but you never know).

Most read closings suffer a similar fate. The closing is the climax of a speech, and it should be repeatedly practiced until you can deliver it confidently and emphatically. Never read your closing—ever.

SIX DYNAMIC CLOSINGS

You have mulled it over and decided you prefer to close to roaring applause rather than to jeers and yawns. Wise decision. So how do you craft a closing that will do that? Look for ways to close that are fresh, surprising, and unforgettable. Here are six exceptional ways to close a presentation, but don't be afraid to experiment:

1. CLOSE WITH A QUOTATION OR A POEM

Apt quotations or poetry, practiced and delivered with confidence, can add the perfect crescendo to any presentation. Constantly gather quotations or short poems that resonate with you, and save them in a notebook, computer file, or shoebox for future use. In principles 5 and 15, and in the recommended resources at the end of the book, you will find lists of sources, including Web sites, that can aid you in your search for the perfect quotation or poem to end your presentation.

2. CLOSE WITH A STORY

Conclude with a relevant story to captivate your audience (principle 13). Dramatic, humorous, surprising, or allegorical stories leave a lasting impression. You can also use the closing to complete a story that you began in your opening or in the body of your presentation. Renowned radio announcer Paul Harvey skillfully uses this technique with his signature closing, "And now you know the rest of the story." He engages his audience with his intriguing tales that slowly unfold until the mystery is solved in the conclusion.

But before you interject just any story, be discriminating. Don't trot out an irrelevant story, no matter how titillating and entertaining you think it might be. That will only befuddle your audience. Make your story brief (no more than two minutes, and ideally less), cogent, applicable, and clear.

Great is the art of beginning, but greater is the art of ending.
HENRY WADSWORTH LONGFELLOW

---

3. CLOSE WITH A CHALLENGE

I blush even to mention this next piece of advice, for fear you will think, "Why does he belabor the obvious?" Sadly, since this axiomatic principle is ignored so frequently, I must state it clearly: *If you want audience members to take action, you have to ask.* The closing is the time to ask. (Glaringly insightful, right?)

Audience members must clearly understand what you want them to do, so don't waffle. If you have laid out your position convincingly, they will act, but only if you ask. Challenge them to get involved: "Chocoholics, they have banished us from the grade school cafeterias; they scorn us at Weight Watchers conventions; we have even become the scapegoat for society's rampant obesity. It is time that we draw a line in the cookie crumbs, grab our Kit Kats and Ben & Jerry's *Chunky Monkey*, and proclaim: 'Enough! We are spitting mad, and we are not going to be bullied any more!'" What self-respecting chocoholic would not answer that call to arms?

Tell them you're ending, and they'll be all yours. Even the weakest tip-off, "In conclusion," or one of its bland variations, snaps people awake.
WILLIAM PARKHURST

---

4. CLOSE BY EMPHASIZING AN EARLIER POINT

Conclude by answering a question you asked earlier in the presentation, or by repeating a quotation, statement, or observation that you previously made. This is an excellent way to reinforce your message, because most audiences need to hear a point repeated several times before they retain it.

For example, if you posed a question in the opening—"If you could ask your grandfather only one question, what would it be?"—answer it in the closing: "I would ask this: 'Grandpa, what is the most valuable lesson you have learned in the past ninety-five years?'" This closing wraps up your message in a tidy little package for your audience.

5. CLOSE WITH A QUESTION

Close with a rhetorical question, or a series of questions, that will cause your audience to pause and reflect. Audiences today want to participate in the speaking experience, and your questions will engage them in your talk. For example: "Let me ask you this, ladies and gentlemen: The Department of Education spent twenty-seven million dollars last year studying whether reality television shows based on dimwits immersing themselves in a mammoth drum brimming with maggots are intellectually stimulating for our children. Now, is that a prudent use of our tax dollars?" The persuasiveness of your presentation should lead your audience to only one answer: the position that you have been advocating (the maggot insanity must stop!).

6. Close with Artistry

At times, the tone and content of your message may call for an emotional, poignant closing. General Douglas MacArthur's closing in his moving farewell address to the cadets at the United States Military Academy illustrates this technique brilliantly:

> In my dreams I hear again the crash of guns, the rattle of musketry, the strange mournful mutter of the battlefield. But in the evening of my memory always I come back to West Point. Always there echoes and re-echoes: duty, honor, country.
>
> Today marks my final roll call with you. But I want you to know that when I cross over the river, my last conscious thoughts will be of the Corps and the Corps and the Corps.
>
> I bid you farewell.[1]

The closing is your final opportunity to summarize your message for your audience, so craft it carefully. Your goal is to leave your message ringing in the ears of everyone in the room.

Make your final words unforgettable. Don't pray for divine inspiration or anticipate that your conclusion will magically appear out of thin air as you are caught up in the moment. That is unlikely to happen. Raise your right hand, and vow never to be a packer, randomizer, rigid reader, or skedaddler. Know exactly what you will say, and say it with absolute confidence. It is your last shot with your audience, so make it your best shot.

PART IV

PRACTICE FOR PERFECTION

YOU HAVE METICULOUSLY RESEARCHED, drafted, and revised your presentation, and you are raring to speak. Now just fill the seats, pick up a microphone, and—Poof!—you are ready to amaze the gathered masses, right? Not quite. Not before you complete another crucial step: focused practice.

Practice is the best of all instructors.
PUBLIUS SYRUS

Do I hear you protesting, "Wait, I am an expert, and I have mastered my topic, so do I *really* need to practice?" Yes, because to deliver an exceptional presentation without practice, you need to be extraordinarily good, and most of us (even you, most likely) are not extraordinarily good. Even virtuoso speakers, who have delivered thousands of speeches, constantly critique, hone, and practice their delivery. What ultimately distinguishes their speeches from so many forgettable ones? Practice, practice, and (did I mention?) practice.

Almost everyone can stand before an audience and listlessly share information. If you are lucky, you may even reach an audience on an intellectual level by doing that (assuming that they hang around long enough to hear what you have to say). But you will seldom touch them on an emotional level. If you really want to make a lasting impression, move both the minds *and* the hearts of your listeners. You cannot do that without practice. Part IV provides a game plan on how to practice to attain extraordinary results.

POLISH WITH PRACTICE

Excellence is an art won by training and habituation.
We are what we repeatedly do. Excellence,
therefore, is not an act but a habit.

—ARISTOTLE

Do you recall the valuable lifesaver we attempted to use when we played games as children? If we whiffed with a wild swing, lobbed up an air ball, or emerged from the water, gasping for air, yards short of our underwater goal, we pleaded: "Do over, do over, I call a do over!" Typically, our fellow zealous competitors jeered and howled, "No way, Butterfingers!" or "Too bad, Choker Boy!"

Well, here is a bit of sobering news: Many of your former playmates are now in your audience. And here is the harsh reality of speaking: There are no do overs (or mulligans, for you golf aficionados). You have only one chance to make a favorable impression with every audience. If you whiff, fumble, or choke, you have squandered your opportunity.

Worse, audiences will rarely understand or appreciate—and they may not even care about—all the time and effort you devoted to researching, drafting, and preparing your speech. Even if your brain is bursting with insights, that knowledge is useless if you fail to convey your information in a logical, compelling manner. What they care about in exchange for the most valuable commodity they can give you—their time—is what you say and how you say it. Your challenge is to distill all your expertise into a succinct, cogent speech.

So, with all those hurdles to leap, do you think you ought to practice?

Speaking is a learned skill, and as with any learned skill (tennis, hopscotch, tiddlywinks), the truly dramatic improvements result from practice. There is no substitute—not your bravado (even blustering has limits), not your shamelessness, not even your innate gift for gab. Reading about the skills required to make a dynamic presentation (such as those in the speaking bible you are currently holding) and watching and imitating exceptional speakers (principle 8) will help immensely. But that passive approach will get you only so far; you will master the skills necessary to speak with confidence only through focused practice.

TWELVE PRACTICE POINTERS

Obviously (at least, I hope it is obvious by now), it is essential that you lay the proper foundation for every speech—thorough research, logical organization, fastidious drafting and redrafting—because even practice cannot salvage a speech's fundamental flaws. But assuming that your speech is ready for prime time, how do you prepare to speak with authority and conviction?

Talking and eloquence are not the same: to speak,
and to speak well, are two things.
BEN JONSON

Since you do not enjoy the do-over option (and wouldn't we all love to have a few of those treasures lying around?), you have resolved to practice. But how can you ensure that you are practicing effectively? Should you painstakingly memorize the speech until you are mumbling it in your sleep? Should you read it aloud at least one hundred times? Should you resort to writing the speech on your hands and arms for easy reference? No, none of those approaches is the answer.

Haphazard practice wastes time, and it will produce, at best, haphazard results. What you need is a plan, and—Presto!—here it is. Use these pointers to practice productively. Where noted, several of the tips are covered more extensively in subsequent principles, but they are mentioned here for handy reference:

1. MAKE THE LAYOUT USEFUL

First, configure the speech into a functional format for practicing. I realize that the tree-hugging conservationists might fly into conniptions with what I am about to say, but start by being extravagant with your paper. Don't try to cram your entire speech into a space the size of a Post-it Note; you will go bleary-eyed deciphering it as you practice.

Triple-space your text; highlight your key concepts in boldface, italics, or underlining, to ensure that you address them; and use a 16- to 18-point font, so you can easily see the text. Leave ample space in the margins to write those fleeting, random thoughts that arise as you practice the speech ("This is poppycock!" "Really?" "In English, please!"). These spontaneous observations will be very useful as you continue to edit the presentation. More on this in principle 18.

Preparedness heralds opportunity.
ENGLISH PROVERB

---

2. REPEATEDLY RECITE THE SPEECH

Begin reciting your speech out loud, in a conversational tone (think human being, not robot). Recite it repeatedly until it flows smoothly. At this juncture, you will probably be reading your speech, but that is fine— no one will punish you. You are simply finding out how it sounds as you deliver it. Then quiz yourself: Does it sound natural or jerky? Are there any clunky, unwieldy sentences? Is it verbose? You most likely will need to tweak, edit, or maybe whittle down entire sections before you resume your practice.

3. MARK THE TEXT

Next, grab your red pen (or crayon), and edit your speech by inserting notes in the text. For instance, if you tend to speak faster than an auctioneer, put a slash between words to remind yourself to slow your delivery at certain key junctures; write delivery cues to yourself throughout the speech ("PAUSE," "SLOW," "SMILE," and "BREATHE"—yes, remind yourself to breathe); or draw an eyeball (not too ghoulish), to remind yourself to maintain eye contact with your audience and not focus on your notes.

Consider color-coding the text to reflect the moods or tones in your delivery: yellow for a lighthearted mood, blue for somber, and red for passionate. But don't go berserk with your color scheme. This is not the time to unleash your suppressed artistic flair. If your color-coded notes resemble a rainbow, you will have defeated the purpose of highlighting for easy reference, and bedlam will ensue as you wonder: "Is that highlighting red or orange?" "Green means faster, doesn't it? Or does it mean slower?" Avoid that, and choose no more than three colors for your notes.

These cues will prompt you not only in what to say, but also in how to say it for greatest impact.

4. GRADUATE FROM THE SCRIPT TO PROMPT WORDS

Practice your speech many times using the full text, but do not plan on using the complete text when you actually deliver it to your audience. Why? Because when you are standing before your audience and slightly anxious, the text becomes an alluring crutch, regardless of how many times you have practiced it. It can become addictive.

When you feel comfortable with your material, reduce the text to an outline, and follow the same procedure of making helpful notations. After you have practiced presenting using the outline, move to note cards, where you should follow the same practice and editing procedures. Finally, graduate to using only prompt words to remind you of the topic or idea you intend to discuss next (for example, "WALDO QUOTE," "BALLOON STORY," "SPANKING LESSON"). Just remember that this weaning off your notes does not happen in one day; it takes time (*yet more* discouraging news for procrastinators!).

Using this technique will ensure that you cover the key points and ideas, and will help solidify the presentation in your mind. Rely less on notes with each recitation. Ultimately, you should be able to deliver the speech fluidly and confidently, looking primarily, if not exclusively, at your audience. Continue practicing until you can deliver your entire speech without fumbling, mispronouncing words, butchering syntax, or losing your train of thought.

We cannot make it rain, but we can see to it
that the rain falls on prepared soil.
HENRI J. M. NOUWEN

---

5. PRACTICE WITH DISTRACTIONS

In the *ideal* speaking world, it would be as quiet as a monastery when you spoke, your audience would be engrossed in your talk, and no one would flinch until you had concluded. You silly dreamer!

In the *real* speaking world, it is typically noisy, and sometimes chaotic, when you speak. Distractions are inevitable: People pirouette in and out of the room; buffoons in the audience jabber away, oblivious to you; cell phones shatter the peace; the waitstaff bangs and slings trays and dishes as though they were competing in an Olympic sport; hacking, sneezing, and nose-blowing are rampant; and that shifty microphone screeches at the most inopportune moment. Protest the unfairness of it all if that is cathartic for you, but plan on this hubbub.

Practice delivering your speech under tumultuous conditions, such as having your children wrestling at your feet, Skippy, the wonder dog, yapping for your attention, or the television blaring some drivel. Becoming accustomed to dealing with distractions as you practice, and remaining poised throughout, will mentally prepare you to deal with them during your actual presentation. Otherwise, you may unravel with the first disruption, which is never a pretty spectacle.

6. Do Not Memorize

Do not memorize the entire speech—ever. You will sound mechanical and vapid. Worse, you may eventually freeze. When that happens, your brain will degenerate to mush, you will babble like a baby, and death will seem like a welcome relief. Enough said for now, but much more on this topic in principle 19.

7. Videotape Your Practice Sessions

While practicing, videotape and analyze your presentation. Why? Because the camera never lies, although sometimes you might wish it would. It zeros in on all your idiosyncrasies. But before you whine too loudly, rest assured that the videotape is just as likely to bolster your confidence by spotting your speaking strengths. To master this tool, use the guidelines set out in principle 21.

However much thou art read in theory, if
thou hast no practice, thou art ignorant.

Sa'di

---

8. Forge Ahead While Practicing

As you become more comfortable with your delivery, refrain from stopping or repeating yourself when you flub a line or stumble over a portion of the speech—and you certainly will do both. Why forge ahead? Because in every speech, no matter how much you have practiced, you will surprise yourself by saying something unexpected ("Where did *that* thought come from?") and express a word, phrase, or idea differently from what you had planned. These mental lapses are an unavoidable consequence of speaking, and they actually add spark and vitality to your speech.

But if you constantly stop and scold yourself for your lapse ("You moron!") or start over ("Speech, Take 7, From the Top, Action!"), intent on delivering the speech verbatim, you will have the same Pavlovian response when you are speaking in front of your audience.

Instead of stopping and fussing, just continue speaking until you get back on track. Become accustomed to delivering your presentation based on its ideas and concepts rather than its exact words. The result will be a more conversational, natural presentation, not merely a precise, mechanical recitation of a script.

Chance favors only the prepared mind.
LOUIS PASTEUR

---

9. STAND, MOVE, AND GESTURE AS YOU SPEAK

As you practice your speech, stand, move, and gesture (principles 24 and 25). If you only practice your delivery while plopped down in your supple leather chair, elbows braced on your desk, gripping the text while twirling a pen, you will be entering unfamiliar territory when you actually deliver the presentation without these security blankets. You will encounter a much different speaking experience when you step to the lectern and confront a sea of faces.

Create a realistic speaking experience by standing and moving around. Focus on an imaginary audience; glance at your notes only periodically. Replicate as nearly as possible the experience of speaking to an audience. (If you want to simulate the whole shebang, dress up in your Sunday finest when you practice.)

10. PRACTICE WITH YOUR VISUAL AIDS

Visual aids clarify and reinforce your message, but they can also sabotage your talk with lightning speed in countless ways. If you intend to use any type of visual aid during your presentation, practice with it (see principles 37 and 38). Your visual aid will affect virtually every aspect of the presentation: your movement, timing, positioning, and interaction with the audience. Unless you relish public embarrassment as you blow a fuse battling with (or sometimes cursing at) inanimate objects, practice with these fiendish tools. You will be thankful you did (and so will your audience).

11. MONITOR THE TIME

Three simple rules: First, when you are in the final stages of rehearsing, time your presentation, and fit it within the prescribed time limits (being mindful that shorter is almost always preferable). Second, if you will be fielding questions during or after the presentation, allow additional time in your planning; if you use all your time speaking without allowing time for questions, you may frustrate your audience. Finally, if you anticipate laughter or applause as you speak (and what speaker does not want both?), budget time for that. Time limits are sacrosanct; exceed them at your peril. More on this pointer in principle 33.

You prepare the ground so that a lucky accident can happen.
SIDNEY LUMET

---

12. TEST THE PRESENTATION

You are feeling plucky and a little bullish. You have buffed the speech and fine-tuned your delivery, and now you are thumping your intrepid chest and chanting, "Bring on the audience!" For those *really* significant speeches, however—say, those where either a gazillion dollars or your job hangs in the balance—consider one additional step: Test it.

Deliver your speech to a carefully selected focus group. Present it to people whose opinions you trust and who will provide meaningful, constructive feedback. Their insights can be invaluable. Ask them: "Is my message clear?" "Are my stories and examples vivid?" "Is the speech logically organized?" "Should I slash material?" "Do I seem to exude confidence?"

"Is my delivery energetic or feeble?" "Were any mannerisms distracting?" And most importantly: "How can I improve the presentation?"

Assess the feedback, and dismiss such inane comments as "Lose twenty pounds, Tubby" or "Tell some yo'-mama's-so-ugly jokes." But if the input is valid, revise your talk and continue practicing. Smooth out the kinks before the live presentation.

There you have it: the quintessential practice plan (am I thumping my swollen chest now?). Start with this twelve-point plan, and experiment to devise a scheme that works best for you. Most importantly, practice. It may not make you perfect, but it will propel you much closer to the Promised Land: a first-rate presentation.

Master Your Notes

Speak as though it were the last sentence allowed you.

—Elias Canetti

I n a perfect speaking world, you would stand to speak, and your words would cascade out freely, effortlessly, and eloquently. You would deliver your message from your heart and dazzle your audience without the need for any notes. But then, reality crashes in on your "perfect speaking world" party.

In the real world, that fanciful scenario is unrealistic for most speakers. Why? Because, let's be honest: Speaking to any audience can be intimidating. If you are anything like me, facing one without a safety net of notes can nearly immobilize you. You risk losing your train of thought, and in your heightened state of speaking anxiety, your memory can play wicked games. Sometimes you cannot remember what you just said or what you planned to say next; in extreme cases, you might not even be able to remember your name or why you are standing before the audience. Notes can help you maintain your focus and, if you are in dire straits, rescue you from your mental quicksand.

Speakers often struggle to find the perfect formula for using notes. One speaker lugs his entire presentation to the lectern; another transposes his presentation, verbatim, onto note cards and marches to the lectern with a fistful in his hand. Both of these speakers are determined never to venture from their script. They don't, and as a result, their presentations sound mechanical. Worse, even before they begin speaking, their audience is already dreading it. They have concluded that speakers who need the entire speech or a bundle of notes must be unprepared, or that their speeches will be tedious, or both. They are usually right.

Eight Tips on Using Notes Effectively

Since most of us will use notes when we speak, here is how to use them most profitably.

1. Shun the Verbatim Script

It is tempting to take your entire presentation to the lectern, but resist this temptation. Why? Invariably, the entire typed-up script of your speech becomes alluring when you are standing at the lectern, particularly if you flub a line—and you will—or temporarily forget a point—a distinct possibility. The script is like a siren beckoning you toward the jagged rocks ("Look at me, read me, fixate on me!"). A quick glance will deteriorate into a protracted stare, and before long, you will be drawn into full-blown reading. Within moments after you begin reading, your audience will slip into daydreamlike mode, and jolting them back to reality during your speech will be a challenging task. Even the very best speakers have succumbed to the Script Siren's temptation.

Never underestimate your power to change yourself;
never overestimate your power to change others.
H. Jackson Brown, Jr.

Remember, you are a *speaker,* not a reader. Leave the script at your seat. I know, for some, that very thought is unthinkable. But if you are prepared to speak, you will not crumble into tiny pieces without your entire speech, I promise.

2. USE A SINGLE SHEET OF PAPER OR NOTE CARDS

Some speakers prefer to speak from a one-page outline of their presentation, so that they can add last-minute notes in the margins, they can easily highlight key words or phrases, and they do not have to slide note cards as they speak.

Most speakers prefer three-by-five-inch note cards, with one or two points per card. If you are a note-card devotee, you enjoy distinct advantages: You can place your notes in your hand or pull them from your jacket pocket discreetly, without alerting your audience that you have notes. Also, your note cards will fit on any lectern. Most importantly, because each card contains only key words or concepts, you cannot rely on them excessively, so you will have better eye contact with your audience.

Experiment with different outline and note techniques until you find a system that works for you.

3. MAKE YOUR NOTES LEGIBLE

"What happened?" you wonder as you squint to read your notes. The words on your note cards were perfectly legible when you reviewed them, sitting at your desk in the solitude of your well-lit office. Now, as you are standing before an audience in a dim banquet room, the words seem microscopic.

Here is some excellent tactical advice: Pray for the best speaking conditions, but plan on the worst. I have had to improvise in some of my presentations where the lectern was of a size suitable for a munchkin, and where it seemed as though only candles were illuminating the gloomy auditorium. Like a conscientious Boy Scout, be prepared.

Set your notes in a large font size (at least 18-point), and use only one side of the paper or note card. If you must handwrite your notes (and you really should avoid that option), print clearly—no cursive, no scrawl—with dark ink, in large letters. Leave wide margins and ample space between the lines. Don't cram words together; this is not the time to fret about trees lost from using excessive paper. The combination of your anxiety, poor lighting, and your need to pick up points quickly will render tiny print useless.

4. Number Your Note Cards

Number your note cards, because either they will become disorganized as you review them, or (far more likely) the dreaded Note Gremlin will snatch them out of your hand and scatter them everywhere just as you are about to speak. You will not recall fondly those awkward moments of silence as your audience stared at you fumbling to organize your note cards.

Also, mark any nonessential note cards, so that you know what points to skip if you are pressed for time (principle 33). To remind yourself that the point on that card is expendable in a time crunch, make a simple note in the corner: "DROP."

The fellow who thinks he knows it all is especially
annoying to those of us who do.
Harold Coffin

---

5. Isolate Quotes or Critical Information

You may occasionally want to share some critical information with your audience, such as a quote, a shocking fact, or a complex statistic. You need to guarantee that you deliver this information precisely, so devote a separate note card just for it. You may even want to pick up the card and read from it, to alert your audience that the point is important. You are not cheating if you read this type of information.

6. Practice Using Your Notes

Pristine outlines or notes sound great in theory, but if you have not practiced using them, you will not know where to glance when you are standing before your audience. Then you will waste valuable time scanning your notes, groping for the words or ideas that will trigger your next thought. As you stare at your notes during your word hunt, you will soon begin talking simply to break the silence, and before long, you will be having a monologue moment with your notes. Avoid that.

Practice your presentation with the same notes you plan to use while speaking (principle 17). You need to know exactly where the key words or ideas appear on the paper; practice will help you become accustomed to pinpointing that spot immediately, with a single glance.

7. SLIDE YOUR NOTE CARDS

Ideally, you want to deliver your speech without alerting your audience that you are relying on notes. But some speakers flip their cards with genuine gusto, eliminating any doubt that they are using notes.

Be subtle. Simply slide (don't flip) each card to the side as you finish using it, while maintaining eye contact with your listeners. Practice doing this, so that your notes never become a distraction. (And your reliance on notes can be your little secret.)

8. TALK TO YOUR AUDIENCE, NOT TO YOUR NOTES

No matter how you use your notes, remember to always focus on your listeners. If you continue speaking while you are glancing down, all your vocal power will be directed toward the lectern rather than projected out toward them. Even worse, if you spend more time talking to your notes than talking to your listeners, they might feel slighted, and soon they will begin to whisper about your peculiar relationship with your notes. Goodness knows where that will lead!

If you need to sneak a peek at your notes, do the following: 1. Pause (in other words, stop speaking). 2. Glance down at your notes. 3. Collect your thoughts. 4. Lift your head. 5. Reestablish eye contact with your listeners. 6. Then, and only then, resume speaking.

Since you will in all likelihood use notes for most of your presentations, let out a sigh of relief, because they are allowed. Just master them. Never let those little demons become a crutch or create a barrier between you and your audience. If you rely on them excessively—or worse, if you read them—your audience will quickly become catatonic. That will not bode well for your success. But if you use your notes wisely, they can be a valuable component in delivering a dynamic speech.

PRINCIPLE 19

MINIMIZE MEMORIZATION

I have never seen a human being who more perfectly
represented the modern conception of a robot.

—WINSTON CHURCHILL

Memorize your speech—but only if you aspire to sound like a robot. Why? If you speak by rote, you typically sound impersonal and detached. It seems as if you are reading to your audience—and you *are* reading to them, from the speech that you have engraved on a plaque in your memory. Do audiences leap for joy at the prospect of speakers *reading* to them? Unless your audience is composed of kindergartners, I doubt it.

The typical memorized speech lacks energy and any sense of spontaneity. As they listen to a memorized speech, listeners feel sedated, as though they have been drugged. No one relishes that prospect. Most listeners are astute; they can spot a memorized speech from one hundred yards: "Look over there, I see a rote talk headed our way! Run for cover!"

A speaker rarely connects with her audience while reciting a memorized speech. She is more concerned with what she will say next, and she is not interested in how her audience might be receiving her message. It is apparent to everyone but the oblivious speaker that her audience is bored silly. Most audiences, upon hearing a memorized speech, will mentally (or worse, physically) straggle off—quickly.

But this consequence of memorizing pales in comparison to the worst risk: going blank. I have visited that land; it is scary, and—believe me—you don't want to go there.

Perhaps my friend Clyde's harrowing tale will convince you. He had begun memorizing his speeches as a child, because some well-meaning teacher had repeatedly patted him on the head and praised him as a gifted memorizer; Clyde felt warm and fuzzy basking in that adulation. As an adult he continued to memorize his speeches (it had always worked splendidly after all), until one day his speaking world collapsed around him. I witnessed the implosion. It was pitiful.

One ought, every day at least, to hear a little song,
read a good poem, see a fine picture, and, if it
were possible, speak a few reasonable words.
JOHANN WOLFGANG VON GOETHE

He was speaking before several hundred people at a luncheon, and three minutes into his speech, he abruptly stopped, smack-dab in the middle of a sentence. He was mentally paralyzed, unable to utter the next word, or any word for that matter (although he did seem to be whimpering a prayer). The silence in the audience was eerie. Clyde's eyes darted to the ceiling as his mind whirred, desperately searching for his bearings in the mental script. His bewildered audience fidgeted and gawked at this spectacle.

His shoulders slumped, and he dejectedly dropped the microphone to his side. Five, ten, twenty seconds passed; you could almost hear the clock ticking. After approximately thirty seconds (which must have seemed like thirty minutes to him), he resumed speaking, *precisely* where he had stopped, in the middle of the sentence. Immediately after his speech, according to informed sources, Clyde entered a Speaker Protection Program, and he is now enjoying his cloistered life as a monk somewhere in Quebec.

Imagine that you are standing before an audience, with hundreds of people staring at you, anxiously awaiting your next words. Now stop reading, and imagine standing silently for thirty seconds while your mind is blank. You cannot remember your next words; you are not even sure you remember your name. Unless you have ice in your veins, that prospect should horrify you, and cause you to swear off memorizing.

Do I hear a dissenting voice? "But actors memorize their lines, and they are amazing speakers—right?" Many are, but here is the big fat distinction: They are professionals, who have devoted a lifetime to mastering the speaking craft. They can polish their delivery until it sounds conversational. Most of us do not have unlimited time that we can spend practicing our speeches. Only a handful of speakers in the world (seven, by last count) can make a memorized speech sound natural—and then only when they don't go blank.

FIVE PARTS OF A SPEECH TO MEMORIZE

The following may sound like a contradiction of what I just said (vacillation is healthy at times), but there are a few limited exceptions to the No Memorization Edict. Although you should never memorize your entire speech (ponder Clyde's excruciating experience if you are still undecided), you can and should memorize *portions* of your presentation. Although that advice may seem paradoxical (and may make you indecisive, if not bewildered), it is not, because sections of your speech are so critical to your ultimate success that, to ensure that your delivery and timing are flawless, you should memorize them. Here is the select list:

1. THE OPENING

Memorize your opening (principle 11). Once you begin speaking, you have a tiny window of opportunity to engage your audience and to convince them to listen. If you hesitate, misspeak, or muse during that period, your audience will quickly conclude that you are unprepared and will move on to more pressing issues (such as their favorite daydreams or their lunch plans). And if you botch your opening, your confidence will vanish for the remainder of the presentation.

There should be no hesitation, uncertainty, or waffling about what will tumble out when you first open your mouth. Do not speak impulsively. Memorize *exactly* what you will say in the opening, look at your audience, and deliver the words effortlessly.

2. QUOTATIONS

Memorize shorter quotations (I know, I know—more work, but definitely worth the added effort). Apt quotations add sparkle to every speech, enhance your credibility, and impress most audiences (principle 15). If you memorize the quotations, you will sound eloquent and well prepared, and every audience appreciates when a speaker honors them by preparing.

Sometimes (and these times should be rare), your quotation is a real whopper, too long to memorize. Then practice reading it repeatedly, committing as much of it as possible to memory, so that when you share it with your audience, you seldom need to refer to it.

Courage is the power to let go of the familiar.

RAYMOND LINDQUIST

---

3. PUNCH LINES

Memorize your punch lines. Humor typically succeeds when the punch line (the surprising twist, the startling revelation, the pithy observation) is reeled off with perfect timing. If you stammer, break eye contact, repeat yourself, or—Horrors!—forget the punch line, the humor generally flops.

For example, let's pluck a punch line from the abundant treasure trove of lawyer-bashing humor: "Q: How do you save a drowning lawyer? A: Take your foot off his head." Now, if you botch the punch line ("A: Take your foot off his foot"), you will confuse your audience, the humor will fizzle, and the silence will be disconcerting if not mortifying. Memorize those knee-slappers.

4. KEY POINTS

Memorize your key points and examples (if they are not too complex or lengthy), such as a shocking statistic, your underlying premise, or your call to action. Every speaker fondly hopes that his listeners will perch on the edge of their seats, listen with rapt attention, and squirrel his every word away in a cranny of their memories. Unfortunately, that will not usually happen, so you need to help them understand and remember the central points and examples. You increase the likelihood of that happening if you memorize and deliver them with conviction, with your eyes firmly fixed on your audience.

5. THE CLOSING

Memorize your closing (principle 16). You should close your speech with authority, not reading, not bungling words, and not improvising. Your closing is your final opportunity to connect with your audience and leave a lasting, favorable impression. That will not happen if you are focusing on your notes, introducing new ideas, fumbling for thoughts, or just winging it. Memorize your closing, and practice it until it flows naturally. Know it and nail it.

Be extremely selective about what you memorize, and never memorize the entire speech. The limitations inherent in memorizing your entire speech far surpass any perceived advantages. Audiences want to hear a presentation that entertains and engages them, not a robot mechanically reciting a script. And what more can I say about the risks of freezing and forgetting your memorized speech? It is a nightmarish experience, so avoid it. Clyde concurs.

ELIMINATE DISTRACTIONS

Rowing harder doesn't help if the boat
is headed in the wrong direction.

—KENICHI OHMAE

Let's be honest: Speaking can be a daunting task. For some speakers, anxiety surges at the mere prospect of speaking. ("I can't breathe!" "My heart is thumping right out of my chest!") Because of your anxiety, you sometimes unconsciously engage in bizarre behavior while speaking: You might mutter, gnaw your lips, tug on your clothing, fidget, fiddle with your notes (or anything else you can grab), stare at the ceiling (praying for divine intervention, perhaps?), or hypnotically sway as if you were standing on the bow of a ship at sea.

SEVEN DISTRACTING SINS TO AVOID

You should exude confidence whenever you speak (principle 30), so eliminate mannerisms that undermine your message. You will spot many of them as you analyze videotapes of your presentations (principle 21), but here are seven of the most common and distracting idiosyncrasies you should mercilessly eradicate. Just call them the Seven Sins.

1. LECTERN CLINGING

A lectern lover caresses, clings to, and hides behind that hulking block of wood. Without it shielding her from her audience, she feels exposed and vulnerable.

If you plant yourself behind a mammoth lectern, your audience may see only your head cautiously peering over the crest and perhaps a sporadic waggle of your hand, venturing out before quickly retreating. The lectern has become a physical and psychological barrier between you and your audience.

The sole purpose of a lectern is to hold your notes and writing instruments, not to prop you up or hide you. Lectern dependency highlights your nervousness and prohibits any meaningful movement or gesturing. If you are a lectern lover, it is time to sever the ties with your inanimate friend. Just step away. You will be fine, I promise.

All things are difficult before they are easy.
THOMAS FULLER

---

2. BOBBING AND WEAVING

A bob-and-weave speaker perpetually moves while speaking for no apparent reason other than to dissipate his nervous energy. He awkwardly shuffles and slides around, stepping from side to side, back and forth, or even in a triangular pattern.

Unfortunately, dancing does not render you invisible; your audience still sees you. And your nervous movement distracts them from your message. Instead of shuffling about, stand erect. Plant yourself confidently in a wide stance, with your shoulders squared to your audience, and your knees slightly bent (principle 24). Move only with a purpose—for example, to signal a transition from one point to another, to emphasize a key idea, or to convey an emotion. Shimmy and shake on the ballroom floor, not when you are speaking.

3. Playing with Jewelry, Clothing, or Writing Instruments

A high-style speaker is festooned with garish bracelets and necklaces, and rings adorn her every finger. She looks like a jewelry infomercial spokesperson. Her flashy ornaments are constantly jangling or banging against the lectern, and she cannot resist fiddling with them. Speaking is not the time to make a fashion statement, so jettison the jewelry.

Yet another speaker has a peculiar fascination with his clothing or his writing instruments when he speaks. He nervously twirls his pointer like a baton, smoothes and tugs at his clothes, adjusts his glasses, or clicks his pen until he just about drives his audience nutty. Beyond being distracting, these quirks send a blaring message to the audience: "I am scared silly." Eliminate them.

Bad habits are easier to abandon
today than tomorrow.
Yiddish saying

---

4. Wringing, Twisting, or Slapping Your Body

We seldom smack or punish ourselves in our daily conversations (at least, I hope you don't), but some speakers abuse themselves in front of an audience. As they speak, they unconsciously wring and contort their fingers, hands, and arms; pop their knuckles; knead their faces; scratch assorted itches; or clean their ears—yes, it happens, and I have videotapes to prove it.

One speaker repeatedly slapped her leg so viciously as she spoke that I feared for her safety. She had no idea she was doing it, and she adamantly denied that it was occurring until she saw it on videotape—and found walloping bruises on her leg. Your mannerisms when speaking should never become a distraction or, worse, a health hazard.

5. Jamming Your Hands in Your Pockets

Sometimes a speaker will burrow his hands deep into his jacket or pants pockets while speaking. To keep his hands occupied while in their temporary home, he might jangle what sounds like a gigantic piggy bank full of pennies. This approach resolves the perplexing quandary of what to do with those annoying appendages (your arms and hands) that you are obliged to bring with you every time you speak, but it severely restricts your ability to gesture effectively, and it distracts the audience. They focus on the jingling and not your message. Placing your hands in your pockets also closes you in, making you appear more like a wooden puppet than a dynamic speaker.

To keep your listeners focused on you, you should use animated (but never excessive or erratic) body language and gestures (principle 25). Once you get fully engaged in your talk, your gestures will come naturally, so don't imprison your hands in your pockets. Bring them out to play.

Habit is habit, and not to be flung out of the window by any man, but coaxed downstairs a step at a time.

Mark Twain

---

6. Grooming Your Hair

A speaker with a wild or disheveled hairstyle often finds her hair flopping in her face as she speaks. She flips, tucks, and even blows the locks away, but within seconds, they return. Another speaker might choose to groom himself as he speaks by running his fingers through his hair.

Before you speak, arrange your hair in a way that will not interfere with your presentation or annoy your audience. Think hairclips, gel, or bows; or for a really drastic fashion statement, consider shaving your dome. Just stop playing with your hair.

7. USING UNNECESSARY FILLER WORDS

Meaningless verbal clutter permeates many speeches, even those by very accomplished speakers. Rather than simply pausing between sentences or thoughts, these speakers segue by using such crutch words as "uh," "um," "and," "er," "all right," "you know," "so," "like," and "okay." These empty utterances grate on listeners. Purge them from your speeches. Instead, pause, be silent, collect your thoughts, and then continue (principle 23). You do not want to become the Wizard of "Ahs."

The Seven Sins are the most common eccentricities, but there are more, trust me, so add to your list as you find them. If you discover distracting intruders, write notes in the text of your speech to remind yourself: "No hand wringing," "Stop grooming," "Never pet the lectern," "Plant, don't rock," and "No leg slapping." Be ever vigilant, because these vexing oddities can insidiously creep into your speeches. If you allow one of them to hang around, unchecked, for a few speeches, the next thing you know—Woe is you!—you have yourself a full-blown habit. Before that happens, ruthlessly root it out.

CRITIQUE WITH
A CAMERA

Experience enables you to recognize a
mistake when you make it again.

—FRANKLIN P. JONES

The camera reveals all: the good, the bad, and the perfectly wretched. As you view a tape of your speech, you may wonder, "Who is that person jabbering away?" "Who is that person making that droning noise?" "Who is that marionette? Certainly not me!" Yes, that's you, and that is exactly what your audience sees and hears.

Videotaping helps neophyte and professional speakers alike polish all aspects of their presentations—timing, pacing, pausing, vocal variety, gesturing, body language, and eye contact—the whole enchilada. I always videotape presentations made by the university students and business professionals I coach. They often cower, wail, and gnash their teeth at this prospect.

I don't do this to torture them or because I am hard-hearted (Jell-O Boy feels their pain, believe me). I do this because revealing their quirks to them is very instructive. Without the videotape, I can repeatedly tell them about their distracting idiosyncrasies: "Stop caressing the lectern; people are beginning to gossip." "Don't stare at your belly button while you speak." They hear what I've said, and they even nod in agreement . . . and then they proceed to caress and stare anyway. But the videotape is often an epiphany. There is no better way for speakers to understand how effectively—or how ineffectively—they are communicating than by seeing for themselves.

Men's natures are alike; it is their habits that carry them far apart.
CONFUCIUS

Allow me to confess: For many years, I had the unconscious habit of stroking my necktie as I spoke. This ritualistic tie fetish puzzled and amused my audiences. Unaware of my bizarre habit, I mistakenly concluded, as the audience members stared at me: "Hallelujah! I am one fine speaker. They love me!" Of course, my audiences were really thinking: "What a weirdo!"

I don't know why, when, or where I developed this neurotic quirk (therapists were equally baffled). But the first time I saw it on videotape, I was so distressed that I was unable to focus on anything I said or did in the speech, because the truth was crushing: I was a kooky tie stroker. Videotaping my subsequent speeches helped me break the habit.

A video camera is an invaluable ally in your perpetual battle to eliminate annoying mannerisms that undercut your presentations. Seeing the unassailable truth on tape is often surprising—and occasionally shocking—but it is always educational. With that education, you will be able to eliminate all the distractions before you step up to the lectern. And here's the bonus: You can later destroy all the evidence of your really strange and embarrassing idiosyncrasies (or at least lock the tapes in a Swiss bank vault).

Before you become overwhelmed with videotaping angst, keep in mind that the camera is a learning tool, not a device for shattering your fragile speaking psyche. Any bad habit that you might have has probably crept into your talks unconsciously. Once you identify it, you can eradicate it.

And here is another nice bonus: You are just as likely to be pleasantly surprised, if not overjoyed, at what you observe. While speaking, you might have felt as though your face were burning, your knees were knocking, and you were on the verge of melting into a puddle, yet the tape might well depict a confident, poised speaker. Watching a video of your presentation can actually bolster your confidence. Like everyone else, you have speaking strengths, and you will see them when you study the video.

Any man is liable to err, but only a fool persists in error.
CICERO

SIX TIPS TO CAPITALIZE ON RECORDING

You have secured a vault for the videotapes, you have steeled yourself, and you are willing to plunge in and videotape your speeches. How can you extract the greatest benefit from this exercise? Here are six exceptional ideas:

1. BE OBJECTIVE

As you review the video, resist any temptation to berate yourself unmercifully: "No, no, no, you blockhead! The word is 'gizmo,' not 'gadget'!" Get a grip on yourself. If you are not careful, you can quickly become your own worst enemy.

Analyze objectively, and ask yourself questions such as the following: "Do my eyes dart furtively around the room, avoiding everyone?" "Do I anxiously rock from side to side like a metronome?" "Am I moving naturally, or do I look as stiff as an iron poker?" "Do I sound warm and friendly, or pompous and bored?" "Do I screech?" "Am I chattering or droning?" "Do I project?" And, of course: "Am I massaging my tie, blouse, or any other piece of clothing?"

In critiquing your presentation, also give yourself credit for what you did right. Relish every success, large and small: purposeful movement, fewer twitches, a conversational tone, a beaming smile, enhanced eye contact, a confident demeanor—soak it all in.

2. Focus on the Speech and the Delivery

Concentrate only on the speech and your delivery; don't fixate on factors that are not relevant to the effectiveness of your speech, such as your bulbous nose or those extra ten pounds (okay, maybe fifteen) that you have been lugging around. Irrelevant analysis is neither constructive nor beneficial. Instead, focus on the criteria in the previous tip, and analyze why your speech worked or, perhaps, why it missed the mark. Avoid the personal, extreme makeover analysis.

Experience is not what happens to you; it is
what you do with what happens to you.
Aldous Huxley

---

3. Capture Various Perspectives

Entice a friend to help you videotape your speeches, with the promise of an apple pie (or a new Mercedes if you are really desperate for her help); and threaten to bean her with a wooden spoon if she mocks you.

Why not just switch on the camera and let it roll? Here's why: Every time you speak, you are communicating with your audience, not only with your words but also with your facial expressions, your eye contact, and your body language, so you need to critique every aspect of your delivery. When speaking in front of an unattended camera, you cannot record all these views, especially as you move around.

Ask your camera buddy to zoom in on your face, eyes, hands, and feet, and to capture your gestures and other movements throughout the speech. Instruct her to focus on any disruptive mannerisms. She should even tape your audience, too (to help you gauge their reaction to your speech and see if they are dozing, doodling, or drumming their fingers while you speak).

4. COMPARE PRESENTATIONS

Compare and contrast your presentations to determine if any new eccentricities or distractions have surfaced. You will also be able to measure your progress, and if you have been following the blueprint outlined in this book, you should be pleasantly surprised at the dramatic improvements you have made. Your accomplishments will come gradually, in incremental steps, not instantaneously. Put in the effort, and you will reap the benefits.

A man who never makes enny blunders
seldum makes enny good hits.
JOSH BILLINGS

---

5. ALLOW TIME FOR ADJUSTMENTS

Allow enough time to review the videotape, to recover if the speech was a dud (smelling salts help), and to rectify the problems. Some adjustments may be simple (move periodically, stop flopping onto the lectern, stop scratching yourself, stop biting your lips) and some more involved (experiment with vocal variety, incorporate more expansive gestures, sustain your eye contact). But if you wait to review the video until an hour before you are scheduled to speak, it is probably too late to make any meaningful changes. And most of us do not produce our best work under a dire deadline.

6. BE REALISTIC

Do not expect perfection, because no presentation is flawless—not those given by professionals and, odds are, not yours. Speaking confidently is a learned skill, so don't anticipate miracles overnight. Don't be obsessive (or compulsive, for that matter) about addressing every problem immediately. ("Next speech, I'll make these fifty-nine improvements!")

If you attempt to fix a barrelful of challenges at one time, you will be overwhelmed and frustrated. Instead, analyze the videotape, decide where to best focus your energies, and continue to tinker. Target three goals for your next talk, and once you have rectified them, tackle another three. Gradually you will chip away at your list, until—Behold!—an exceptional speaker will emerge from the cocoon.

Learn in order to teach and to practice.
TALMUD

You will benefit enormously from videotaping and critiquing your presentations. If you are honest (but not brutal), objective, and receptive, you will learn more in several video sessions than most speakers learn in several years, and you will avoid many mortifying speaking moments. That bonus alone is priceless. Excellent speakers understand and harness the incredible power of the video camera. You should too.

PROJECT VOCAL POWER

*Eloquence lies as much in the tone of the voice, in the eyes,
and in the speaker's manner, as in his choice of words.*

—FRANÇOIS, DUC DE LA ROCHEFOUCAULD

Raise your hand if you have heard any of the following speakers:

- The *plodder*, who speaks at a painfully ponderous, halting pace, pausing frequently, methodically weighing every word as if it were profound beyond belief
- The *jabberer*, who races lickety-split through her speech, never pausing and seldom breathing, talking so fast that her listeners fear for her welfare
- The *screecher*, who sounds so high-pitched and strident that her listeners fear for *their* welfare
- The *droner*, who tediously hums along, sounding lifeless and bored and, as a result, boring his audience

I see quite a few hands. It is a chore to listen to these speakers even if it is a titillating topic.

Now raise your hand if you have heard a speaker who uses his voice to engage his audience, who sounds natural and relaxed, and who varies the pacing of his delivery. Or how about a speaker who employs vocal variety and energy, in a manner that is congruent with her message? Not as many hands, I see, and for good reason: Very few speakers do this. Most speakers barely scratch the surface of their vocal potential.

You can make dramatic strides toward enhancing your power as a speaker by learning to use your voice more effectively. Ironically, in a one-on-one conversation, you probably speak in a natural, relaxed manner, without giving it any thought. The person to whom you are speaking can close his or her eyes and still know exactly how you feel: excited, passionate, angry, disgusted, frustrated, indifferent, or relaxed.

But, unfortunately, an amazing transformation often occurs when you stand to speak: Your normal manner of speaking becomes abnormal, and you can sound diffident, monotonous, strident, or unnatural. Or perhaps you have become—drum roll, please—the authoritative-sounding Speaker, someone brimming with Seriousness and Pomposity. It is not long before the audience says, "Enough of you."

Enthusiasm begets enthusiasm.
HENRY WADSWORTH LONGFELLOW

EIGHT VOCAL POWER SECRETS

All right, you prefer to sound confident and natural. You might be asking, "How do I do that?" Good question, so here are eight excellent ideas:

1. WARM UP YOUR VOICE

If you were to bounce out of bed (or tumble out, for you sleepyheads), grab a microphone, and immediately begin speaking, your voice would sound raspy, discordant, and probably a little scary. Why? Because your vocal cords are not warmed up.

Before you speak, always warm up your vocal cords; otherwise, you risk straining them. Hum a few bars of a song (avoid gangster rap), or deliver a portion of your speech to an imaginary audience (the one that gave you seven curtain calls, remember?). If you are tense before you speak (and some of you do look a little taut and ashen), this warm-up will relax you and help prepare your voice to speak.

2. LISTEN TO YOUR VOICE

Enhancing your vocal power calls for cold, callous analysis, so stop whining, "I hate my voice" or "I sound like a dope." We are going to fix that. Remember our good friend, the one we met in principle 21, Mr. Camera (or his cousin, Mr. Audio Recorder)? Let's usher him back onto the stage and put him to work.

Record your presentations, and analyze how you sound. Ask yourself the following critical questions: "Would listeners know how I felt if they had only heard my presentation without actually seeing me speak?" "Do I emphasize key words or thoughts in my delivery?" "Is my voice congruent with my message—angry, calm, or self-assured?" "Do I sound like the type of person I would like to listen to?" Make vocal adjustments to address any shortcomings.

There are some people who leave impressions not so lasting as the imprint of an oar upon the water.

KATE CHOPIN

---

3. DON'T MUMBLE

Occasionally a speaker gets lost in Speakerland and forgets that he is standing before an audience. As he weighs his thoughts or inspects his notes, he becomes introspective and begins to mumble. He seems to be carrying on a fascinating monologue with himself.

If you talk to yourself regularly, counseling might help. In the meantime, be aware that when you are in the spotlight, your audience is focusing on you at all times. And they can hear you. Pause, collect your thoughts, look at your audience—and only then, speak.

4. NEITHER PLOD NOR JABBER

At the beginning of this principle, I introduced you to the plodder, that speaker who trudges along, pausing awkwardly and frequently. His pauses make him appear uncertain or even dense. His delivery is halting, sometimes unfolding at the speed of cold molasses. It is maddening to the audience ("Jeez, hurry up!" they silently implore).

A plodder also sounds like a stuffed shirt, intoxicated with his own self-importance. If the plodder characterization sounds anything like you, you may be taking yourself much too seriously. The historians will contact you in due course, when it's time to memorialize your scholarly musings; until then, zip up the pace a little.

I also introduced you to the antithesis of the plodder: the jabberer, who spews words so rapidly that no one can understand her. Listeners can neither process nor absorb the message; indeed, they can hardly catch their breath as the jabberer races along. Listeners are suspicious of this fast-talker, assuming that she must be trying to slip something by them. Consciously force yourself to slow down and interpose pauses (principle 23).

Experiment until you find a speaking rate that is neither too fast nor too slow.

5. EXPAND YOUR VOCAL RANGE

Slip into your imaginary physician's smock (okay, grab a stethoscope, too), and graph your voice the way an electrocardiograph monitors the activity of a heart—with high, low, and middle ranges. If your voice remains in a limited vocal range for a protracted period, like a droner, it lulls your audience into a drowsy state. They simply cannot focus on your message.

Because of the anxiety that speaking causes, you might also sound shrill or high-pitched. If you do this too often or stay up there too long, you officially join the Screecher Club. A squeaky-sounding speaker does not instill confidence in most audiences. Screeching is usually caused by nervousness and improper breathing. If you are struggling with the pitch of your voice, practice some of the suggested breathing exercises that are discussed in the recommended resources listed at the end of the book. Aim for a natural, conversational pitch.

Also, don't constantly rant and rave at your audience, in an effort to persuade them. That is seldom effective. Irritating, yes, persuasive, no. And don't continually speak in hushed tones, almost whispering your words, because your audience will decide you are a wimp, unconvinced of your own position.

In summary, a limited vocal range dilutes your message. To maintain your audience's attention and emphasize your key concepts, vary both the pitch and the volume at which you speak. Now, take off the smock. We have work to do.

6. Experiment with Different Voices

This is a great vocal exercise: Practice incorporating the dialogue of different characters in your presentation: Tweedledum and Tweedledee, Mutt and Jeff—you get the point. For example, tell a story involving a surly taxi driver (but sanitize the language) or a jilted lover (*really* sanitize that language). Attempt to capture their emotions in your voice: surprise, joy, antipathy, bitterness, or frustration. Using different voices will force you outside of your limited and comfortable vocal patterns.

Man never rises to great truths without enthusiasm.
Marquis de Luc de Clapiers Vauvenargues

---

7. Adjust Your Voice to Your Environment

Adapt your vocal volume to your environment, considering such factors as the size of the room (a tiny conference room versus a grand ballroom), what other activities are occurring in the room while you are speaking (meals being served, audience members milling around), and the acoustics in the room (high ceilings, hard surfaces). For example, you should project your voice much differently if you are in a quiet conference room than if you are speaking on the steps of City Hall with horns blaring and the agitated crowd threatening to crack your knee-caps. Know beforehand what conditions you will find where you are speaking, so you can be prepared (principle 26).

8. SOUND ENTHUSIASTIC

Do not expect your audience to get excited about your message if you are not. A lifeless speaker moves no one, because he himself sounds unmoved. If you are a droner, one of those passionless speakers who merely shares facts ("Just the facts, Ma'am"), your listeners will be yearning for a glimmer of a real person, any sign that blood might be flowing in the veins of the bionic man they are witnessing. If you are periodically banging cymbals to wake up your audience, you need to add a little zing to your voice—Pronto!

Sound enthusiastic! Use your voice to express the same passion that you had when you shared how your college basketball team won the national championship, or the elation you felt when you told your family about your promotion to Chief Muckety-Muck. Your enthusiasm will be contagious with the audience.

Only passions, great passions, can elevate the soul to great things.
DENIS DIDEROT

Study professional speakers and historic speeches if you want to see how some of the masters harness the power of their voices. Explore the History Channel's Web site (www.historychannel.com/speeches); it contains over a hundred of the greatest speeches of all time. You can also search the Web sites listed in principle 8 and review the recommended resources listed at the end of this book for additional examples.

Use the magnificent and complex instrument of your voice to enchant and amaze your audiences. Separate yourself from the gaggle of plodders, jabberers, screechers, and droners, and vow never to rejoin them. Why? Your audiences will thank you, and your deliberate projection of vocal power will make a colossal difference in every presentation. You may not get those seven curtain calls right away, but start making your presentations sparkle with vocal energy, and you will have a much better chance.

Capitalize on Potent Pauses

The most precious things in speeches are pauses.

—Ralph Richardson

A journalist once asked Isaac Stern, one of the world's preeminent violinists, what distinguishes the great violinists from the merely proficient, when all of them play the correct notes in the proper order. His response was insightful: "The important thing is not the notes. It's the intervals between the notes."[1]

Pausing—those intervals between the words—is also an excellent strategy when speaking. In fact, here is a sobering truth: A timely pause is often more compelling than anything you might have said to fill up the silence. Why? *Less said is often more.* I'm sorry if that lets a little air out of your speaking ego, but it's true.

You should pause at many junctures in your speech, for various reasons: to make transitions in mood or topic; to emphasize critical points; to alert your audience that you are about to share something significant; to heighten their suspense; to enable them to reflect; and to enable them to laugh. Simply stop talking, and reap the enormous benefits.

So, why don't more speakers capitalize on the powerful pause? Two reasons: First, there is a spectrum of fear associated with speaking. At one end of the spectrum, speaking can make you mildly anxious ("My heart is racing"); at the other end, you can become completely terrified ("End my misery—shoot me, please!"). When you are anxious, you might tend to rattle on because your overriding concern is to finish the speech as quickly as possible, minimize the damage to your self-esteem and reputation, and bolt away from the watchful eyes of your audience. Pausing would only prolong your agony.

Silence is wisdom where speaking is folly.
WILLIAM PENN

I have seen this in the courtroom. Allow me to illustrate. I once prepared my skittish witness (let's call him Sparky) to testify at trial. I repeatedly advised him to answer my critical question directly: "Sparky, just testify that 'it was three-fifteen p.m.,' and then stop talking. All right?" Sparky smiled and nodded in agreement with my simple instruction.

When the fateful moment arrived, I asked the question at trial; Sparky responded and then, just as we had planned, paused. But almost immediately, with everyone staring at him, he began to squirm. Under the unbearable weight of, what was apparently to him, the lengthy silence (approximately two seconds), he quickly crumbled and started blathering away: "It was three-fifteen p.m. . . . . I know, because I was screeching out of the Gulp & Guzzle Tavern parking lot after knocking back eight or nine beers with the boys. . . ." Pausing had become an alien concept to the suddenly chatty Sparky. I quickly settled that case.

The second reason for not pausing: You failed to plan to pause. Your mind might be blazing with ideas, and you cannot identify the crucial ones, so you don't discriminate. You attempt to cram a twenty-five-minute speech into a ten-minute slot; there is no time for pausing ("Not a second to lose!"), because you are on a mission to cover as much ground as possible.

Former Vice President Al Gore did this during his acceptance speech at the 2000 Democratic National Convention in Los Angeles. Throughout the speech, he trampled on the laughter and applause of his adoring audience because he was intent on completing the speech during prime-time television. As a result, he was often forced to repeat himself, and he blunted the impact of his message.

Sometimes you have to be silent to be heard.
STANISLAW J. LEC

NINE WAYS TO PAUSE WITH IMPACT

If pausing makes sense to you (and I hope it does), consider this plan. Don't just haphazardly pause for the sake of pausing ("Bingo, got another pause squeezed in!"), because that will make your delivery jerky. Instead, pause at specific junctures in the speech. Here are nine exceptional ways to benefit from the power of the pause.

1. ALLOW TIME FOR PAUSES

Speech time limits are sacrosanct (principle 33), which is a rule many speakers flout. If you fail to allow time for pausing, you will either trample the time limits, or you will speak too rapidly, trying to cram everything in. Neither approach is prudent. As you practice and time your presentation, budget time for pausing.

2. PRACTICE PAUSING

Pausing may seem unnatural, especially when all you *really* want to do is wrap it up quickly and scram. So as you rehearse your speech, practice pausing to replicate as nearly as possible every aspect of your delivery. Because you are likely to speak faster if you are anxious, write the word "PAUSE" in the text or on your note cards.

3. PAUSE BEFORE YOU BEGIN

If you are eager to tear into your speech, and you begin chattering before the welcoming applause has subsided, rein yourself in, Impatient

One. Let your audience size you up and get comfortable with you. You want to project confidence from the moment you are introduced (principle 30), and pausing helps you do just that.

Step up to the lectern, smile, and pause before you utter your first word. Wait until you have your audience's undivided attention (usually two to three seconds). Your pause alerts them: "I am confident, and you do not intimidate me." (Even if they do intimidate you, you will never have to tell them.)

Silence is not always a sign of wisdom,
but babbling is ever a mark of folly.
BENJAMIN FRANKLIN

---

4. PAUSE WHEN SHARING COMPLEX DETAILS

Listeners lose their directions easily, and it is your job as their tour guide to hold their attention and to keep them focused. Evaluate both your listeners (principle 6) and your speech, and determine whether they will understand your topic, or whether it is likely to fly right over their puzzled heads. The language and terminology you use daily (academic, legal, technical, or scientific mumbo jumbo, for example) may baffle many listeners ("The gizmo interfaces with the whatchamacallit, which, of course, controls the thingamajig . . . *blather, blather*").

Although you understand all the subtle nuances of your topic, your listeners might not. Before you begin to share complicated or technical data, pause. If the complexity of the topic warrants, consider pausing *and also* alerting them that what you are about to say might be confusing. With this preface, your listeners will concentrate carefully on what follows—something they might not have done if you had simply launched into your complexities without pausing and alerting them. Also, pause *after* you have shared the information, to enable them to digest it. Everyone may not grasp your technical data, but pausing certainly improves the odds.

5. PAUSE BEFORE AND AFTER QUOTATIONS

You have already seen the benefits of sprinkling quotations throughout your presentations (principle 15). To highlight each of these pearls of wisdom, pause both before and after you deliver it. Enable your listeners to reflect upon the quotation's import. If you zip right through the quote without pausing, you diminish its impact; in fact, your listeners may not even realize that you shared a quotation.

Trust the man who hesitates in his speech.
GEORGE SANTAYANA

---

6. PAUSE AFTER YOU ASK A QUESTION

You will engage every audience if you ask questions, but—and this is important—only if you pause immediately after asking them. If you pose a question and then speed ahead without pausing, you signal to your audience that you really did not expect them to think about or answer it, so they will do neither. Do that repeatedly, and you communicate to them that you do not care about their perspective. Soon they will be ignoring all your questions (and maybe ignoring you). If you want your listeners to contemplate your questions, pause.

7. PAUSE WHEN THEY LAUGH

If you take a stab at humor, as you should, and—Praise the day!— your audience laughs, be still. Do not talk. Just smile, pause, and enjoy the moment, because, trust me, sometimes the silence following your punch line is eerie. I know that eerie silence all too well.

Never stifle the laughter of your audience. If you keep talking while they are laughing, they will not hear you. Even worse, your talking will cause the laughter to die down much more quickly than it otherwise would have. So just pause, relish the laughter, and think: "They like me; they *really, really* like me."

8. PAUSE TO CREATE SUSPENSE

Pause before you disclose a critical fact, to build suspense: "I could not believe it when, sobbing, he confessed: [PAUSE] 'Yes, I jammed my thumb into the bottom of each of the chocolates, searching for caramels. I am so ashamed!'" A pause before a revelation alerts your audience to pay close attention. And once again, if you really want to magnify the impact, pause *after* you disclose the critical information as well.

The deepest rivers flow with the least sound.

QUINTUS CURTIUS RUFUS

---

9. PAUSE WHEN YOU CONCLUDE

Don't be one of those speakers who is so anxious to skedaddle as she approaches her conclusion that she begins packing up her materials and walking away as she mumbles her final words. This will send the message that you are eager to conclude, and you will end with a resounding thud. Your closing is critical (principle 16), so to heighten the dramatic impact of your message and to convey your confidence, do the following: Just before you utter your final words, and again afterward, pause.

Well-timed silence hath more eloquence than speech.

MARTIN FARQUHAR TUPPER

Judiciously weave pauses into your speech. If you pause too often, your speech will become tiresome and choppy. And if you never pause during your breakneck delivery, the full force of the message will be diminished. But well-placed pauses will highlight critical points and send an unmistakable message to your audience: "I am self-assured." It works for Isaac Stern, and it will work for you, so pause and capitalize on those critical intervals between the words.

PRINCIPLE 24

STAND TALL

*[D]o not let [fear] into your
house. . . . Stand up straight.*

—JOHN CHEEVER

Contrast the following two speakers: After being introduced, Sluggo Sammy lethargically shuffles to the front of the room like a big oaf. His shoulders are slumped, his spine curved, and his energy apparently depleted. He props himself against the lectern, virtually draping himself over it. His eyes are riveted on his notes rather than on his audience ("What audience?" he wonders). Sammy stifles a gaping yawn, and his gestures are feeble. He seems so limp that you fear that at any moment he will crumple to the floor.

Enter speaker two, Perky Peggy. She confidently strides to the lectern, quickly arranges her notes, and then steps away from the lectern. She smiles, pauses, and establishes immediate eye contact with her listeners. Her shoulders are back, and her feet are firmly planted. She leans toward her listeners to engage them.

As a member of the audience, you have not heard one word from either speaker, but answer these questions: What are your immediate impressions? Who appears to be more confident, more professional? Are you thinking, "Whoa! Sluggo Sammy will surely have a doozie of a presentation. I can't wait!" I doubt it.

Unless you are Sluggo Sammy's mother, you dread his talk. His body language is screaming: "I am a wet dishrag!" Maybe that is an inaccurate and unfair assessment, but the audience is likely to immediately form that conclusion. Sluggo Sammy has handicapped himself from the outset. In stark contrast, Perky Peggy's demeanor, posture, and stance instantly command their attention and arouse their interest.

This world belongs to the energetical.
ALEXIS DE TOCQUEVILLE

Every audience will choose an energetic speaker, one who approaches the task of speaking with gusto and passion, over one who seems to approach it as pure drudgery—*every* time. Your audience is evaluating you, from the moment they first see you. Your body language and demeanor speak volumes, signaling whether you are excited to be speaking or whether you are completely indifferent and maybe even bored. Listeners are remarkably perceptive, so your nonverbal communication is critical to the success of your presentation. In fact, it may have a greater impact on your listeners than what you actually say.

If you apathetically trudge to the lectern, slouch, and violate all the rules of posture that your mother drilled into your head since childhood ("Stand up, or you'll become a hunchback!" "Chin up, Mopey Face!"), you are signaling to your audience that there are dozens of places you would rather be at that moment. You are constantly communicating with your body language, so be careful what message you send.

EIGHT GUIDELINES FOR POSTURE AND MOVEMENT

All right, so you want to join the perky club—a wise choice. How should you position yourself and move around in front of your audience to convey confidence? Here are eight outstanding suggestions:

1. REMOVE PHYSICAL BARRIERS

Any object between you and your audience becomes a physical and psychological barrier. The usual suspects: the mammoth lectern, of course, but also the microphone stand, a desk or table, a pad of paper, a writing instrument (not much cover there), and even your intertwined fingers and folded arms. As a speaker, you want to seem accessible, confident, and trustworthy, so strip away all these barriers. Stand tall, remove the barriers, and let the audience see all of you.

2. NEVER PLANT YOURSELF IN ONE SPOT

Sometimes a speaker remains riveted to one spot for the entire presentation ("I ain't movin', no way, no how!"). Like a prospector in the Gold Rush, he has staked his claim to a plot of stage, and he will guard it just as fiercely. Oh, he may glance to the left or right, and if he is feeling especially spunky, he may even pivot at the hips. But his feet might as well be buried in cement.

Can you say, "R-I-G-I-D"? Loosen up! It will not matter if you are revealing the secret formula for concocting Coca-Cola or sharing your exploits climbing Mount Everest in your swimsuit; it will be extremely difficult for you to maintain your audience's attention if you have become, essentially, an inanimate object. Move around (but heed the next three guidelines).

3. NEVER PACE

Sometimes a speaker will nervously pace back and forth like a caged zoo animal anxiously awaiting a feeding. Perhaps she has deluded herself that constant movement renders her invisible. Are you anything like her? Sorry, your audience still sees you. Your perpetual pacing contributes nothing to your speech and eliminates any doubts that your audience might have had that you are nervous. Avoid the zoo-animal syndrome.

4. NEVER DANCE

Then there is the speaker who suffers from that peculiar malady, Happy Feet. His feet are perpetually moving as he speaks. Sometimes they are sliding side to side or back and forth; other times they step in a rhythmic, repetitive pattern. Occasionally, the speaker just bounces and taps his feet. All this occurs for the sole purpose of dissipating nervous energy. Take command of your feet, and restrict your dancing to the dance floor.

5. MOVE WITH A PURPOSE

As you practice your presentation, consciously decide when you should move—for example, when you make a transition from one story or point to the next, when you segue from your analysis of the problem into your proposed solution, when you want to signal a change in the mood of your presentation, when you need to illustrate distance or location, or when you are portraying a conversation between several individuals.

You can also move when you are covering less significant information, but then, when you want your audience to really concentrate on the words you are about to share with them, stop, pause (principle 23), plant yourself, and deliver your point. The contrast between your movement and your sudden stop helps ensure that your audience will focus on you at a critical point in your speech.

Purposeful movement helps project a confident image.

Self-assurance reassures others.
GARRY WILLS

---

6. STAND WITH CONVICTION

You want to exude confidence whenever you speak, so make sure your body cooperates. Position yourself in the following manner: Assume a spot in the center of the stage. Align your feet with the outside of your shoulders; pressing your feet together will appear unnatural (even worse, you may teeter and possibly tumble over, never a great confidence booster). Pull your shoulders back, and keep them squared up with your audience. Let your arms drape at your sides. Shift your weight slightly forward onto the balls of your feet. Slightly bend your knees; if you lock them, you restrict your blood flow (and increase your chances of fainting, yet another way to undermine your fragile speaking psyche).

7. FACE YOUR AUDIENCE

Speakers who use visual aids often fall into the habit of orienting themselves toward the visual aid rather than toward the audience. When you speak, look primarily at your listeners to engage them in your presentation. Step toward them to signal that you want their attention and to communicate the message that they do not intimidate you. Avoid turning your back on them, because you will lose eye contact and miss all the vital signals they are sending: nods of agreement and note taking, or puzzled looks and spitballs flying across the room. Face the crowd.

8. STUDY YOUR MOVEMENTS ON VIDEOTAPE

Time to break out Mr. Video Camera again (it is a genuine love/hate relationship with him, isn't it?). Begin recording from the moment you approach the lectern, and don't stop until you return to your seat. Then study the tape. Scrutinize your body language, and ask: "Do I stride to the front of the room with confidence?" "Do I fidget, rock, or shift my weight?" "Are my shoulders back and squared to the audience?" "Do I move fluidly, or do I appear as stiff as a board?" "Do I lean toward the audience, or am I constantly retreating and plastering myself against the wall at the front of the room?"

Next, turn the sound off, and fast-forward the video, always an enlightening and sometimes an entertaining exercise that will reveal whether you are hypnotically swaying side to side or back and forth, and whether any of your movements seem annoyingly repetitive. Don't blame Mr. Video Camera, because he is just the messenger. Your audience is seeing exactly what he records, so ensure that your nonverbal body language is commanding.

Nothing is stable. Nothing absolute.
All is fluid and changeable.
There is an endless "becoming."
BENJAMIN N. CARDOZO

Stiff, lethargic, or erratic body language undermines your authority as a speaker. Be aware of the message you are sending to your audience. Trust me: They will give Perky Peggy their undivided attention, and they will cringe and groan when Sluggo Sammy shuffles to the front of the room to speak. Listening to a slouching, spiritless speaker looms as a chore. Engage your audience with animated, purposeful, and confident body language.

GESTURE WITH CONVICTION

Suit the action to the word,
the word to the action.

—WILLIAM SHAKESPEARE

It is the mother of all speaking bugaboos, *the* burning issue for many speakers. It torments neophyte speakers and even vexes some speaking pros. Some agonize over it and suffer sleepless nights; some turn to drink; others pray for divine inspiration to unravel the mystery. The perplexing question: "How in the world do I gesture?" Many would pay a king's ransom for a magic potion, Gestures in a Bottle.

The irony is that in daily conversations, you gesture freely and naturally, without the slightest hesitation. Your hands and arms flow with your words as you speak. You are animated, relaxed, and engaged in your exchange. You make chopping motions with your hand to get across your point, jab your finger into your palm to drive home your message, and even pound your fist for emphasis. And you do this without even thinking about it.

But some mysterious metamorphosis occurs in those fateful few steps from your warm seat in the audience to the loneliness of the lectern. Anxiety grips you, and suddenly—Poof!—you are immobilized. Your gesturing becomes positively anemic, or you become as rigid as a plank of wood—and that will not impress your audience.

So how do some speakers attempt to address the gesturing conundrum? In peculiar ways—most of them unnatural, and some of them remarkably bad: One speaker clutches the lectern with a white-knuckled viselike grip. Another speaker locks his hands at his belly. Still another speaker plasters her elbows against her ribs (in a position aptly described as Velcro Elbows). There is also the speaker who fiercely clasps his hands behind him (protecting his buttocks) in a formal military stance. Another folds her hands below her waist in a modest fig-leaf position that conjures up images of Adam and Eve. Yet another tightly crosses her arms in an authoritative, defiant stance. And finally we have the speaker who simply crams his hands deep, deep, *deep* into his pockets; those hands never see daylight for the duration of the speech.

Problem solved, right? No, problem compounded. Each of these "solutions" in the all-star lineup of gesturing don'ts will severely handicap you as a speaker and will undermine the confident image you want to project. Why? You appear puckered up, wimpy, robotically stiff, and ridiculously tense. In the worst case, rigor mortis seems imminent.

So what is the solution, you ask? You may snort in disdain at the pure simplicity of the answer, but more than twenty-five years in the speaking arena have convinced me of its validity: *Forget about yourself, and focus on the audience.* That's it.

Men trust their ears less than their eyes.
HERODOTUS

Speakers who are tied in knots about their gesturing are typically focusing on how they appear *to* the audience rather than how their message is received *by* the audience. Consider every presentation as something that you want to say, to people who want to hear it. Take the focus off you, and place it on your audience (principle 29). The critical question should never be, "How do I gesture?" Rather it should be, "How do

I connect with my audience?" Answer that, and you will resolve the gesturing puzzle.

EIGHT GESTURING TIPS

Those of you suffering gesturing phobia might be thinking (or obsessing): "Fine, but can you give me specific gesturing guidance?" Certainly. Help is on the way in the subsequent paragraphs, and the real bonus: The gesturing solution does not involve pain, medication, or hypnosis. To help you transform your handicap into a genuine asset, here are eight gesturing nuggets of wisdom.

1. BELIEVE IN YOUR MESSAGE

First, never approach any presentation with the attitude that it is "just another speech." Why? Because it never is. If you think it is, don't speak. If you can't say what you have to say with enthusiasm and conviction, perhaps you simply should not be saying it at all. If you don't believe your message is important, neither will the audience; you will indeed just be reciting "another rote speech" that will leave your listeners yawning.

Instead, develop the mind-set that your listeners need and want to hear what you have to say. And they actually do. They are there to hear you speak for any variety of reasons: to be informed, to be persuaded, or perhaps to be motivated. They do not want to waste their time listening to a detached bore. Become engrossed in and excited about your message, and your gesturing self-consciousness will melt away.

2. MAKE THE GESTURE FIT THE EMOTION

Your gestures should match your emotions and accentuate your message: more restrained if your message is informational, more animated if you are selling or persuading. For instance, suppose that you had been passed over for a promotion—for the ninth time—and you were justifiably livid. If, as you pleaded your case to the honchos on the promotion review panel, you gestured with a puny wave of your hand, you would be belying your anger. Instead, you should wave your arms, pound your fist, or twirl away in disgust. (Just don't go berserk if you want to be around to be passed over the tenth time.)

3. Never Cling to the Lectern

Some of you (and you know who you are) cower behind that hulking lectern (many of which are about the size of Noah's Ark) and fiercely clamp it (fearing perhaps that you might be swept away in the Great Flood if you loosen your grip). As a result, your movements are limited to head bobbing and shoulder shrugging—gestures hardly likely to enhance your message.

Okay, Lectern Lovers, try this: Take a step back, so that you will have to stretch your arms forward to grasp your wooden friend. The stretch may feel awkward (as it should), but it will remind you that lectern hugging is forbidden.

Now, if you are really feeling spunky, periodically move to the side of the lectern as you speak, so your audience can see you. The sky will not fall, I promise. You may even feel remarkably liberated. Don't worry: If you start to wobble on your newfound speaking legs, you can dart back in a pinch to the safety of Mother Lectern.

Gestures and facial expressions do indeed communicate, as anyone can prove by turning off the sound on a television set and asking the watchers to characterize the speakers from the pictures alone.
Peter Farb

---

4. Drop Your Arms to Your Sides

Your arms are useful for emphasizing key points as you speak. Unfortunately, if you are busy nearly massaging your hands raw, if you cross your arms in front of your chest, or if you press your elbows against your ribs, you cannot use your arms in any meaningful way.

Instead of handicapping yourself, simply drop your arms to your sides, so that as you become engaged in sharing your message with your audience, your arms are in a position to gesture naturally.

5. INCORPORATE PLANNED GESTURES

In dire straits, if you are really struggling with your gestures, incorporate a few planned gestures into your presentation. For instance, you might try holding your hand up, displaying three fingers, and counting off while you tell the audience the three reasons why you should never be compelled to speak: "First, the written word is intrinsically beautiful; second, speaking is cruel and unusual torture; and third, sweating profusely from anxiety as I speak is not glamorous."

As you begin to discuss each point in detail, gesture again: "Let's discuss point one, the beauty of the written word. . . ." But be careful: You do not want to look like a marionette gesturing, so practice this technique until it seems natural, not jerky or mechanical. Your comfort level will rise with practice.

6. ADD VARIETY TO YOUR GESTURES

Repetitive gestures quickly become monotonous. They seem choreographed and predictable. Their impact, and the audience's attention, quickly plummets. And since many audiences have a limited attention span, you must use every tool in your speaking arsenal to keep them engaged. Spice up your presentation with a little gesturing variety: sweeping your arms, raising your hand, or counting off your points on your fingers.

7. MAKE THE GESTURES FIT THE SPACE

Diminutive gestures may be effective if you are speaking in smaller venues, such as a classroom or boardroom, but they will be lost in a larger setting, such as a cavernous hotel ballroom. In that type of mammoth arena, your gestures must be expansive and sweeping. Find out about the facility where you will be speaking (principle 26), and practice using the same type of gestures you will need to use in that size venue.

8. STUDY YOUR GESTURING ON VIDEOTAPE

Analyze the videotapes of your presentations (principle 21), both from your practice sessions and from your speeches before audiences. This is an excellent way to root out any wimpy or ineffective gestures. Be warned, however: Sit down and breathe deeply before you begin watching, because this gesturing analysis can be downright scary. You may gasp in dismay and even hyperventilate at your lifeless gestures. The good news: The sooner you identify any lame or distracting gestures, the easier it is to banish them, preferably before they blossom into full-blown habits.

Every act of conscious learning requires the willingness
to suffer an injury to one's self-esteem.
THOMAS SZASZ

For more detailed information on gesturing and nonverbal communication, see the recommended resources at the end of this book, which offer advice and exercises to help you conquer your gesturing phobia.

Your goal is to gesture with authority and conviction. Purposeful and commanding gestures will enhance your presentation and convey your emotions in a way that words alone cannot. They will make you stand out like a real person in a world deadened by robotic speakers. No one likes watching a speaker who displays all the gesturing flexibility of an iron statue. Until the Gestures in a Bottle potion hits the market, concentrate on the audience and how you can effectively connect with them. Do that, and the gestures will soon flow naturally.

PART V

FOCUS ON THE DETAILS

AT LAST, IT IS NEARLY SHOWTIME. It has been an arduous journey, with many zigs and an occasional frustrating zag along the way. But you made it. You have revised and polished the text of your speech, repeatedly practiced and refined its delivery, and videotaped and critiqued it. You are ready to speak and amaze the throngs.

A word is dead
when it's said,
some say. I say it just
begins to live
that day.
EMILY DICKINSON

So, with all the grunt work accomplished, all you need to do is show up at the designated time and place, let the words flow, and a stellar performance is virtually guaranteed—right?

Sorry, there is more work to be done (I know—will it ever end?). Specifically, you have to attend to all the critical details that, if not addressed, could potentially diminish your effectiveness at best and undermine your speech at worst. Part V outlines the steps you should take to make sure that you anticipate and plan for everything when you speak.

PRINCIPLE 26

PLAN CAREFULLY

A man's accomplishments in life are the cumulative
effect of his attention to detail.

—JOHN FOSTER DULLES

Do details *really* matter? After all, isn't the message all that really counts? Well, as Clint Eastwood would say: "[Y]ou've got to ask yourself one question: Do I feel lucky? Well, do ya'. . . ?"

If luck is not always on your side, then remember this: There are *no* insignificant details. Ignore them, and you will at least heighten your anxiety. But overlook the wrong detail, and your presentation may implode before your very eyes. From my perspective as a speaking implosion expert, I assure you: A speaking disaster is one gut-wrenching experience you want to avoid.

In a perfect world, your only job as a speaker would be, appropriately enough, to speak. You would arrive at the designated speaking location and find an ideal environment. The room would be arranged exactly as you had requested; the temperature would be cool and comfortable; soothing classical music would be wafting through the room; and the AV equipment would work flawlessly. Best of all, an eager assistant would be at your beck and call, scrambling to address your slightest desire. You would be treated like royalty, because after all, you are (drum roll, please): The Speaker. That, my friends, is a speaker's utopia.

Now, back in the *real* speaking world, it *very rarely* works that smoothly. "Never" might be an overstatement, but not by much. It is very risky to simply show up at the last minute to speak, expecting that all the details have been handled (because they rarely are) or that you will have time to address them (because you seldom do). You are just as likely to arrive at the venue and encounter bedlam: saunalike conditions, no AV equipment, no lectern, nothing you previously requested, and—worst of all—no eager assistant, no meeting host, and nary a human being in sight.

If you leave the details to others, you may find yourself minutes before your presentation wildly scrambling around, sweating like a pack mule, hoisting cumbersome chairs, shoving unwieldy tables, and juggling a cornucopia of unimaginable problems. In this frenzied state, you will invariably overlook something. And rest assured: Your oversight will eventually surface at the most inopportune moment—such as smack-dab in the middle of your presentation.

So, do ya' feel lucky?

An individual who is observed to be inconstant to his plans,
or perhaps carry on his affairs without any plan at all, is
marked at once, by all prudent people, as a speedy
victim of his own unsteadiness and folly.
ALEXANDER HAMILTON

The best advice for every speaker, in any speaking situation, is this: Leave nothing to chance. Assume that if you do not personally handle the details, or personally see that they are handled, they will not be handled. That cynical view may not jibe with your sincere belief that people will always do what they promise to do, but that kind of Pollyannaish faith is sorely misplaced when you are the speaker.

And here is the worst part: When your presentation flops, your audience will fault *you*, not the people behind the curtain and not those who failed to deliver. Instead, they will blame you for everything: the screeching microphone, the botched introduction, and the sweltering conditions in the room. Everything. Protest the unfairness until you are blue in the face, but don't be surprised when the disappointed masses turn surly on you. Audiences expect results, not excuses.

TEN THINGS YOU NEED TO KNOW FOR EVERY SPEECH

So, besides wailing and gnashing your teeth, what can you do to ensure that neglected details do not undermine your speech? If you are prudent, you will use the extensive checklist set forth in principle 28 when preparing for every speech, particularly the critical ones (like when your job hangs in the balance). But the following ten items deserve special attention, because if treated cavalierly, they have a proven record of sabotaging speeches with lightning speed.

1. KNOW WHO IS IN CHARGE

Determine who is responsible for handling all the issues (and there will be many) that arise between the date when you agree to speak and the date when you actually speak. Make that person your new best friend. That expert can answer questions, provide support, and help you avert calamities. Shamelessly fawn if necessary, and resort to candy bribes in a pinch.

2. KNOW IF PLANS HAVE CHANGED

Particularly when you make speaking arrangements months in advance, circumstances can and often do change. What might change? The size of the audience, the topic you are expected to address, the length of time you are expected to speak, or the location or time of your presentation. Sometimes the plans have changed (say, for instance, the meeting at which you were the keynote speaker has been canceled), and—Surprise!— no one has bothered to tell you. Nothing will dampen your enthusiasm for speaking faster than staring at a room full of empty seats when you were scheduled to speak. Stay abreast of all developments.

3. KNOW THE HEAD COUNT

The size of the audience will dictate how you should prepare for many aspects of your presentation, such as which visual aids will be suitable, the number of handouts you should prepare, your need for a microphone, and how the room will be arranged. Addressing an intimate gathering of thirty people poses an entirely different set of challenges than does speaking to a boisterous crowd of five hundred.

Plans must be simple and flexible. . . . They should be made by the people who are going to execute them.
GEORGE S. PATTON

---

4. KNOW THE TERRAIN

Know the terrain where you will be speaking. Know, for example, whether you will have theater seating in rows or chairs at tables? Why do you need to know this? You want your audience to be as close to you as possible, so you can interact with them, field their questions, and read their reactions. (On the other hand, if you anticipate that your message will cause a violent response, you may prefer to speak by teleconference—from another country.)

Certain room conditions cannot be remedied, such as inherent acoustical limitations or columns that might interfere with sight lines. Even if you cannot correct these problems, if you are aware of them before your presentation, you can mentally prepare to deal with them when you speak.

5. KNOW THE LECTERN OPTIONS

Preferred option: no lectern, just a table for notes, so you can freely move about. Second option: a tiny lectern, similar to a music stand, suitable for holding only a few notes and your favorite pen. Worst option: a hulking mound of wood about the size of New Hampshire.

A massive lectern will dwarf you as the speaker and severely limit your visibility, your gesturing, and your body language. If that is your only option, insist that you have enough microphone cable and available space to stray away from it and move about the stage. And if all else fails, bring a shiny, sharpened ax to whittle down Mr. Lectern.

6. KNOW YOUR MICROPHONE NEEDS

How best to describe microphones? All unique, most unreliable, and every single, sneaky one anxious to betray you as you speak. Principle 35 provides a list of microphone rules. If your presentation requires you to use a microphone, don't skim that chapter. Rip it out, laminate it, and even put it under your pillow if it will help you absorb the rules.

We're all, it seems, saving ourselves for the senior prom.
But many of us forget that somewhere along
the line we must learn to dance.
ALAN HARRINGTON

---

7. KNOW THE VISUAL-AID RULES

It is a statistical dead heat which can gut a presentation faster: microphones or visual aids. Visual aids present a sweeping array of challenges; the rules for using them are discussed in detail in principles 36, 37, and 38. The salient points: Ensure well before the masses arrive that the visual aids are in the room and working. Set aside ample time for testing them. Recalcitrant visual aids torpedo hundreds of presentations every day, and in all likelihood, at this very moment, they are sinking a few speakers. Don't trust them.

8. KNOW WHEN YOU ARE SPEAKING

You need to know the time of day when you will be speaking. Content-heavy presentations work best in the morning when attention levels are at their highest. At the end of the day or following a meal, attention plunges dramatically, so if you are speaking then, eliminate 30–50 percent of your content (I know, I know—it's all fabulous material, but some of it has to go, sorry).

Speaking during a meal can be especially challenging. You will be required to compete for your audience's attention with scrumptious desserts or the clanging of dishes as the waitstaff clears the tables. You need to mentally prepare for these distractions.

I was once scheduled to speak at a luncheon, presumably after the meal had ended. Unfortunately, the members of this audience had apparently not eaten a solid meal in over a week, judging by the zeal with which they were attacking the food. With shirtsleeves rolled up, they were devouring everything in sight. In the middle of this feast, while the audience members were gorging themselves, my introducer leaned over to me, his jowls firmly packed with food. As he wiped the gravy off his chin, he mumbled, "We're running behind, and . . . [Chew] we promised you thirty minutes for your talk. [Chew] So, why don't I go ahead and introduce you now? [Swallow] You can begin speaking while we're eating."

As I observed the ravenous crowd, I knew not only that my message would be ignored, but also that the audience members would resent my insensitive intrusion on what appeared to be a truly religious eating experience. Without any hesitation, I replied, "No, why don't you allow them to finish? I will adjust the time of my speech to meet your schedule."

Did that require instantaneous adjustments to my speech that were a wee bit unnerving? Certainly. But as a result, this particular audience was more receptive, because I was not competing with a meal for their attention. Perhaps a portion of my message stuck. I will never know for sure, however, since they were clamoring for a second dessert when I left.

9. KNOW WHO ELSE IS SPEAKING

If others are speaking with you on the program, ask these questions: "What are their topics?" "How long will they speak?" "When are they scheduled to speak?" Why? Because you may encounter a boorish speaker with a swollen head who will unilaterally decide that he prefers your topic to his; he will switch topics with you but neglect to inform you. Or perhaps he will determine that his allotted time is inadequate for someone of his stature—after all, the audience cannot possibly hear too much from him—so he will flout the time limits, gobbling up large chunks of your time.

Unless you relish dancing on the head of a pin with hundreds of people watching, or unless you are remarkably gifted at improvising, know these risks beforehand and plan accordingly.

To know things well, we must know them in detail.

FRANÇOIS, DUC DE LA ROCHEFOUCAULD

---

10. KNOW WHO WILL INTRODUCE YOU

Never—that is, *N-E-V-E-R*—let anyone "wing it" on your introduction. Not your grade school buddy, not your boss, not even your rabbi. Surrendering control over your introduction is a recipe for disaster. Invariably, some nitwit will botch it if given the chance. This issue warrants an entire principle (principle 27), because it is critical. For now, just remember one word: *never.*

Nagging details can make or break every presentation. Gamble at the roulette wheel, at the racetrack, or in the office pool, but never while preparing to speak. A confession: I have felt lucky a few times, and I ignored the details. I was confident that my wealth of speaking experience would save me from any calamity. I was wrong. Don't gamble in the speaking arena.

PRINCIPLE 27

PREPARE YOUR
INTRODUCTION

*What makes a plan capable of producing results is the
commitment of key people to work on specific tasks.*

—PETER F. DRUCKER

You have carefully crafted, honed, and practiced your presentation, and in mere moments, you will stand to speak and mesmerize the audience. But then you realize—Oops!—you forgot to prepare the script that your host will use to introduce you.

Not a problem. You can just scribble a few ideas on a scrap of paper and pass it to your introducer (a big mistake), or you can simply tell him or her: "Go ahead and say whatever you want. You know me" (a mammoth mistake). Why is each of these solutions a mistake? Because the introduction sets the tone for the speech. An exceptional introduction will generate interest and excitement, but a bad one can sully the entire speech. Don't stumble before you even begin.

Do I hear a dissenting voice? I know what you are thinking: "It is *just* an introduction. No big deal." Wrong. It is a huge deal, because introductions are regularly bungled. They suffer a greater than 50-percent failure rate, and here is how: An inept introducer may mispronounce your name: "Mr. Chocker? Mr. Clucker? Mr. Chuckster? Whatever—the speaker." He may mutilate the introduction in his vain struggle to pronounce words containing more than three syllables. She may randomly select tidbits from the introduction that you carefully crafted: "Let me see what's important here . . ." He may deliver the introduction like a perfect zombie, which is unlikely to entice your audience to hang around. Or she may improvise: "One thing you may not know about Buck . . ."—words that will surely send chills down Buck's spine.

And what is the result of those introduction debacles? Your audience may be laughing for the wrong reasons; they may be disoriented, scratching their heads, wondering who you are and why they should listen; or they may be focusing on the blunder rather than on your critical first words. You have been handicapped before you open your mouth to speak. You will need to waste valuable time cleaning up the mess, establishing your qualifications, and refocusing your audience.

Here is a simple rule: Never take a chance on something so important to the success of your presentation. Your introduction should answer the following three questions for each audience member: "What is the topic?" "Why does this topic matter to me?" And, "What qualifies this speaker to address this topic?" Your audience should know these answers before you begin speaking, because you have ensured that your introducer has told them.

No plan originated by another will be as
sympathetically handled as one's own plan.
CONRAD H. LANZA

EIGHT CRITICAL INTRODUCTION RULES

Use your introduction to entice your audience to listen. These are the rules for doing that:

1. PREPARE YOUR INTRODUCTION

Carefully craft the introduction yourself. Never allow your introducer to improvise: "Our speaker today is Ms. Chatterbox. I don't know what she has to say, but I bet she will be interesting—at least, I hope so. Give her a rousing round of applause!" Few audiences will be giddy with anticipation to hear poor Ms. Chatterbox. Your introducer should say exactly what you want him or her to say—nothing more, nothing less.

2. Tailor Your Introduction to the Presentation

Every presentation has a purpose (and if yours doesn't, then you must have skipped principle 9—shame on you!). Tailor your introduction with that purpose in mind. Focus on your qualifications or experiences that are relevant to your presentation. For instance, an audience of homeowners worried about spiraling tax assessments in their subdivision will care deeply about the speaker's expertise gained while she worked in the county tax assessor's office; they will care very little about her prize-winning recipe for succulent salmon.

If you are making an entertaining after-dinner presentation, your introduction should set the tone for your speech and alert your audience that they will have fun: "Our speaker graduated in the bottom ten percent of his college class, but he no longer has to stand on interstate exits holding a sign that reads 'Will Clean Gutters for Food!' He is encouraged by these advances in his career."

Brevity is the sister of talent.
Anton Chekhov

---

3. Make It Brief

Resist the urge to use your introduction to chronicle all your stellar achievements over the past thirty years. Here is the litmus test: If your introduction is longer than your speech, pare it down—about 90 percent. Make it relevant, informative, enticing, and above all, brief. Generally, it should not exceed one page in large font, and always keep in mind that shorter is better.

4. DEFUSE HOSTILITY

If you know beforehand that the audience is hostile, use the introduction to defuse the hostility. For example, if you are speaking to the Plastic Bag Society of America about the glories of paper sacks, your introduction might read: "Our speaker today realizes that many of us are utterly contemptuous of paper sacks and are frankly suspicious of their advocates. But Jim Bob grew up in a family of plastic bag aficionados, so he understands the challenges confronting us. He believes we can peacefully coexist."

This more conciliatory approach may not convert the plastic bag purists to your way of thinking, but it may slightly blunt their hostility. And they may be less likely to seethe and sling hard objects at you.

5. TYPE YOUR INTRODUCTION

Always prepare your introduction in a large font size (18-point), and triple-space the text, to make it easy for the person introducing you to read it. Do this for three reasons: Your handwriting is probably not as fabulous as you imagine; the lighting in caves is brighter than some lectern lamps; and you do not want the blind-as-a-mole introducer squinting and craning his neck to decipher the microscopic words crammed on the page. Help the introducer do his job.

6. EXHORT THE INTRODUCER TO PRACTICE

It seems like so very little to ask of the person introducing you to practice your introduction beforehand, and then deliver it in a somewhat natural manner, exactly as it was prepared. That is a perfectly reasonable expectation, right? Apparently not, because it seldom happens. Introducers stumble herky-jerky through the introduction, mispronouncing words, skipping vital details, or delivering it like a perfect cyborg. So, how do you avoid that?

Give your introducer a copy of the introduction days prior to your presentation. Stress the importance of her responsibility to set the right tone for your speech. Ask her (plead and threaten mayhem if necessary) to review and practice the introduction until she can comfortably recite it and not sound like a crashing bore. Finally, emphasize that veering off the script is not an option (see rule 7). Assert yourself.

Are these steps overkill? You may think so, right up until some bonehead butchers your introduction or launches into a monologue you have never heard and hoped you would never hear when being introduced.

7. RESTRAIN THE INTRODUCER

You want an introduction, not a comedy routine. The unrestrained introducer often aspires to be witty, but there is a huge problem: He's not. Worse, his inane comments are typically directed at you. For example, he may share embarrassing personal information you had hoped to forget: "We used to call Charles 'Chowdown Chuck' in the good ole fraternity, because that boy could cram down five chili dogs in mere seconds."

I was once introduced by a bozo who, sneering, tossed aside the introduction I had meticulously prepared for him and instead delivered this snappy witticism: "I would like to introduce David Dempsey, because, well, that's his name. Please give him a round of applause." Strangulation, anyone?

These introductions undermine your professional image and leave your audience clueless. Muzzle the comedic introducers.

It is by the goodness of God that we have in our country
three unspeakably precious things: freedom of speech,
freedom of conscience, and the prudence never
to practice either of them.
MARK TWAIN

---

8. BRING EXTRA COPIES

Even if you have delivered your introduction to your introducer several days before you are scheduled to speak (which you should), bring several extra copies with you when you speak. Why? Because other than car keys, nothing on the face of the earth is lost more frequently.

Your introduction should pique your audience's interest in your presentation and signal that an expert is about to speak. There is too much at stake for you to cross your fingers and hope for the best. It is okay to trust your banker, trust your partner, and trust your priest—provided they are not introducing you. But never trust an unprepared or unrestrained introducer. You will regret it if you do.

PRINCIPLE 28

CHECK YOUR CHECKLIST

Your plan should foresee and provide for
a next step in case of success or failure.

—B. H. LIDDELL HART

With apologies to Charles Dickens, I have seen the best of times, and I have seen the worst of times speaking. Allow me to share the worst.

I had agreed to speak to over one hundred prominent business executives ("The Hotshots Roundtable" or something like that) at 7:00 a.m. in a private dining room of an Atlanta restaurant. Weeks before my speaking engagement, I had painstakingly addressed all the details, and several days before the event, I reconfirmed everything. The host was affable and accommodating. He repeatedly assured me that I was in the hands of a professional, with many years of event-planning experience. His exact words: "Relax. This is not my first rodeo." Thus soothed, I trusted that he would do what he said he would do. Big mistake.

At 6:00 a.m. on the day of the presentation, our agreed meeting time, my host was nowhere to be found. That, however, was the least of my worries, because the room was a disaster. It had been the scene of a gluttonous bachelor party the evening before, which appeared to have ended only a few moments earlier. The putrid stench of cigars, beer, and anchovy pizza permeated the air, and plastic cups, confetti, and garments of every type littered the room. The revelers had apparently showered each other and the room with beer, because I had to peel my shoes from the sticky floor. Chairs and tables were toppled, soggy banners with inspiring messages ("Your Life Is Over, Loser Boy!") hung limply from the walls, and the strobe light above the dance floor was still spinning.

With my heart pounding and my throat constricting in panic, I tracked down the restaurant manager, who was sleepy, unshaven, and slumped over the counter, gulping coffee. He had attended the party, and he assured me that it was "one fine wingding!" I explained that we had less than one hour to convert the den of iniquity into some semblance of a meeting room. Unfazed, he smiled and glibly stated, "No problem, man! The cleaning crew should be arriving around 6:30 or *thereabouts.*" To convey my exasperation with his nonchalance, I considered wrapping my hands around his neck.

I had two choices: Bolt out of the front door and move to another state, or roll up my sleeves and get to work. I plunged in with wild-eyed frenzy. I fashioned a lectern out of plastic milk crates and propped it on the head table. I covered the empty beer kegs with greasy tablecloths and tossed the pizza remnants in a closet. I raced around the room like a whirling dervish, dragging tables, heaving chairs, and gathering trash. Practicing law suddenly seemed appealing again.

In Fair Weather prepare for foul.
THOMAS FULLER

The good news: I survived. The bad news: It was a mediocre presentation under barely tolerable conditions, and that was my fault. Why? As the speaker, I was responsible for everything related to my presentation.

You are responsible for everything when you are the speaker, too. If your listeners are uncomfortable, if the visual aids are difficult to see, if the handouts look unprofessional, or even if a strobe light is flashing—your listeners ultimately blame you. That may be unfair, and you can squawk and howl all you want, but it is a fact. Audiences want results, not excuses, and this is particularly true of business audiences who are investing their valuable time listening to your presentation.

Exceptional speakers obsessively address every detail that affects their presentations. They do everything to ensure that each presentation is a roaring success. Sometimes it will not work out the way you had planned, and you may need to hold the program together with a little baling wire and duct tape, but that is exactly what you must do. Canceling is never an option—ever. And you must do your best to keep any problems behind the curtain:

> As a presenter, you are the actor, the director, and usually the crew. The audience must always have the feeling—from you—that it's effortless.[1]

THE PERFECT PRESENTATION CHECKLIST

I am going to wildly assume that you would prefer to avoid a speaking debacle like mine, so I have set forth below an exhaustive list of issues you should consider before every presentation. Admittedly, not every item on this checklist will apply to every presentation, but the checklist will help guarantee that you at least consider every detail. You may scoff at some of these suggestions as excessive, merely the musings of a worrywart. I would have felt the same way, too, prior to my dining-room disaster.

Let me recommend that, as you work through the checklist, you get commitments from people in writing. That is excellent advice, because such written commitments will eliminate confusion and clarify who is responsible for which task. Enlist others to help, and delegate tasks, but never forget that you are in charge of, and ultimately responsible for, everything.

1. PREPRESENTATION DETAILS

By addressing the following items as early as possible before your speech, you can adapt your speech to the real circumstances you will face, and you can prepare appropriate visual aids or handouts.

- Who will pay your speaker's fee if one will be paid, and when will it be paid?
- Who will pay for such expenses as handouts, travel, hotel accommodations, and equipment and vehicle rental? When will these expenses be paid?
- Who is responsible for all AV requirements?
- Who is responsible for copying and distributing your written materials?
- Who is responsible for handling your speaking requirements, such as setting up the room (principle 26) and testing the microphone (principle 35)?
- When and how will attendees be notified of the meeting (printed invitations sent in the mail, e-mail distribution, Web site posting)?
- What time will you speak?
- How much time will you have for your speech (principle 33), including Q & A (principle 34)?
- How long is the entire program?
- How many people are expected to attend?
- Who are the other speakers on the program, what are their topics, and how long are their presentations (principle 33)?
- Will any other business be addressed during the meeting?
- Will meals be served before, during, or after your presentation?

2. PROGRAM ASSISTANT DETAILS

Make sure you have contact information (including office, home, and cell phone numbers, and an e-mail address) for everyone involved in the program, including:

- The host
- Alternative contacts to the host, such as an assistant
- The person who will introduce you
- A technician to assist with AV requirements and problems
- A building engineer or a building manager to assist you with technical problems with the room (building access, lighting, temperature)
- A contact with building security

3. BUILDING DETAILS

Answer the following questions, to become familiar with all the details of the facility where you will speak:

- Is it easy to find the building?
- Will directions to the meeting room be sent to the attendees or posted on a Web site?
- Are there traffic challenges around the building (congestion, limited access) that might delay the arrival time of your attendees?
- Is public transportation available and accessible?
- Is there adequate parking?
- Are there parking fees?
- Is valet parking available?
- What are the details of ingress and egress (stairs, elevators, alternate routes, emergency exits)?
- Is there wheelchair accessibility?
- Are there security or safety issues?
- Will you or the attendees need building security clearance?
- Are the building personnel and security guards familiar with the meeting details?
- Will you have access to the meeting room outside normal business hours, to set up and practice?

- Are there copying and faxing facilities on-site?
- Are the restroom facilities convenient to the room?
- Are there accommodations for smokers?
- Are there vending machines, or is there a snack shop?
- Are there lunch facilities in the building or within walking distance?

4. MEETING ROOM DETAILS

Study the room where you will speak, and eliminate potential problems. If they cannot be fixed because of inherent structural limitations (poor lighting, a column obstructing views), prepare mentally to work around those limitations.

- What is the size of the room?
- Does the room have adequate seating capacity?
- Has the room been arranged with tables and chairs according to your specifications?
- Will extra chairs be removed?
- Are rows sectioned off to encourage attendees to sit toward the front of the room?
- Is there ample aisle space?
- Will each audience member have an unobstructed view?
- Does the room have a stage or raised platform?
- Can you move easily off the stage and into the audience?
- Is the requested lectern properly placed?
- Are there tables for your notes, books, writing instruments, and handouts?
- Is there a sign-in table, with a registration list and a program agenda?
- Will whiteboards or chalkboards be available?
- Is there any AV equipment in the room?
- Are electrical outlets reasonably accessible?

- Have you mastered the lighting controls for the room?
- Will there be adequate heating and air conditioning, so that the room will be comfortable?
- Are there separate thermostat controls for the room?
- Will there be sunlight glare at any time during the day, and if so, will you be able to lower the blinds or shades?
- Are there any unavoidable distractions (lights, traffic noise, scenic views)?
- Have avoidable distractions been addressed (intercom system muted, signage posted on doors for the meeting in progress)?
- Is there a place for coats and bags?
- Will audience members have water glasses and pitchers?

5. EQUIPMENT DETAILS

You need to assure yourself that any equipment you plan on using will be working properly (Part VII). Make sure that you have tested and retested the equipment (right before you retest it again), and that you have all the accessories and emergency supplies readily available.

- Do you have the microphone you requested?
- Does the microphone cable enable you to move about freely?
- Have you conducted a sound check on the microphone (principle 35)?
- Has all visual aid equipment been tested (principles 37 and 38)?
- Is the equipment situated properly?
- Do you have a backup laptop computer?
- Are your laptop computers compatible and tested?
- Do you have an extra computer mouse?
- Is your computer battery charged?
- Are there additional cables for the computer, projector, and VCR or DVD player?

- Do you have extra extension cords and three-pronged electrical adapters?
- Do you have extra lightbulbs for all the equipment that needs them?
- Have you tested the remote controls for all the equipment?
- Do you have new batteries for all the equipment?
- Have the video monitors been tested?
- Is there a surge protector for your equipment?
- Can the audience see the flip chart, screen, video monitor, and meeting room boards (principle 37)?
- Are all videotapes and CDs properly cued?
- What is your fallback plan if the equipment fails?
- Is there a separate backup floppy disc or CD with the entire program and handouts saved on it?

6. SUPPLY DETAILS

Bring all the tools and supplies you will need before and during the program. Use this checklist so that you do not overlook anything:

- A printed agenda
- Additional photocopy-ready handouts
- Name tags and place cards on the tables for the attendees
- Extra business cards
- Extra copies of your introduction (principle 27)
- Duct tape for taping down carpets and cords (and, in a pinch, for holding the program together)
- Fresh markers for the flip chart, whiteboards, and name tags
- Adequate paper for your flip chart
- Thumbtacks and masking tape for hanging sheets of paper
- Erasers and cleaner for the chalkboards and whiteboards
- A laser pointer
- Pens and highlighters

- Post-it Notes in various sizes
- Paper clips and binder clips
- Stapler and staples
- A clock or large watch to monitor the time (principle 33)
- Bottled water for you
- Throat lozenges for you
- Food for you (energy bars, raisins, nuts) to eat during the breaks

---

The final test of a plan is its execution.
UNITED STATES ARMY FIELD MANUAL

I know exactly what you are thinking. Yes, this is a lot to consider, and yes, some of these items will not apply to every meeting. And sometimes, despite your utmost efforts, even exceptional plans go awry. But your goal is to avoid unexpected surprises that will heighten your anxiety and diminish the impact of, or completely undermine, your speech.

So, obsess over the details. Anticipate everything, and overlook nothing. The details make a monumental difference. And if your host ever utters the words, "Relax. This is not my first rodeo," sound the alarm.

PART VI

DAZZLE WITH DELIVERY

As A CHILD (before the advent of electronic games and MTV), I played for hours with a nifty device about the size of a notebook, called an Etch A Sketch. I used two plastic knobs to move a stylus horizontally or vertically to sketch any picture I wanted with the black aluminum powder on the screen. But the real beauty of this toy was this: If I disliked what I had drawn, I simply picked up the box and shook it; that cleared the screen, and it was ready for me to start over.

Three things matter in a speech: who says it,
how he says it, and what he says—and,
of the three, the last matters the least.

JOHN MORLEY

You do not enjoy a similar luxury when speaking. Every time you speak, you have *one* chance to make a lasting impression. If you fail to deliver your message with confidence and conviction, all your hard work will be for naught. You have no ability to quickly wipe the slate clean.

Part VI discusses the techniques that will help you dazzle the crowd with your delivery.

FOCUS ON YOUR AUDIENCE

Some writers take to drink,
others take to audiences.

—GORE VIDAL

Do you focus on your audience when you speak—*really* focus—or
does every audience look alike to you, just another sea of blank faces?
Be honest (it's okay, you don't have to share your answer with anyone).

All right, it's test time. Perform an honest self-assessment now, by
asking yourself the following questions: "When I speak,"

- "Do my listeners sometimes seem detached or disinterested?"

- "Do I respond to nonverbal body language from my listeners, or do
  I unwaveringly stick to my script?"

- "Do I analyze how my listeners are reacting, or do I concentrate primarily on what I have said and on what I will say next?"

- "Do I attempt to involve my listeners in the presentation through
  questions or audience participation, or is it always just a monologue?"

- "Do I *really* listen to and process their questions, or am I more concerned about sounding authoritative?"

- "Am I primarily concerned about looking and sounding good?"

Study your listeners, and they will let you know how you are doing. If your speech is clicking, they will send unequivocal signals that acclaim, "Exceptional presentation!" What type of signals? Nods of agreement, rapt attention to your words and to your visual aids, sitting upright and leaning forward, feverish note taking, and smiling faces. When that happens, the sky is bluer, the birds are chirping, and—Ta Da! blare the horns—you have entered the speaker's Promised Land. Pat yourself on the back, and cherish the memory. You may need to recall that moment on another day, when it feels as though you are plodding along in wet sand as you speak.

I do not object to people looking at their watches when I am speaking. But I strongly object when they start shaking them to make certain they are still going.

LORD BIRKETT

Let's look at one of those wet-sand days, when your presentation is flopping and you are just not connecting with your listeners. Then their signals are unmistakably telling you that you are on the fast train to nowhere: rampant fidgeting; furtive (or blatant) watch glancing; wincing; furrowed brows; distressed, puzzled, or downright antagonistic stares; clinched jaws; or defiantly folded arms. If you speak frequently, tackle challenging topics, or face such tough audiences as lawyers, doctors, or grade school children, you will encounter these signals. As painful as the signals might be, don't ignore them.

Never forget your primary purpose in speaking: to connect. It does not matter whether you are trying to sell, persuade, inform, inspire, or entertain; if you don't connect, you might as well not have spoken.

Understand that every audience is tuned to a single frequency: WII-FM ("What's in it for me?"). They want to know how listening to you will benefit them, so you had better answer that question—and stay tuned to their frequency. Throughout your presentation, broadcast a static-free message to your listeners that you understand their perspective and that they are important. Do everything in your power to genuinely connect.

Joel Weldon, a very successful professional speaker, describes his interaction with his listeners this way:

> By the time I'm introduced, all the preparation is done and there is no thought given to the material, the ideas, stories, examples, or the humor. My entire conscious focus is on the audience. I'm watching the audience, thinking what they are thinking, attempting to experience what they are experiencing. I'm looking for people who are buying in, signs of resistance, or things that might have passed over them that need to be restated in a simpler, clearer way.[1]

EIGHT WAYS TO READ AND REACT TO YOUR AUDIENCE

So, what do you do when you feel like you are dying on the platform, when it seems like your speaking world is crumbling all around you? How do you react? Do you: (1) Ignore the signs, drop your chin, and barrel ahead? (2) Conclude that the audience is the problem? (3) Just talk louder and faster? (4) Disregard the audience and conduct a titillating monologue with your notes or with your PowerPoint slides? Or (5) wrap it up quickly, dart away, and hope to preserve a smidgen of dignity? None of those choices bodes well for your long-term speaking prospects.

The correct answer: Get attuned to your audience and the messages they are sending you, and react to those messages. Here are eight excellent ways to accomplish that:

1. ELIMINATE DISRUPTIONS

If something or someone is interfering with your message, pause and address the problem. Crossing your fingers and wishing the problem away, talking louder, or simply ignoring it never helps. Ask the industrious waiters who are banging dishes to stop, or the buffoons in the third row who are yakking to put a lid on it. Politely suggest that you might bop them in the nose if they refuse (a variation of the "Speak softly, and carry a big stick" slogan).

Your listeners will appreciate it, and you will increase the probability that your message will be received. Taking control of distracting situations also demonstrates that you are confident and that you are concerned about their ability to hear your important message.

There is always a single ear in the audience,
to which we address ourselves.
HENRY DAVID THOREAU

---

2. SOLICIT QUESTIONS

The following recommendation may sound like pure heresy to the legions of speakers who memorize *every* speech (who, incidentally, are encouraged to reread—and memorize, if necessary—principle 19). Periodically deviate from your prepared text to solicit audience input. For example, pause and ask: "I realize that I blazed through that material, and it might have been somewhat confusing. What questions do you have?"

Audiences today want and expect an interactive presentation, and they are typically eager to participate and share ideas. Straying from the script is an exceptional way to accomplish that and to minimize confusion. Principle 34 delves into the intricacies of Q & A participation.

But here is the stipulation: Solicit questions only if you are willing to listen to them. Don't start thinking about what you will say next while the questioner is speaking. If you begin responding before you have a clear understanding of the question, you will gain little insight, probably alienate a few listeners, and merely compound your problems. Pause, listen, process, and only then respond.

3. REFER TO A SPECIFIC AUDIENCE MEMBER OR EVENT

Periodically refer to someone in the audience by name (assuming that you won't embarrass him or her): "I was speaking to Mr. Big Wheel this morning about your competitor's products." And also refer to recent events that occurred in the organization, such as a banner year in sales, an industry honor, or an upcoming retirement. Gather information about your audience from various sources (principles 6 and 7).

If you demonstrate that you have gone out of your way to customize your message for that particular audience—in other words, that this is not just another "canned speech"—you heighten their interest and enhance your credibility. Just be careful not to reveal confidential information ("Mr. Big Wheel really regrets that he will have to can two hundred of you today") if you hope to speak to that group again.

4. PAUSE TO ALLOW FOR LAUGHTER AND EMOTIONS

If your listeners are laughing, stop talking and let them laugh (principle 23). Savor this moment, because at other times the silence after your witty lines can be deafening.

If some listeners are emotionally upset, honor that moment as well. Pause and acknowledge their feelings: "I know this is upsetting to some of you, and that is understandable." Pausing and allowing for an emotional response shows that you respect your listeners, and it also gives you a chance to collect your thoughts.

5. TAKE A SHORT BREAK

If it appears that the energy in the room is waning (gaping yawns, glazed looks), take a short break. Encourage everyone to stand, stretch, and check his or her neighbor's pulse for signs of life—you get the point.

Don't get your feelings hurt, because you may not be the source of the problem. They may be drowsy because it has been a long day, because the room is too warm, or because that triple cheese lasagna they ate at lunch is taking its toll. The speaking time you lose by taking a break will be offset by the heightened attention of your listeners for the remainder of your presentation. And next time, specify salads, melba toast, and caffeinated drinks for lunch.

6. BREAK THE PATTERN

If your audience seems numb (eyes are rolling back, heads are drooping, doodling is rampant), be honest: You may be the problem (I know, hard to imagine). Maybe your delivery has grown tedious; maybe you have overwhelmed your audience with information; maybe the topic is complex or boring; or maybe your energy has waned. Whatever the reason, it is time to change courses quickly and spice it up.

What can you do? Pause, vary the pacing, change your volume or tone, move around, step toward the audience, expand your gestures, incorporate a slide or video, refer to the handout, engage in some audience participation exercises, or ask questions. Do anything (within the bounds of good taste) to snap them back to attention and to refocus them.

I have just got a new theory of eternity.
ALBERT EINSTEIN
(after listening to a long-winded speech)

---

7. SHORTEN THE PRESENTATION

Sometimes your audience has already sat through several presentations by the time you speak, and they are satiated with information. They have had enough, and they are sliding into full-scale shutdown. If you are facing that situation, you could be sharing the winning numbers in the Mega-Millions Lottery for the drawing that will occur the next day, but they don't care and won't listen. It's time to employ a quick exit strategy. Try this.

Slash a portion of your prepared presentation, and address only the key points. Let your audience know that you are doing this: "I was scheduled to speak for one hour, but I realize that you have already been inundated with information. So if you will just give me your attention for fifteen minutes, I will highlight four points that are particularly important to *you* [audience focus always], and then stop. If you have questions, I will be available to speak with you individually afterward, or you may e-mail your questions to me at the address in the handout." Your audience will appreciate your sensitivity, and they will typically return the favor by focusing on what you have to say.

There can be no fairer ambition than to excel in talk;
to be affable, gay, ready, clear, and welcome.
ROBERT LOUIS STEVENSON

---

8. ACCEPT THE INEVITABLE

You have tried everything to connect, but the audience vibes are still distinctly negative: locked jaws, rigid body language, heads shaking in disagreement, or—worst of all—the evil eye. What then?

First, recognize that no matter how eloquent you are, you will not always sway everyone, so stop trying. Acknowledge those who disagree with you, and thank them for their willingness to listen to your viewpoint (which, of course, as you know, is the correct one).

Second, solicit the naysayers' input. You may not convert them to your way of thinking, but it affords them an opportunity to vent, it livens up the program, and it sends the message to everyone that you are confident in your position. But avoid this option if you feel it will result in chaos.

Finally, resign yourself to the reality that you sometimes just encounter a bad audience. Some audiences are unreceptive, grumpy, and convinced that you could not possibly have anything valuable to share with them. Smile, do the best you can under the circumstances, and go home. No presentation is final or fatal. But—and this is important— don't use the "it was a bad audience" rationalization unless you know that you have done *everything* possible to guarantee an exceptional presentation.

Concentrate on connecting with your audience. Always remember the frequency that every listener is tuned into: WII-FM. You may not like the signals the audience is sending you, and you must be nimble whenever you decide to deviate from your prepared comments. But if you stay focused on your audience, you greatly enhance the chances that your message will be understood and favorably received. And after all, isn't that the primary reason for speaking?

ACT CONFIDENT

Whether you believe you can do a thing
or not, you are right.

—HENRY FORD

I could not wait to finally hear Professor Muck-a-Muck speak. He was the preeminent authority in his field, an esteemed Ivy League professor who had written several treatises on his expertise. He had even appeared on *The Oprah Winfrey Show,* so I knew he stood at the pinnacle of his profession. I arrived early, determined to secure a front-row seat. As I stepped into the auditorium, I was tingling with anticipation. He was already on stage, and what I saw shocked me.

Professor Muck-a-Muck exuded fear. He was wringing his hands, scribbling notes, and frantically flipping pages in the mounds of books scattered around the head table. He appeared to be researching his talk at the last minute. Sweat dripped off his forehead, which he repeatedly mopped. Old Muck-a-Muck was fighting a colossal battle with his glasses, which repeatedly slid down his wet nose only to be shoved back into place. Occasionally, he would glance apprehensively and furtively at people who were trickling into the auditorium, but this seemed only to exacerbate his anxiety and quicken his pace. He looked like a condemned man. I feared he might injure himself before he began speaking. His pretalk behavior was both comical and pathetic.

This was hardly the image I had expected. Before he uttered his first word, I had formed a negative opinion. I began to question his qualifications, based solely on his appearance and conduct—unfair, and probably inaccurate, but I could not help myself. And I was not alone. From the bewildered looks around the room, it was apparent that others shared my surprise.

Every time you speak, remember this: You are communicating with your audience from the moment they first see you. They immediately begin to evaluate you and form conclusions based on your appearance and conduct. I know that contradicts the admonition we heard repeatedly as children: "Never judge a book by its cover." Sorry, we may have learned it, but most don't apply it, and neither will your audience.

Your audience expects you to be a self-assured expert when you speak, so you had better look, sound, and act confident, poised, and focused. You immediately place yourself at a huge disadvantage if you resemble a milquetoast, a disheveled pack rat, or—worst of all—a Professor Muck-a-Muck. All of the following mannerisms undercut your confident image:

- Pacing or swaying for no apparent purpose
- Fidgeting
- Clinging tightly to the lectern
- Clasping, shuffling, or rattling your notes
- Sweating profusely
- Emitting strange sighs or grunts
- Darting your eyes
- Staring at the floor, ceiling, or out the window
- Licking, biting, or sucking your lips
- Contorting your hands
- Touching, rubbing, or scratching your face (or other body parts)
- Fiddling with your hair
- Twirling your rings or other jewelry

- Adjusting your clothing or glasses
- And (my favorite): Stroking your tie

Audience members quickly zero in on all these distracting quirks. Soon, they forget your message and simply enjoy the spectacle that you have become.

EIGHT WAYS TO PROJECT CONFIDENCE

Here are eight steps guaranteed to enhance your confidence *and* to send the unmistakable message to your listeners that you are self-assured:

1. DRESS UP AND STRIP DOWN

Audiences expect speakers to look clean, polished, and professional. You risk undermining your credibility by wearing flashy, trendy, or sloppy clothing when you speak. What are the rules for appropriate dress?

- Be one of the best-dressed people in the room.
- Dress conservatively and professionally. If you want your listeners to take you seriously, save your snazzy purple shirt, cartoon-character necktie, leather miniskirt, fishnet nylons, argyle socks, or white buck shoes for a really big date night.
- Shine your shoes (or pray that patent leather becomes fashionable). Audience members notice.
- Empty your pockets. You look slovenly if your jacket or pants pockets are jammed with a week's worth of receipts, your jumbo key chain, or a bursting wallet the size of a ham sandwich.
- Remove your technology. Do not march to the front of the room with your cell phone, pager, calculator, iPod, BlackBerry, or any other technology draped on your pants.
- Minimize jewelry. Layers of necklaces, rows of bracelets, and fingers covered with gaudy rings distract your audience and become an alluring diversion for you to play with as you speak.

2. MINGLE AND GREET

Arrive early, mingle with the audience members, and introduce yourself before you speak. Let them know that you are genuinely excited and honored to be speaking to them. Why? It relaxes you, it gives you a few friendly faces in the audience (you can never have too many of those), and it heightens their interest in your talk. But avoid any alcohol during your meet-and-greet session; that is the first step on the treacherous slope to a speaking calamity.

Knowing is not enough, we must apply.
Willing is not enough, we must do.
JOHANN WOLFGANG VON GOETHE

---

3. DO NOT REVIEW OR EDIT YOUR NOTES

When you are about to speak, you should already know what you are going to say. If you are unprepared when the curtain is about to rise (Perish the thought! Is it possible that you skipped principles 1–29?), forget about reviewing or editing your notes. It is now too little, too late. Despite all your success working under self-inflicted, dire deadlines in college, desperate cramming will seldom improve any speech; it will probably only exacerbate your anxiety. It also alerts your audience that you are unprepared. Give it your best shot, deal with the repercussions, and properly prepare for the next speech.

4. PAUSE BEFORE YOU BEGIN

Some speakers begin jabbering the minute their name is announced—before the applause has subsided, sometimes before they even reach the microphone—as if the speech were a race to jam in the most words in the time allotted. This behavior sends one unmistakable message: "Man, oh man, I am one Nervous Nellie!"

Instead, approach the lectern with confidence, arrange your notes quickly, and pause before beginning (principle 23). Let your introducer return to her seat, and wait for everyone to quiet down. Insist on total silence and your audience's undivided attention before you begin. Opening in this manner signals: "I am confident and poised. You, Dear Audience, do not intimidate me."

5. DO NOT APOLOGIZE

If you are unprepared to speak, do not apologize. You don't need to; it will probably be obvious that you are unprepared, and your apology will not improve the speech. Resist the urge to appeal to your audience's sympathy at this stage, because such an appeal only undercuts your credibility and highlights the problem. Do the best you can under the circumstances, and learn from the experience. (And cross your heart and vow to always prepare in the future.)

We shall never know all the good
that a simple smile can do.
MOTHER TERESA

---

6. MONITOR YOUR FACIAL MESSAGE

Your facial expressions should send the message that you are genuinely delighted to be speaking. I have to constantly remind myself to smile when I speak, because I get engrossed in my talk, and I look like a perfect grump. To remind yourself to enjoy the process, make notes on your text (a smiley face or the word "SMILE" will work).

Even worse than a grouch is Mr. Pomposity. You know, the pontificator who stares down his nose at you through his bifocal reading glasses, who frowns while he condescendingly lectures, and who harrumphs repeatedly. Spare us. Nothing alienates an audience faster than some blowhard who patronizes the audience. Act that way, and your speech is kaput. Period.

7. CONNECT WITH EYE CONTACT

Your audience can see you. Do you see them? If so, actually look at them. Establish and sustain eye contact with as many audience members as possible. Once again, this signals that you are confident. To learn exactly how to capitalize on using your eyes to connect, see the seven eye-contact secrets in principle 32.

8. DEFUSE HOSTILITY WHENEVER POSSIBLE

If your audience is hostile toward you, acknowledge the animosity and attempt to neutralize it. You might say, "I recognize that many of you disagree with me on this issue. Thank you for your willingness to listen. I hope I can persuade you, but perhaps we will simply have to agree to disagree." There are two advantages in doing this: You are showing respect for your listeners and their opposing (and, of course, woefully misinformed) viewpoint, and you are communicating to them that you are not afraid of contrary opinions.

Your listeners are watching and judging you all the time. Are you sending the right message, that you are confident, friendly, and prepared? Or are you signaling that you are puffed up, petrified, or disorganized? Don't undermine your credibility. The nonverbal signals are often more powerful than anything you say (just ask Professor Muck-a-Muck). Let your actions and words convey one message: "I own the stage!"

PERSUADE WITH PASSION

The eloquent man is he who is no beautiful speaker,
but who is inwardly and desperately
drunk with a certain belief.

—RALPH WALDO EMERSON

A persuasive speaker is passionate about his message. Within seconds after he begins, his listeners lean forward in their seats, drawn in by his compelling delivery. He speaks with contagious energy, animated body language, sustained eye contact, and captivating vocal power. His style is always dynamic. But more importantly, he moves his listeners because he himself is moved. He is passionate about his ideas and is determined to reach his listeners.

What about you? If you are not on fire with your message, don't expect your listeners to do cartwheels with excitement.

"Does passion really matter?" you might ask. Absolutely, and here is why: It makes a huge difference in how you connect with your audience. Especially if your primary purpose is to persuade, in an intensely competitive marketplace, any edge is significant. If you can ignite your audience with your passion and conviction, you are far more likely to be persuasive.

The benefits of honing your skills as a persuasive speaker are tremendous. You are viewed as an expert, your status as a leader soars, and you motivate your listeners to act on, or at least carefully consider, your viewpoint. And let's be honest: A persuasive speaker sells more of his products, ideas, and services, and (if I might be crassly commercial for a moment) that often translates into cold, hard cash. That should be a particularly compelling incentive if you ever hope to have that jet-black Ferrari parked in your garage.

Persuasion is achieved when the orator's speech is so spoken as to make us think him credible; when the speech stirs our emotions; when the speaker provides logical arguments.

ARISTOTLE

So, how do you become an exceptional persuasive speaker? It is time to pull out the playbook of the masters again (remember, it is all right to emulate the best). Start by studying the consummate persuaders: motivational speakers. Anyone who has attended a motivational rally has likely been swept up in the groundswell of enthusiasm. Before long, you have shelled out hundreds of dollars for books, tapes, DVDs, posters, and assorted paraphernalia guaranteed to revolutionize your life and divulge all the secrets that made Bill Gates obscenely rich. These speakers do more than just share words; they infuse their messages with passion.

Consider the following insights from a few professional speakers at the pinnacle of their profession, Anthony Robbins, Dr. Wayne W. Dyer, and Mark Victor Hansen:

I would say that the most important key to speaking is not to be perfect or to know exactly what you're going to say or how you're going to say it. But rather, that you have incredible passion about what you're speaking about. Your emotional intensity is what people will remember.[1]

I speak to an audience in the same way I would speak to somebody in the living room of my home. From my heart, with integrity, and with enthusiasm. . . . [I]f you are truly enthusiastic about what you are thinking about, and not acting out a role, not playing "rent-a-speaker," not being an actor, not delivering a script . . . [if] you are enthusiastically, excitedly delivering your talk, it will come across.[2]

Great speakers have a calling within them to communicate; they communicate exceedingly well. They are absolutely passionate and intense. They have the eye of the tiger, the magnificent obsession. I can tell within thirty seconds of meeting someone whether they're on purpose toward some goal, because they start spilling over with effervescent enthusiasm about it.[3]

Passion is what distinguishes these exceptionally persuasive speakers from the majority of speakers—those who may know their topic, who may even have strong convictions, but whose delivery is lifeless. I often question whether some speakers have blood pumping in their veins as they methodically grind along. A dry, pedantic recitation of facts may be informative, but who is going to listen? Speak like that, and you will neither be persuasive nor interesting, and it is likely that your listeners will not hear most of what you say. They will simply check out. And, you won't have to worry about scheduling subsequent speaking engagements; audiences will avoid you like a plague.

Speech that leads not to action, still more that hinder it, is a nuisance on the earth.
THOMAS CARLYLE

THREE STYLES OF PERSUASION

So you want to genuinely connect with your audience and be a truly persuasive speaker? You need an effective method for channeling your passion. There are three proven styles of persuasion: empirical or logical, psychological, and personal. Each style is described below. Work with me: This is as close as I come to psychological gibberish in the book, so I will make it quick.

1. EMPIRICAL OR LOGICAL PERSUASION

With empirical or logical persuasion, you sway your listeners to accept a particular point of view with inductive reasoning (empirical persuasion) or deductive reasoning (logical persuasion). A few examples may help.

With inductive reasoning, you first present all the facts and reasoning and then ask your listeners to take a particular course of action. For example, let's say Tiny Tim has been summoned to the principal's office because of his involvement in a playground scuffle. In pleading for clemency, Tiny Tim might argue: "I was sitting there [fact], absorbed in the titillating tales of Cicero in my book *Latin for Nerds* [fact], when that half-wit Buster shoved me down [fact], snatched my lunch [fact], and stomped on my banana [fact]. Everyone knows Buster is a bully [fact]. I was only defending myself when I beaned him with my backpack [logic]. So, I say, hurl Buster into detention, and toss away the key [call to action]."

A speech has two parts. Necessarily, you state your case, and you prove it.

ARISTOTLE

With deductive reasoning, on the other hand, Tiny Tim would begin with the result he wants: 1. The playground should be saved from hooligans, and all hooligans who disrupt the playground should be sentenced to decades of detention without leniency. 2. Anyone who stomps on bananas of a nerdy student reading the tales of Cicero is a hooligan. 3. I am a nerdy student. 4. Buster stomped on my banana while I was absorbed in reading *Latin for Nerds*. 5. Therefore, Buster is a hooligan. 6. Therefore, Buster should be sentenced to decades of detention.

Both inductive and deductive reasoning are effective, and Buster will enjoy many years cleaning erasers and scraping gum off desks after school.

2. PSYCHOLOGICAL PERSUASION

With psychological persuasion, you appeal to the self-interest of your listeners (the WII-FM—"What's in it for me?"—radio frequency we discussed earlier, remember?). For your appeal to be effective, you need to know why the action you are proposing benefits them. Always answer the following question first: "If my listeners act as I request, will it satisfy one or more of their basic needs or interests—*biological* (hunger, thirst, sleep); *security* (money, protection, a sense of order); *affiliation* (family, love, friendship, association with a particular organization); or *recognition* (success, pride, doing the right thing)?"

At the risk of stating the obvious, understand that psychological persuasion works only if you have researched your audience (principles 6 and 7) and you can answer their WII-FM question. Know your audience—their likes, dislikes, goals, history, experiences, hopes, the whole shebang—and you will enjoy a huge advantage when attempting to persuade.

———

Speech is power: speech is to persuade, to convert, to compel.
RALPH WALDO EMERSON

———

3. PERSONAL PERSUASION

A personal appeal is based on a speaker's reputation, credibility, or influence. For example, a president with a high approval rating can persuade the public to act in a particular way, sometimes even if many of the citizens do not agree that it is in their best interests.

Following the terrorist attacks on the World Trade Center and the Pentagon on September 11, 2001, President George W. Bush enjoyed widespread personal appeal and support from the majority of Americans (his job performance approval rating exceeded 80 percent). Over the next several months, President Bush was able to spend some of that political capital persuading most of the public that our national interests justified costly and dangerous military action in Iraq. He was persuading through his personal appeal.

In contrast, though former President Bill Clinton is very charismatic, the public was skeptical of his call for military action in the Middle East during his presidency, because it came during his impeachment process when his reputation and credibility had been sullied.

Personal appeal can be very powerful when attempting to persuade, so look for ways to burnish your reputation and credibility. (Stomping on a nerd's banana will not help.)

Nothing great in the world has been
accomplished without passion.
GEORG HEGEL

Use any or all of these styles of persuasion when delivering your message. When coupled with your passionate delivery, they greatly enhance your chances of persuading your listeners. Study all the secrets of speaking with passion that are listed in the recommended resources at the end of the book. And don't forget to review recordings of memorable persuasive presentations, both current and historical (principle 8).

If you want to persuade your listeners, speak with genuine passion and conviction. Don't expect your audience to be persuaded, excited, or even interested if you drably deliver a string of platitudes; you might as well save your listeners the trouble by letting them nap at home rather than in your audience. Instead, communicate with a "magnificent obsession" to share your message. Do that, and you will move the hearts and minds of your listeners—and truly persuade.

LOOK 'EM IN THE EYE

Eyes can speak and eyes can understand.

—GEORGE CHAPMAN

Listeners today are not content to tag along passively wherever the speaker leads them. They want to be part of the speaking experience. No matter how many people are in the room, each listener wants to feel as if the speaker were talking directly to him or her. One of the best ways to produce this feeling requires a bit of courage: Look directly into the eyes of your listeners, and speak with confidence and conviction. Do that, and you not only enhance your chances of connecting with your listeners, you also send a tacit message: "You can trust me."

Many speakers seem oblivious to the audience and rarely look at them in any meaningful way throughout the entire presentation. Let's meet five typical eye-contact transgressors:

- The *gazer,* who pensively stares out the window (fascinated by any activity in the parking lot) or at the back wall (transfixed with the wonder of a beige wall)

- The *sweeper,* who rhythmically and hypnotically sweeps her eyes back and forth across her audience, never sustaining eye contact for an instant

- The *transfixer*, who becomes mesmerized by his notes, studying them as if they were the Holy Grail
- The *worshiper*, who focuses primarily on the floor (maybe hoping the earth will swallow her and deliver her from her plight) or on the ceiling (maybe hoping for divine intervention)
- The *navel ogler*, perhaps the most entertaining of the lot, who delivers his presentation with a bowed head, staring directly at his belly button

If you belong to any of these clubs, it is time to resign your membership.

If you accept the premise that eye contact is essential (and you should), why do so many speakers look anywhere and everywhere *except* at the audience? Let's examine the typical excuses.

First there is the speaker who focuses primarily on her notes, because she is unprepared and has no idea what to say next. She has no time to be troubled with her audience, because she is desperately searching for her next words. If you are unprepared, don't expect to engage your audience with your message.

Then there is the speaker who gets the jitters from speaking. He fears that he might crumple into a blubbering mass if he were actually to *look* at someone. Sorry, but as painful as it might be for you skittish ones to glance at your audience periodically, avoiding eye contact actually exacerbates your anxiety and alerts your audience that you are tense.

Finally, there is the speaker who is just indifferent or pompous; she considers her audience a huge annoyance, just lucky to be graced by her presence. That attitude alienates any audience within seconds, so instead of avoiding eye contact, this speaker should avoid showing up, thereby sparing everyone from a wretched experience.

One thing is certain: If you are not using your eye contact to create a positive connection with your audience, you are squandering a golden opportunity and diminishing your effectiveness. Avoiding eye contact makes it far more challenging to inform, persuade, inspire, or entertain any audience.

Seven Eye-Contact Secrets

If you appeared on the list of eye-contact transgressors (let's be honest, we have all made cameo appearances), and the excuses seem feeble (as they should), consider these seven excellent ways to enhance your delivery and convey self-assurance and sincerity with your eye contact:

1. Get Ready

Without belaboring the point (all right, only slightly belaboring the point), be prepared. If you are well prepared, you can focus on your audience rather than concentrating on your notes, the memorized script in your head, or that apparently intriguing spot on the back wall. Enough said.

2. Make Friends

Speaking can be intimidating (now, there is a revelation, right?). You are alone in front of the audience, staring at a sea of faces, and grappling with that old hobgoblin: Fear. So, what should you do? Before you speak, work the crowd like an eager politician. Enthusiastically introduce yourself to the audience members as they enter the room, and thank them for attending. Show a genuine interest in them, and they will reciprocate with undivided attention. When your audience is brimming with smiling, attentive faces, it is much easier to establish eye contact.

3. Connect Before You Speak

If you begin speaking before you have visually connected with your audience ("What audience?"), trumpets will blare and a heavenly voice will proclaim: "Scaredy-cat!" Instead of dashing into your speech, do the following: After you have been introduced, assume a commanding stance, pause, breathe, smile, and—this is important—look at your audience. They will not bite. With your eyes, send the unmistakable message "I am confident, and you will enjoy this." Then, and only then, begin speaking. That will quiet those trumpets.

4. READ AND REACT

If you are preoccupied with your notes, the ceiling tiles, your shoes, or your belly button, you will miss those harbingers of trouble that are evident throughout the room: droopy eyelids, furtive glances, skeptical expressions, and rampant note passing.

But if you are attuned to your audience, you can pick up on these signals and react (take a break, ask a question, vary your delivery). If you miss the signals because you never look at your audience, your speaking ship may be headed for the bottom of the deep blue sea, and you will not realize it until it is much too late. Stay focused on the vital passengers on the speaking voyage, the audience members (principle 29).

The eyes have one language everywhere.
GEORGE HERBERT

---

5. SUSTAIN EYE CONTACT

If your eyes dart about or drift aimlessly around the room, landing everywhere except on your audience, that audience will conclude that you are shifty, unwilling to look at them when you speak. Shiftiness is not a desirable speaker attribute. And unless you are a hypnotist, intent on lulling your audience into a trance, don't rhythmically sweep your eye contact back and forth across the room.

Try to establish and sustain eye contact, for a few seconds at least, with as many people as possible. In smaller settings, you should establish eye contact several times with each listener. But be careful not to stare intently, because that might intimidate the listener. Even worse, some listeners may become defiant if you stare, and they will reciprocate by menacingly staring back. Menacing glares can cause your knees to buckle, so avoid stare downs with your audience.

6. Divide a Large Audience into Sections

If you are speaking to a large audience, establishing eye contact can be challenging (so many faces, so little time). Try this: Divide the room into quarters, speak to each section of the room for a short period, and attempt to make eye contact with as many people as possible in that section. Then shift to another section. Most audience members in the general vicinity of your gaze will believe you are looking only at them, and you never have to tell them otherwise.

7. Deliver Key Points to Individuals

Identify the significant points in your speech (poignant quotes, startling revelations, challenges, or calls to action). When you approach each of these points, pause, plant yourself, and then deliver the words slowly and with emphasis while looking directly at one individual in the audience.

This will make your delivery more forceful, and you will seem more sincere. Repeat this practice with each key point, focusing on a different audience member each time. (If you repeatedly look at the same individual, others will feel slighted, and gossip will run amok.)

To speak much is one thing;
to speak well another.
Sophocles

If you really want to connect with your audience, maintain eye contact with them. Don't gaze, sweep, transfix, worship, or—worst of all—ogle your navel (or anyone else's navel, for that matter). Let your eyes send a message of utter self-assurance and trustworthiness.

Adhere to the Time Allotted

One never repents of having spoken too little,
but often of having spoken too much.

—Philippe de Commynes

Have you encountered the inconsiderate windbag speaker who believes that his audience cannot hear enough from him? He rambles on and on *and on,* flouting the prescribed time limit for his presentation as if it were merely a suggestion. He is wrong, of course. He may never want to stop talking, but his listeners feel otherwise. At times, they want to stand up and shout, "Enough!" Hell hath no fury like an audience scorned.

Listeners are not renowned for their patience. We want everything fast. How fast? It is telling that we can now get married at a drive-through window. Don't encroach on your audience's precious time. The inviolable rule regarding time: Speak for the scheduled amount of time—or less—and sit down.

I once attended a presentation entitled "Ten Secrets to Ridiculous Riches." It was about seven secrets too many. The financial wizard was scheduled to speak for twenty minutes, but when he reached that landmark, he was still yammering about Secret Number Three ("To become rich, spend less, and earn more . . ." or something equally astute). Unfazed by the time, he continued to trudge along until he mercifully concluded at forty-five minutes.

Had the blabbermouth bothered to glance at his audience after twenty minutes, he would have seen listeners impatiently flipping ahead in the handout, glaring at the clock (and at him), and restlessly squirming. Clearly we were irked by this intrusion on our time. After he blew by the twenty-minute barrier with no glimmer of light at the end of the speaking tunnel, attention and patience began to plummet. At thirty minutes, listeners were openly grousing; at forty minutes, we were preparing to storm the stage and toss him off.

The less said, the better.
JANE AUSTEN

Brevity is beautiful when you are speaking. Always strive to deliver your message in a memorable way, in the fewest words possible. Typically audiences are delighted whenever a speaker concludes early. They are likely to hail you as an outstanding speaker if you cut it short; end early on Friday afternoon, and they may deify you.

SEVEN RULES ABOUT SPEAKING TIME

Adhere to the following guidelines to ensure that you are not flying right through the speaking stop sign and agitating your listeners:

1. TIME IT

When you are practicing your speech (you are practicing, right?), time it *after* you have made your final revisions. If you time it during the drafting phase, as you are adding and deleting material, you will get a distorted idea of its length. Your goal is to make your delivery fit into the time allotted. If it does not, continue tinkering.

Be flexible, because various factors may impact your time: You may be anxious (yes, even you) when you speak, which may cause you to jabber or to forget a few thoughts. You may get caught up in the spirit of the moment and insert new comments. Or—Thank goodness!—your audience may laugh at a few of your witticisms. All of this affects your time, so don't be absurdly inflexible ("Okay, I will complete my opening at two minutes and fifteen seconds, wrap up point three at nine minutes and thirty seconds, and finish with ten seconds to spare"). Unless you are an accountant, that type of unrealistic, mathematical precision shackles you, so build a little leeway into your time frames.

———————

Have more than thou showest, speak less than thou knowest.
WILLIAM SHAKESPEARE

———————

2. PREPARE TO JETTISON

Time not only the entire speech but also each section. Why? Because you could be forced to jettison portions of your speech (a point, a story, an example) to meet time constraints—for example, if the program runs late (not uncommon), if your audience's attention, for any variety of reasons, has become very limited (again, not uncommon), or if a prior gasbag has monopolized your time (a capital offense).

In any of those events, you should cut your speech short. Even if you did not cause the timing problems, you will be regarded as the culprit if you encroach on your audience's sacred times: lunch, scheduled breaks, or quitting time all spring to mind.

Alert your audience that you are shortening your speech to respect their time, and offer to be available afterward to address any questions. You will then bask in the warm glow of your audience's admiration.

———————

Far more numerous was the herd of such,
who think too little, and who talk too much.
JOHN DRYDEN

———————

3. CONTROL THE MEETING FLOW

Begin your presentation on time, and if there are breaks during your presentation, reconvene on time. Why? You can assume that the attendees, like children, will test your authority. If they determine that you are a wimp, and that the times you announced are merely suggestions, they will cavalierly disregard them, knowing that they can arrive late and not miss anything important. These stragglers invariably arrive with a noisy flourish and cause a commotion as they squeeze into their middle seats (they *always* have middle seats), stomping on everyone's toes along the way and loudly apologizing ("Oops! Sorry, sorry").

If audience members arrive late, ignore them. Continue speaking unless they become so disruptive that you must pause and allow them to get settled. Reward those who arrived on time by not repeating what you have already said.

4. MONITOR YOUR TIME AS YOU SPEAK

Monitor your time, because it evaporates quickly, and it is very easy to lose track of time in the midst of your presentation. Place a large watch on the lectern, locate a wall clock that is visible from the stage, or designate an audience member to periodically but discreetly signal how much time you have remaining. Avoid glancing at the watch you are wearing while you are speaking, because that sends the unspoken message that you are either bored or anxious to bolt.

The secret of being a bore . . . is to tell everything.
VOLTAIRE

---

5. KEEP 'EM POSTED

Let your listeners know that you are sensitive to the time constraints. This builds audience rapport, always a worthy goal. The bonus for you is that they are much more likely to pay attention.

Such comments as "In the fifteen minutes I have with you today . . . ," "In the final few minutes, I would like to discuss . . . ," or "Let me be brief . . ." signal that you respect your listeners' time. But here is the caveat: After you make any of those announcements, you had better abide by them. Never raise expectations with promises you don't intend to keep, because your audience will be miffed and will feel betrayed. And, as you know, "Hell hath no fury . . . ."

———

I should be glad, if I could flatter myself that I came
as near to the central idea of the occasion, in
two hours, as you did in two minutes.
EDWARD EVERETT TO ABRAHAM LINCOLN

———

6. Do Not Exceed Your Audience's Attention Span

Under most circumstances, the attention of your audience members tends to dwindle after ten minutes, and nearly vanishes after twenty minutes. If the speaker is a crashing bore, she may be lucky to hold their attention for one minute.

It may seem hard to imagine, but the time races by when you are speaking, so you should distill your message to its essence. I know, all your points are critical, but you may have to sacrifice a few brainy insights if they cause your talk to run long.

I was once intent on impressing a coveted prospect with the depth of my knowledge, so I puffed: "I have ten compelling reasons why you should hire my presentation skills company." Without missing a beat, the prospect leaned forward, wryly smiled, and said: "I'm sure you do, but why don't you just give me your best two?"

This is great advice for speakers, too. Make one lasting impression with a few crisp, direct points rather than creating a haze with a barrage of words. Give them your best points, and then go home.

7. ALLOW TIME FOR QUESTIONS

Before you speak, clarify with your host whether you will be provided additional time to address audience questions, or whether you are expected to answer them within your allotted speaking time (principle 34). Field questions whenever feasible, because it is an excellent way to engage your audience, but have a clear understanding of the time limits. Don't encourage questions without budgeting time for them, because if you run out of time during a Q & A session, your audience will feel cheated and you will seem evasive.

Think before you speak; stop talking
before they say "enough."

SA'DI

Abide by the time limitations in every presentation, unless your audience or your host invites you to continue and you are not encroaching on subsequent speakers' time. Don't get swept away in the heat of the moment and delude yourself that your audience is anxious to hear more. They generally prefer less (a harsh but accurate assessment). Make your points, and then, while your audience is intoxicated with your words, sit down.

TAKE COMMAND
OF "Q&A"

Before I refuse to take your questions,
I have an opening statement.

—PRESIDENT RONALD REAGAN

Here is a bitter truism that those who are rigidly tethered to the speech script do not want to hear: Most speakers do more to inspire, persuade, sell, and inform their listeners by confidently responding to audience questions than by *anything* they say during the prepared speech. I can hear the "say-it-ain't-so" wails of anguish from the disciples who never deviate from the prepared speech. Sorry, it is time to leave that safe cocoon.

These unpredictable question-and-answer sessions give you an excellent opportunity to clarify and reinforce points, elaborate on issues, solidify your expertise, address any misunderstandings, and perhaps persuade those who seem unpersuadable. Yes, you up the anxiety ante when you venture away from the safety of your carefully planned presentation and invite audience input, but the rewards outstrip the risks by a tremendous margin.

A question-and-answer session typically crackles with energy, often generating more interest than the prepared presentation did. What accounts for its appeal? One reason is that the audience members get to participate, which increases interest and learning. Also, during a question-and-answer session, the speaker traipses into uncharted territory. Perhaps it is the same phenomenon that compels us to gawk at a car wreck (be honest, you know you have done that): It is dangerous and unusual. When the questions start flying, everyone, even the drowsiest listener, snaps to attention and perches on the edge of his or her seat, especially if the exchange promises to be heated (such as when the speaker is advocating plunking a halfway house in the audience's bucolic neighborhood).

Now, for the bad news (I know, what a killjoy!): A question-and-answer session is a tremendous opportunity—listen, because this is important—*if,* and *only if,* you are prepared (do you detect a theme developing in this book?). If you are unprepared, the session can quickly become a treacherous minefield, the kind that has doomed even exceptional speakers. If you are unprepared, cower and pray when the questioning barrage begins.

I was gratified to be able to answer promptly,
and I did. I said I didn't know.

MARK TWAIN

There are manifest rewards for deftly handling audience questions. Yet sometimes a speaker devotes not a single forethought to them; he just wings it: "I was just strolling through the Q & A neighborhood, and thought, 'What the heck! Why not take a few questions . . . ?'" That is a sure recipe for disaster. With no planning, this foolhardy speaker is often perplexed by even the most predictable questions. Staggered, he lamely mumbles an unresponsive reply, or he reaches into his handy grab bag of canned answers. If you do that, you can put one gigantic check mark in the squandered-opportunity column. And while you're at it, let a little air out of your "expert" balloon to boot.

SEVENTEEN QUESTION-AND-ANSWER RULES

So, you are willing to add a little zest to your talk with questions. Now what? Unless the prospect of public humiliation exhilarates you, don't enter the Q&A arena without a plan. Here it is. Study these rules before you invite the first question.

1. KNOW THE TERRAIN

Do not simply cross your fingers and fervently hope that your audience will not ask the questions you are dreading. They will. In the same way that a predatory animal can smell fear, an audience has the uncanny ability to zero in with amazing accuracy on just those particular questions. So you had better be prepared, lest you find yourself under the heat of the spotlight, babbling incoherently.

What can you do? Start by knowing as much as possible about your audience before you speak, so you can anticipate their questions and plan your responses (principles 6 and 7). Ask yourself the following questions:

- "Are the questions likely to be pointed and probing or friendly and fluffy?"
- "Do my listeners understand the issues?"
- "What is the opposing position?"
- "What are the strengths of the opposing position?"
- "Am I advocating something that threatens my listeners?"
- "Am I dealing with emotional or inflammatory topics (stem cell research, same-sex marriage, Yankees versus Red Sox)?"
- "What are the weaknesses in my position?" (There are always some.)
- "Should I concede anything in my response?"
- "Do any listeners have a hidden agenda?"
- "How will I respond to provocative or irrelevant questions?"
- "What will I do if an audience member becomes confrontational?"

Know the terrain, your risks, and your vulnerabilities before you solicit questions.

2. Devise a Plan

Before you speak, decide whether you will field questions during or after your prepared speech. In your introduction or in your opening comments, clarify for your audience which approach you will take. Each has inherent advantages and disadvantages.

Accepting questions during the speech typically heightens the interest for everyone, it enables you to immediately gauge your audience's response and level of understanding, and it gives you an opportunity to correct misunderstandings quickly (what seems clear to you may be murky to your audience). This approach can be risky, however, if one of the questions is only marginally related to your topic (it happens) or if it baffles you (this also happens). In addition, the questions might divert your audience's attention from your message. Finally, if you accept questions during the speech, your allotted time can quickly evaporate, so plan accordingly.

On the other hand, if you hold questions until you have completed your speech, you will be able to cover all your points without interruption. Unfortunately, without immediate input from your audience, you limit your ability to evaluate their reaction to your message. Moreover, listeners may forget their questions or be reluctant to raise a question regarding a subject that you covered much earlier.

Either approach will work, but pick your path before you begin to speak.

3. Understand the Question

Here is a simple rule: If you don't understand a question, don't guess and don't answer. No one will think you are a dunce if you ask the questioner to explain or clarify the question. That is definitely preferable to taking a wild stab at it and answering unresponsively. If you are clueless but plunge into a response anyway, you may create confusion; irritate the questioner, who will conclude that you are being evasive or flippant; and irk the other audience members, who may conclude that you are patronizing one of their kindred spirits in the audience. Any of these results will open Pandora's Box for you, so clarify before responding.

4. SCHMOOZE

If you want to encourage questions, create a friendly, nonthreatening atmosphere. Solicit participation with an open-ended invitation for questions: "I know I covered that topic quickly. What questions do you have?" Also acknowledge and thank audience members for their participation: "Thank you for that question." This respectful attitude toward those who ask questions—yes, even when all you really want to do is sock the bozo, whose goal it is to agitate you, in the nose—helps to build audience rapport.

But, avoid saying, "That is an excellent question," because you risk offending others who have already asked a question ("Hey, what about me? My question was better than his!"). Audiences can be hypersensitive, so don't single anyone out for special praise.

Think before you speak, pronounce not imperfectly,
nor bring out your words too hastily
but orderly and distinctly.
GEORGE WASHINGTON

---

5. REPEAT THE QUESTION

If it is a large audience, repeat the question before responding, to ensure that everyone has heard it. The listeners will appreciate your audience focus (principle 29), and you will gain additional time to consider your response. (If you are momentarily stumped, even a few seconds can help while your brain whirs away in a desperate search for a reasonably intelligent thought.)

6. REFRAME THE QUESTION

Occasionally, some ninny in your audience will plop a disjointed, convoluted, or complex question in your lap. Address such queries cautiously, because they can undermine you quickly.

Paraphrase the question if it is confusing: "Let me see if I can restate your question, so I am sure I understand it." If it is a compound question, break it into bite-size segments: "I think you have asked several questions, so let me attempt to respond to each one separately." Finally, if the question is irrelevant, smile, say so, and move on: "Thank you for the question, but that is really beyond the scope of my talk today." Your goal is to respond in a direct, logical fashion and to remain focused. If the question causes your intuitive alarms to sound "Danger! Danger!" proceed warily.

7. BE RESPONSIVE

You seldom persuade your listeners with ambiguity or evasiveness. Stop futzing around, and answer as honestly and as directly as possible. Don't stall, hoping that a pithy comment will pop into your noggin. If you ignore the question, or if you launch into your "speaking points" to rehash your position, your evident elusiveness will undermine your credibility. (On the other hand, if you are honest and responsive, there is a price to pay as well: You will have eliminated your prospects of running for political office.)

Speak properly, and in as few Words as you can,
but always plainly; for the End of Speech is
. . . to be understood.
WILLIAM PENN

---

8. ADMIT IT IF YOU DO NOT KNOW

Some speakers feel that saying "I do not know" will cause them to turn to stone. But it is not merely okay to admit ignorance, it is preferable at times. Unless the question is clearly one that you *should* know the answer to ("Is it not true that Giovanni "The Hatchet Man" Gotti handed you a greasy duffel bag filled with fifty thousand dollars in crisp one-hundred-dollar bills?"), it's perfectly acceptable to respond by saying, "I am sorry, but I don't know the answer. Let me see if I can find out and get back to you."

Understand, however, that there is no substitute for thorough preparation, and if you are intentionally unresponsive ("A greasy duffel bag jammed with cash? Let me think . . . I'm not sure") or cagey ("That depends on what your definition of *is* is"), your audience will quickly become exasperated and you will undermine your credibility.

Teach thy tongue to say,
"I do not know."
MOSES MAIMONIDES

---

9. EXUDE CONFIDENCE WITH YOUR BODY LANGUAGE

Your goal is to exude confidence when you speak (principle 30), so don't forget that when you begin to take questions. Here is a laundry list of what not to do: Don't stand ramrod stiff, clench the lectern with ferocity, recoil, flop over the lectern, prop your chin in your hand, scowl, wince, or draw your face taut. Such body language and facial expressions diminish the message of self-confidence you want to convey, and frighten small children and animals.

Look interested and relaxed. Being prepared (there is that gosh darn Mr. Preparation again!) will do wonders for your confidence and your stage presence.

10. REMAIN COMPOSED

Stay positive and composed despite questions that are antagonistic ("Your position is just double-dumb!"), personal ("I would not expect an insensitive half-wit like you to understand!"), or irrelevant ("Can vegetarians eat animal crackers?"). Do not let hostile questioners provoke an angry response from you. That response is often precisely what they want to accomplish. Rather, be firm but polite. Smile, grit your teeth, and agree to disagree. Shouting invectives may be cathartic, but it is neither helpful nor persuasive.

Our anger and annoyance are more detrimental
to us than the things themselves
which anger or annoy us.
MARCUS AURELIUS

---

11. TARGET THE MAJORITY

You will rarely convince everyone to accept your position, so don't waste valuable time and energy addressing questions from the malcontent minority and attempting to persuade them. Focus instead on the concerns of the majority of your audience. Some members of your audience would not accept your position if it were an edict chiseled in granite and delivered from heaven. Move on confidently, smugly knowing in your heart that they are wrong and you are right.

12. BE BRIEF

Get to the point. Don't ramble, filibuster, or browbeat when responding. This only annoys your listeners, creates confusion, and generates more questions. Your listeners will better understand and remember concise, focused answers. Being brief also enables you to address more questions in the time allotted. Answer succinctly, and let your listeners get on with their lives.

13. FOLLOW UP

After you have responded to a question, occasionally ask a follow-up question, such as "Does that make sense?" or "Does that answer your question?" This demonstrates that you are genuinely interested that the questioner understands your point. But avoid follow-up if it prevents you from addressing questions from other audience members, if the questioner is argumentative, or if you are anxious to move on to the next question (just darn thankful that you were able to mumble something marginally lucid in your answer).

14. MAINTAIN CONTROL OF THE ROOM

Sometimes, multiple conversations or even heated arguments—complete with name-calling, finger-pointing, and fist waving—will erupt during a question-and-answer session. Disruptions can escalate into chaos if you ignore them.

Pause and politely ask those causing the disruption to hold their comments, so that everyone can hear both you and the person asking the question. Allow the agitators to be heard only if you have time on the program and are so inclined. It is your responsibility as a speaker to maintain control of the room. If all else fails, suggest that they settle their disagreement by arm wrestling in the hallway; resort to your crowd-control mace only in dire circumstances.

If you can't answer a man's argument, all is
not lost; you can still call him vile names.
ELBERT HUBBARD

---

15. MONITOR THE TIME

Always adhere to the time allotted for your presentation (principle 33). So, when you are preparing your speech, budget time for questions. If your time on the program has expired, stop. Don't continue to field questions, especially if others are speaking after you. Instead, inform your audience that you will be available to answer all their questions one-on-one out in the hallway or through e-mail.

16. PRACTICE Q & A

Round up all your inquisitive, annoying, and stubborn friends (don't tell them that this combination of characteristics is why they were selected) and role-play. Practice responding to *their* questions. This will hone your ability to think on your feet and to formulate crisp, responsive answers. Have your inquisitors ask every conceivable type of question, because that is exactly what you can expect from your audience: compound, convoluted, and confrontational questions posed by bewildered, inarticulate, and hostile questioners.

Some of the questioners in your audience will have amazingly fertile imaginations; others will have hidden agendas; and still others will just be dunderheads. Inevitably there will be at least one who relishes the sound of her own voice and will welcome any opportunity to merely pontificate. The practice sessions will help you prepare for all of them.

17. STUDY VIDEOTAPES

Compose yourself first; then dive in and analyze videotapes of both your practice sessions and your live presentations involving Q&A. This study may be painful, but it will be profitable, I promise.

Be analytical, and ask yourself these questions: "Was I responsive, or were my answers gibberish?" "Was I focused, or did I blather?" "Did I sound confident, or did I sound confused?" "Did I focus on the questioner, or did I allow my eyes to dart around?" "Did my body language and facial expressions convey poise, or did I look like a crazed, trapped animal?" The videotape reveals exactly what your audience will see, so study it, internalize the lessons, and address any deficiencies.

Deftly fielding questions is a skill you develop only with practice. Study the additional works regarding question-and-answer sessions that are listed in the recommended resources at the back of the book.

Venturing from your script can be unnerving, but you can calm your jitters and minimize the risks with careful planning. Handle questions adroitly, and you will distinguish yourself and embellish your stature and credibility with every audience. But never enter the question-and-answer briar patch unprepared; many speakers have done that, and they have not been heard from since.

PART VII

TALK WITH TOOLS

THE PROCESS OF USING A MICROPHONE looks effortless from the comfort of your seat: Walk up, grab it, and just start yammering. Simple, right? Hardly. That seemingly harmless microphone can sabotage you lickety-split if you are unfamiliar with all of its quirks.

Things seen are mightier than things heard.
ALFRED, LORD TENNYSON

Speakers regularly incorporate visual aids into their presentations, and for good reason: A visual aid can transform a dismal presentation into an extraordinary one. When you use a visual aid in your presentation, your audience is more attentive, learns more, and retains the message longer. But that happens only *if*—and it is a colossal *if*—it is created and used skillfully. When poorly designed or handled clumsily—and it frequently is—a visual aid frazzles the speaker, vexes the audience, and undercuts the presentation. If this happens when you are speaking, you will rue your decision not to have become a cloistered scientist.

Part VII addresses a variety of presentation tools, the advantages and disadvantages of each, the nuts and bolts of fickle Mr. Microphone, and the secrets of using a visual aid flawlessly.

251

PRINCIPLE 35

MASTER THE
MICROPHONE

The wisest thing to do with a fool is to encourage him
to hire a hall and discourse to his fellow citizens.
Nothing chills nonsense like exposure to the air.

—WOODROW WILSON

I know exactly what you are thinking: "What could be difficult about using a microphone? Don't you just flip a switch and start rattling away?" Yes—if you enjoy living dangerously. Microphones harass grizzled veteran speakers, and they can befuddle neophytes. In the worst of times, speaking greenhorns can completely unravel. So that you will recognize your microphone risks, let's start with a quick lineup of the Eight Egregious Microphone Sins. Please step forward as your name is called.

Sin One occurs when a speaker holds the microphone too close to her mouth, nearly inhaling it. This causes her to sound shrill, amplifies her anxious breathing, and produces sounds that terrify small children.

Sin Two occurs when a speaker forgets that his strange sniffling, snorting, and paper-shuffling sounds are fully amplified for his audience.

Sin Three happens when a speaker plants her chin on her chest, focuses on her feet, and speaks directly into the microphone that she is holding right next to her belly button. She might as well be speaking into a bucket.

Sin Four surfaces when a speaker treats his microphone as he would a deadly cobra, clenching it with a steely grip and holding it a stiff-arm away from his mouth. His microphone is useless, and the added drawback: He resembles the Tin Man from *The Wizard of Oz.*

Sin Five crops up when a lanky speaker, rather than pausing and adjusting the microphone stand higher, decides to simply droop down several feet to the microphone's level, which makes him look like a giant slouch.

Sin Six takes place when a speaker gestures wildly during her talk with the hand that is holding the microphone; only haphazardly, whenever the microphone happens to cruise by in the general vicinity of her mouth, does she project a random word or two.

Sin Seven comes into play when the speaker discovers to his misfortune, as he tumbles either to the floor or into the orchestra pit, that—yes, yes indeed—there is a cord attached to the microphone.

And finally, *Sin Eight* (drum roll, please), the worst of all the transgressions for a speaker but, without question, the most entertaining for her audience, is when she forgets that her microphone is on before she steps up to speak, and she broadcasts her juicy observations and scurrilous accusations throughout the room. Her mother cringes in shame, and the speaker wonders where she will find her next job, *gosh darn it!*

So, do you still think that all it takes is a flip of the switch?

THREE MICROPHONE OPTIONS

You might as well resign yourself to the reality that you will need to use a microphone sometime in your speaking career, so you need to know your options. There are three main types of microphones, each with its own inherent advantages and disadvantages (it is never easy, is it?). Let's study each of them.

1. THE FIXED MICROPHONE

As its name implies, a fixed microphone is attached to the lectern. You can typically make minor adjustments in the height of the microphone but not much else. After adjusting the height, you simply turn it on, test it, adjust the volume, and talk. Other than staying close to the microphone as you speak, there is no other fussing required. You are free to gesture with both hands (provided you have not locked your hands in the lectern death grip), and there is no risk of tripping over that pesky microphone cable.

But you pay a hefty price for this apparent simplicity. The biggest drawback is that you are stuck behind the lectern for the entire presentation, a position that saps your power. It is even worse if you find yourself standing behind a hulking monster that required all the lumber from several giant redwood trees to build. This behemoth lectern obscures your audience's view of everything except your bobbing head. That obscuring is a huge disadvantage in every situation, so avoid the fixed microphone whenever possible.

Finally, if you are tall, don't forget Sin Five: Adjust the microphone's height upward, because a slouch seldom projects power or confidence.

A lot of managers aren't bad at public speaking.
But "not bad" ain't good enough.
TOM PETERS

---

2. THE HANDHELD MICROPHONE

You can detach a handheld microphone from the lectern or microphone stand and move about with relative freedom. Once you become proficient with a handheld mike, you can also use it in various ways to enhance your voice. Many professional speakers prefer it for that reason.

But like its relative, the fixed microphone, a handheld microphone suffers inherent limitations. First, since you are holding the mike, you can gesture with only one hand at a time (unless you commit Sin Six, and if you do, you should confess it and resolve to stop). Second, many of these microphones have cables, which limit how far you can wander. Third, you must constantly monitor the microphone cable's location, lest either you step on it, with the resultant loss of slack yanking the microphone from your hand, or you trip over it. Both predicaments will require nimble improvisation by you. Finally, it takes practice to master where and how to hold the microphone to amplify your voice correctly, positioning it neither too close (which produces sounds similar to those made by alley cats) nor too far away (which produces no sounds).

3. THE LAVALIERE MICROPHONE

A lavaliere microphone is a tiny mike that clips to your shirt collar, jacket lapel, or necktie. It has many advantages. You can wander about and gesture freely and naturally with both hands. It is typically cordless, eliminating concern that you might step on or trip over a cable. And you can speak naturally, without constantly monitoring whether you are holding the microphone in the proper position to amplify your voice.

Lavaliere microphones have three drawbacks. First, some are not cordless, which limits your movement and interjects that tripping bugaboo. Second, you need to make sure that your microphone is not attached on some clothing that moves, swishes, or crinkles, because that will produce disturbing noises. And third, you can easily forget that you are wearing this unobtrusive devise; if you do not vigilantly monitor when it is on, your uncensored Sin Eight comments may haunt you.

SEVEN MICROPHONE GUIDELINES

Now you know your options, so let's consider seven pearls of microphone wisdom:

1. PRACTICE WITH A MICROPHONE

Familiarity breeds confidence (or was that contempt, but I digress), so get accustomed to holding the microphone as you practice your presentation. If you don't have a spare mike lying around your office or home (doesn't everyone?), hold a pencil, a rolled-up magazine, or a Tootsie Roll Pop to replicate the feeling.

Holding a mike in place while speaking is not as easy as it might look, so repeatedly practice. Videotape yourself to see whether you are using the microphone correctly (principle 21). If you spot any problems (the microphone careening about wildly, erratic projection, your striking resemblance to a robot), address them and continue practicing until you have mastered the mike.

It is unnatural to stand for long periods with your elbow bent, pressed against your ribs, holding an object next to your mouth. If you have difficulty doing this, try this: Position your elbow against your ribs and have someone tie a string around your rib cage and microphone arm as you practice. That will help you hold the microphone in place and acclimate you to the feeling. But remember to remove the string before you speak to your audience.

———

Speech was given to the ordinary sort of men whereby
to communicate their mind; but to the wise
men, whereby to conceal it.
ROBERT SOUTH

———

2. BEFRIEND AN EXPERT

If the venue where you will be speaking has an on-site AV specialist, track this person down, and enlist his help in testing the sound system, ironing out the glitches, and exorcising the microphone demons. Try to ensure that he will be readily available to help you if the microphone begins to balk when you are speaking. Give him your unconditional love, cash, or both, because it will be one of the best investments you make in your presentation.

3. ALWAYS TEST THE MICROPHONE

Raise your hand if you have been in the audience when some numbskull has trudged to the microphone after his introduction and then repeatedly thumped it with his chubby fingers while reciting the only microphone mantra apparently known to the human race: "Testing, testing, 1-2-3, is this on? Can you hear me?" Unfortunately, we can, and we now realize that we are in the hands of a hack speaker.

Test the microphone well before your audience arrives. Enlist someone to move around the room as you speak, while you are also moving around; listen for dead spots where the microphone sound mysteriously disappears (call that the Bermuda Triangle for Microphones). Tinker with the microphone settings: Does it emit shrill feedback? Do you need to adjust the volume? Do you know where to hold it for ideal projection?

Microphones are notoriously unpredictable, and even identical models can sound noticeably different. Leave nothing to chance: Test it. And stop thumping it.

4. POSITION THE MICROPHONE

To amplify your voice properly, keep the microphone close to your mouth as you speak. Otherwise, you will hear such unsettling catcalls as "Speak up!" "What'd ya say?" "Can't hear you!" As a general rule, position the microphone about three to four inches from your mouth and about one inch below your lower lip, and get used to holding it there for your entire presentation. Your elbow of the arm holding the microphone should be held next to your ribs (not flying around). That will steady the microphone (and disguise your trembling hand).

Be careful not to hold the microphone too close to your mouth, because you might smack your teeth or spit on it. When it is too close, it also creates discordant, shrill sounds that will make your audience cringe. On the other hand, if as you get caught up in the spirit of the moment, you forget you are using a mike and you don't hold it close enough, your voice will fade in and out. That is recommended only if you are weaseling out of sharing bad news and secretly hoping that your audience will not hear you. Experiment until you find the ideal positioning.

5. BE LEERY OF THE CABLE

While you are speaking, that seemingly harmless microphone cable lurks, just waiting for its first opportunity to entangle your feet and wreak havoc. It can quickly transform a confident speaker into a klutz. Use your free hand to control the cable and push it aside. Unless you relish pratfalls, never lose track of that insidious little demon.

6. CONTROL YOUR GESTURES

If you are speaking with a handheld microphone, you can gesture only with your free hand. Since you can hold the microphone in either hand, add a little variety by switching hands periodically.

If you are an avid gesticulator, you might find it difficult to control your gesturing as you become engrossed in your message. If some of your grand gestures send your microphone several feet away from your mouth, your audience may miss the wisdom that you are so energetically imparting. If you speak regularly to groups large enough to require a microphone, consider investing in a lavaliere mike. If it enhances your delivery or helps you avoid even one nightmarish experience, it is a worthwhile investment.

7. ACT "MICROPHONE SAVVY"

Some speakers approach the microphone with absolute trepidation, as though it were about to snap at them. Become comfortable using the microphone. Before your audience arrives, practice removing the mike from its cradle, holding it, moving around with it, and placing it back in the cradle. Practice until it feels and looks perfectly natural.

From the moment you step before a crowd and seize the microphone, every one of your actions should convey a simple message: "I am confident, because I have done this many times." If you can convey that message, your audience will never know that this is your first adventure with fickle Mr. Microphone.

All your diligent work can be washed away in an instant if you botch handling the microphone. If your listeners cannot hear you, if they are constantly distracted by booming, popping, or screeching feedback—frankly, if you commit any of the Eight Egregious Microphone Sins—you may be racing pell-mell toward microphone meltdown, not a place you want to visit. Practicing with the microphone may not make you perfect, but it will have a tremendous positive impact, so get to work.

Capitalize on Visual Aids

*Remember: It is ten times harder to command
the ear than to catch the eye.*

—Duncan Maxwell Anderson

Powerful visual images etch lasting impressions in our minds. Consider the following examples:

- Little John Kennedy, Jr., saluting his father's casket as it passed
- Neil Armstrong stepping onto the lunar surface, taking "one giant leap for mankind"
- East and West Germans drinking champagne together atop the Berlin Wall
- Two commercial jets crashing into the World Trade Center, and the buildings collapsing

Whether you witnessed these events as they unfolded or saw them captured on film, they created indelible impressions.

A visual aid can also have an enormous impact in most speeches, one that often surpasses the effect of anything you might say (yes, even you). It can make complex concepts understandable and mundane topics engaging. It packs the following wallop:

- *Holding your audience's attention.* Let's be honest: Whatever your objective when speaking, you are unlikely to be as effective if your audience is physically present but mentally miles away, or even dozing as you speak. A visual aid increases the chances that they will remain engaged and focused on your message.

- *Reinforcing your message.* The disillusioning truth is that the typical listener will quickly forget much of what you say, sometimes within moments after you say it. But if you toss in a compelling visual aid and employ it skillfully during your presentation, the equation changes. Studies consistently demonstrate that listeners understand and recall points that are reinforced with a visual aid better and longer. How much better and longer? In one study, audience retention increased between 38 and 200 percent when a visual aid complemented the message.[1]

- *Staying on target.* In the unlikely event that you are not as prepared as you should be (never, correct?), the visual aid can substitute for notes, helping *you* remain focused on your message.

But (you just knew there was a *but* coming, right?), don't start haphazardly incorporating visual aids into your presentation without first carefully considering how they might sabotage it. Here are three of the treacherous ways they might do that:

First, if your visual aid becomes monotonous (one tedious slide after another), its impact shrinks. Your audience will quickly start concentrating on any convenient distraction, such as twiddling their thumbs. Soon, both you and the visual aid become an annoyance, and your message is doomed.

Second, if you jam too much information into too little space, display too many complex details, or distract with too many whiz-bang features, you introduce confusion rather than clarity. You should always design your visual aid with your audience in mind (principles 6 and 7). If you overwhelm them with content that is irrelevant to their current needs, or if you dazzle them with impressive effects at the expense of relevant content, your message is doomed.

Finally, if you bungle around when using a visual aid (and bungling around is rampant in the visual aid world), you will drain all the impact out of whatever message you were trying to enhance with that visual aid. You can read more about this in principles 37 and 38, but you must be comfortable handling the visual aid and quickly resolving glitches that inevitably surface during your speech. The glitches can bedevil you if you are unprepared (they are notoriously recalcitrant). Witnessing a visual aid balking and a speaker imploding is painfully awkward for everyone. You do not want to go there, I promise. And if you do (did I mention this already?), your message will be doomed.

Eyes are more accurate witnesses than ears.

HERACLITUS

NINE VISUAL-AID OPTIONS

Speakers enjoy a startling array of visual-aid options, from the simplicity of a snapshot to the complexity of a stunning multimedia extravaganza. This is both a blessing and a curse: All visual aids have both advantages and limitations—advantages that can be enthralling but limitations that can be crippling.

You should carefully select your visual aid, and meticulously plan how you will weave it into your presentation. Your goal is to create suspense, heighten interest, and solidify your message. Examine the list below to select the right visual aid for your presentation. Then master the rules for using a visual aid set forth in principles 37 and 38.

1. HANDOUTS

By having your listeners fill in handouts as you speak, you will reinforce your message and improve listener recollection. Another bonus is that your listeners typically refer to the handouts after the presentation to supplement your message. But this is important: Handouts should *always* be well organized and look professional. If they are disorganized, cluttered, sloppy, or appear to have been created on a 1930s-era mimeograph machine, they reflect poorly on you.

You want to provide rich content in your handouts, but don't go overboard. If they are too detailed (about as lengthy as *War and Peace,* for instance), they become a distraction. Your listeners end up reading them and ignoring you. Being ignored as you speak can be disconcerting; worse, it bruises even the heartiest ego.

2. OBJECTS

Almost anything that you can easily handle and display fits into the object category: a scale model of a building, a baseball bat, a book of artwork, or a water gun (unloaded, please). An object typically commands the immediate attention of your audience, particularly when you skillfully incorporate it into your presentation.

A precaution: Your object should neither be so small that it is nearly invisible to most of the audience (cuff links or a paper clip) nor so hulking that it is unwieldy (a refrigerator or a fifty-gallon barrel of olive oil). Neither choice will enrich your presentation. And as a rule, avoid any visual aid with the potential to cause a hernia as you clumsily attempt to shove it around.

3. PHOTOGRAPHS

A photograph can captivate your audience, but only if the image is clear and large enough to be seen by everyone, including those introverts clustered in the back of the room. If the photograph fits in your wallet, it will be appropriate only for a very small audience—say, two people.

A blurry or tiny photograph only frustrates your audience, and they will quickly lose interest. Consider enlarging and mounting your photographs on stiff foam boards to make them easier to display. And never pass a stack of photographs around as you are speaking, because they—not you—will become the center of attention.

————

Seeing is believing all the world over.
MIGUEL DE CERVANTES

————

4. DIAGRAMS

A diagram—whether you prepare it ahead of time or, assuming you have some rudimentary drawing skills, draw it while you are speaking—can help clarify your message. You can use it to reinforce your points—for example, by showing the hierarchy of an organization, an architectural plan, or vehicle paths during an automobile accident.

But sometimes a diagram looks like a labyrinth of disjointed lines that are more likely to confuse than enlighten. A few determined audience members may attempt to decipher the maze (while concentrating so hard on the puzzle that they miss what you are saying), but many will just give up. Strive for clarity and simplicity.

5. GRAPHS

A graph can be useful when you need to explain a topic loaded with mystifying statistics, mind-numbing data, or technical jargon, especially when your audience is not conversant with the topic. Three popular options:

You can use a *line graph* to depict trends or developments over time, such as your company's dramatic spike in sales immediately after you launched the exciting "Piddle-Paddle" line of cutting-edge swimwear. A *bar graph* can help you illustrate trends and percentages, such as when you want to compare the disparity in the income levels of J. Roland Dough, III, the swaggering, blue-blooded, Ivy League graduate, versus Ralph Sipowitz, a high school dropout. And a *pie graph* can delineate percentages—for example, when you want to clarify the portion of the pastry market cornered by that juggernaut Doughnut Decadence.

Like a diagram, a graph must be visible, simple, and easily under-stood. If it is too complex, it is worse than worthless—and that is bad.

6. THE FLIP CHART

The preceding three visual-aid options—photographs, diagrams, and graphs—can be incorporated into the final four options: the flip chart, overhead transparencies, slides, and electronic presentations.

A flip chart is the workhorse in many presentations, for several good reasons: It is the essence of simplicity, you can use it in a variety of ways, and you do not risk a gut-wrenching electronic snafu. When you write on a flip chart during your presentation, you reinforce your message, and you can record audience input. Also, you can tear off sheets from the chart and post them around the room for repeated reference.

But like all visual aids, the flip chart has a few limitations. It is suit-able only for a small audience—say, of twenty to thirty people. A larger audience will not be able to read the text. And if your scrawl is horren-dous ("Is that cryptography?"), either you will need to entice someone to write the information beforehand, so you can flip to the appropriate page during the presentation, or you will need to enlist a volunteer with stellar handwriting to help you while you speak. Swallow your penman-ship pride, and make sure that your flip chart text is legible.

Eloquence is the power to translate a truth into language
perfectly intelligible to the person to whom you speak.
RALPH WALDO EMERSON

---

7. OVERHEAD TRANSPARENCIES

Although the overhead projector is somewhat outdated technolog-ically (the Pilgrims used this device at the Plymouth town hall meet-ings), it is still regularly used by many speakers because it offers distinct advantages: It is simple to use, you can face your listeners, you can pre-sent information easily to any size group, you can instantaneously record listener input, and you can prepare colorful transparencies before the presentation.

As with all electronic visual aids, you may need to lower the lights in the room, and this can be a dicey proposition, especially if your topic is slightly tiresome or if you tend to drone on (never a good idea with or without a visual aid). You will need to raise the lights periodically to guarantee that your audience does not become drowsy. More on this topic in principles 37 and 38.

8. SLIDES

Slides are an excellent way to reinforce your message and captivate your audience for a long period of time. Unfortunately, even the simple task of loading the slides into a carousel can be unnerving. I have seen them loaded upside down; backward, producing mirror images; and in the wrong order. Also, although it is relatively easy to operate, a slide projector can and does jam, usually at the most inappropriate moment. The typical result is a tug-of-war battle with the projector. The battle is usually entertaining (especially if you are not one of the combatants), but always unprofessional, so try to avoid it.

9. ELECTRONIC PRESENTATIONS

After surveying today's visual-aid market, you may conclude: "So many alluring, snazzy visual-aid toys, and so little time!" You now have at your disposal a huge array of video, DVD, computer, and multimedia visual aids that have the potential to rivet your audience; these are discussed in principle 38. But before you race helter-skelter down this high-tech path, be sure that you know what you're getting yourself into. It can be a perilous journey for any speaker.

We have only scratched the surface, but if you intend to rely on a visual aid in your presentation—and you should—study the recommended resources that are listed at the back of this book.

A visual aid can pack enormous punch when it is carefully designed and skillfully used, but many speakers fail one or both of those requirements. A visual aid should never become a crutch, never substitute for thorough preparation, never be used excessively, and never overwhelm the audience—rules that are ignored far too often. But if you harness its power by knowing and applying the rules described in principles 37 and 38, a visual aid can help make your message unforgettable.

PRINCIPLE 37

KNOW THE
VISUAL–AID RULES

Believe nothing of what you hear,
and only half of what you see.

—ANONYMOUS

You have studied principle 36, carefully selected the ideal visual aid, and now you are hankering to go. All you need to do is schlepp it to the front of the room, prop it up, and Presto! It works like magic, right? Only in fantasyland.

Either you had better know how to use your visual aid proficiently, or you can plan on some embarrassing moments. It takes planning, tenacity, and plenty of practice to ensure that your visual aid complements rather than undermines your talk. Why? Because it is never a question of *whether* something will go awry with your visual aid; it is only a question of *when*. Take every precaution to avoid that experience, because visual-aid calamities can rattle speakers, as the following episode illustrates:

One of my university public speaking students was demonstrating the steps involved in repotting a plant. She carefully laid out her trowel, clay pot, pile of dirt, and plant. Unfortunately, she had not practiced with her visual aid before her speech, and she had overlooked a critical detail: A clay pot has a big, pesky hole in the bottom.

As she spoke, holding up the pot so that it was visible to the entire class, she troweled dirt into it, and just as quickly, the dirt poured onto the table. The logical way to address this untoward development was simply to pause and plug the hole. But there was no logic involved, because she was flustered and her brain was frozen. She elected to handle her perplexing problem in a peculiar manner: by scooping faster—much, *much* faster. She was hell-bent on trying to shovel the dirt into the pot more quickly than it was pouring out, but she was losing the race and growing ever more frenzied. Her rate of delivery quickened, and she ripped through her ten-minute presentation in less than three, winded and ankle deep in dirt. The class was tremendously amused; it's too bad she had not intended to deliver an entertaining speech. She is now a huge fan of silk plants.

Twenty Rules for Using Visual Aids

Scrupulously adhere to the following rules when using a visual aid. Some of them may seem excessive, but you should always plan for the unexpected. I am confident that Murphy's Law was conceived with visual aids in mind, and the likelihood of complications increases the more you rely on complex high-tech gadgetry. This principle addresses the rules applicable to all visual aids; principle 38 covers the unique challenges multimedia visual aids pose.

1. Study the Speaking Venue

The omnipresent "P" word—prepare—surfaces again. Before selecting your visual aid, analyze the room layout to identify any limitations that might adversely affect your using it during the presentation. Ask yourself the following questions:

- "How large is the room?"
- "Are the electrical outlets, screens, and lights easily accessible?"
- "Will the room's sound system, lighting, or acoustics present any challenges?"
- "Are there any barriers in the room (columns, walls, chandeliers) that will obstruct my audience's view?"
- "Will I be speaking on an elevated stage separated from my audience?"

You cannot select or create the appropriate visual aid without specific information about the venue where you will be speaking, so to avoid nasty surprises, answer these questions sooner rather than later.

2. MAKE YOUR VISUAL AID VISIBLE

I know what you are thinking: "Make it visible? What a brilliant concept!" But speakers regularly violate this rule. One speaker will use visual aids that he has jammed with a maze of cryptic words, cluttered points, and minuscule graphs. Another speaker strains mightily to read the itsy-bitsy lettering on her visual aid, even though she is standing right next to it. A third speaker displays objects so small that they could rattle around in a thimble, and he wonders why his audience is not engrossed.

Make your visual aid visible from every vantage point in the room. Your audience will not spend much time concentrating on a minuscule or perplexing visual aid. They will quickly give up and divert their attention to more pressing matters, none of which involve you or your message. Don't guess that your visual aid will be visible; know it. If you cannot assure yourself of its visibility, either replace it or eliminate it from your presentation.

3. MAKE YOUR VISUAL AID PROFESSIONAL

A sloppy, disorganized, or amateurish visual aid damages your professional image and handicaps your presentation. And unless your purpose is pure entertainment and silliness (presenting to an audience comprised of toddlers, for example), avoid hand puppets, cartoons, home videos, or any Halloween costumes. That kind of buffoonery is more likely to annoy than to amuse your audience.

You have one chance to make a lasting, favorable impression, so don't squander it. Your visual aid should convey the following message: "I am a well-prepared expert." If you cannot muster the time, resources, or expertise to create (or have someone create, following your specific directions) professional visual aids, do not use them. No exceptions.

4. Use Vibrant Colors

Judiciously add a smattering of color to your visual aid. From their exposure to television, movies, and the Internet, audiences today are accustomed to bright colors and striking images, so black and white visual aids can seem drab to them.

Use colors to highlight key points, to focus your audience's attention, and to show contrasts on graphs or charts. But don't go wild with dozens of colors; too many colors become distracting. Choose two or three per visual aid. And, avoid the gaudy, fluorescent shades that are visible from a quarter mile away; you don't want to daze the audience members.

5. Design Horizontally

Design your visual aid so that as you reveal a point, your audience reads it from left to right. Why? Because audiences are accustomed to reading material that way, not diagonally or vertically. Don't disorient them; they can do that by themselves.

6. Select Clean Block Lettering and Fonts

Suppress any latent desire to express your individuality or your artistry when you design your visual aid. Fancy calligraphy is generally illegible, and multiple fonts will confuse your viewers.

Use basic, crisp block lettering. That style may seem boring, but being easy to read is far more important than being ornate in the visual-aid world. Use no more than two font styles per visual aid.

The size of the lettering depends on the size of your audience. As a general guide, consider using a 36-point font for titles, 24-point for subtitles, and no smaller than an 18-point for text, but the litmus test is always the same: Is it visible? A visual aid that may be appropriate in a cozy conference room will be impractical in a large ballroom—simple common sense that is consistently flouted.

7. HIGHLIGHT THE KEY CONCEPTS ONLY

Highlight the crucial points in your visual aid, but not every point. I know: "It's all crucial." Perhaps to you, but probably not to your listeners. You will stupefy them with a tsunami of information. Your greater risk is that the essential points will wash right by in that tidal wave and the groggy listeners will not notice them ("What was that? Was it important?").

Another drawback of laying out every topic in detail is that your audience may opt to read the visual aid rather than listen to you. Soon your voice will become only annoying background droning noise.

You should use the visual aid to guide your audience to the essence of your message, and then point it out ("Look, right there: That is crucial!"). Ask yourself these questions when you create your visual aid: "What is the most effective way to make my point with the fewest words and images?" "What are the three to four crucial points my audience *must* remember?" If the information is not crucial, pare it out. Make simplicity and clarity your watchwords.

———

When the eyes say one thing, and the tongue another,
a practiced man relies on the language of the first.
RALPH WALDO EMERSON

———

8. USE SIGNPOSTS

Don't make your listeners work to follow along, because most will not. If your material looks like one big unbroken blob of words and sentences, then it reeks of hard work and boredom—both of which will cause your listeners to zone out. It is your job to guide your listeners through your talk. Do not invite them to stray from the path with a muddled, complicated visual aid. Rather, make it memorable and concise. How?

To focus attention and to facilitate understanding, use numbering, lettering, or bulleting in your visual aid. Limit the number of bullets per slide or page to four or five to minimize the clutter. And limit the number of lines per visual (four to six at most, and less is preferable) if you want your listeners to comprehend your information. Present your information in phrases rather than in complete sentences.

Finally, organize and group the information on the visual aid in the most logical, understandable way: pros versus cons, advantages versus disadvantages, brawny versus brainy.

9. CREATE SUSPENSE

Think of yourself as a master storyteller or a magician (yes, you may have a wand and top hat if you must). Use your visual aid to delight and surprise your audience. To add suspense, heighten the impact, and maintain their fickle attention, carefully orchestrate when and how you will reveal the information. Why?

If you display all the points of your message immediately, rest assured your audience will read ahead; they are headstrong that way. Soon, they will lose interest in your presentation, because they already know exactly what you intend to say. Alternatively, if you fail to hide the points that you previously discussed, your audience may lag behind while you have moved ahead to your next point. Either occurrence guarantees that they will not be focused on what you are saying when you are saying it.

Reveal your points only as you make them. For example, if you have a bulleted list entitled "**Seven Fashion Blunders**," highlight blunder number one ("**White Shoes and Black Socks: A Deadly Duo**") only while you address it, and only as long as you want your audience to focus on that point. Conclude your discussion of that fashion faux pas and hide it before you highlight blunder number two ("**Gold Chains and Hairy Chests: A Tacky Twosome**").

10. PROOFREAD THE MATERIALS

Surely everyone proofreads any material that will be displayed to an audience, right? *Surely not.* Few oversights will undermine your professional image and credibility more quickly than typographical or grammatical mistakes. You can profusely apologize, curse the gremlins in your computer, look petty and blame everyone else, even engage in self-deprecating humor as a face-saving last resort, but you are unlikely to recover from this embarrassing setback.

Before you unveil your visual aid to the world, have several qualified people proof it. And then have several more do it. It takes far longer to undo the damage created by sloppy work than to get it right the first time.

11. LIMIT THE NUMBER OF VISUAL AIDS

Speakers sometimes look like circus ringmasters as they ricochet from one visual aid to the next—PowerPoint slides, handouts, flip charts, videos, whiteboards, and models. Adding such layers of complexity to your presentation will exacerbate your anxiety and diminish the overall impact of all of the visual aids. Select one or two clear, concise visual aids to use during your presentation. If you still have the urge to multitask, join the circus or take up juggling as a hobby.

It is quality rather than quantity that matters.
LUCIUS ANNAEUS SENECA

---

12. PRACTICE WITH YOUR VISUAL AID

When your visual aid works flawlessly, it can amaze your audience, reinforce your message, and make you look like a real genius. And after a few flawless presentations, you can easily delude yourself into believing that visual aids are your reliable, loyal friends and that you can always trust them. Sorry, but they will betray you eventually, and no amount of sniveling, cursing, or head banging will save you from your plight. Master the visual aid *before* you make your presentation—unless living on the edge of disaster exhilarates you.

Repeatedly practice your entire presentation using your visual aid exactly as you intend to use it when you speak. Iron out all the logistics: the timing, where you will stand, and how you will display the visual aid.

Practice flipping the pages, playing the videos, writing on the transparencies, and changing the slides. It should seem effortless when you are speaking. If possible, practice using the visual aid in the room where you will make your presentation. That experience will enhance your confidence when you speak, because you will have eliminated surprises and challenges.

13. PROTECT YOUR VISUAL AID

Protect the visual aid you have so painstakingly created. Store it in a dry, secure place before your talk; do not stack it in your garage or broom closet, or sling it in the car trunk next to your gym bag full of sweaty clothes. Photographs, posters, and charts are easily damaged: Edges become tattered, pristine charts become soiled, and greasy smudges mysteriously appear. A sloppy visual aid undermines your professional image.

One speaker stored his charts in a tube for several weeks before he spoke, and then he whipped them out during his presentation. He spent the remainder of his talk tethered to his display stand, using one hand to hold down the obstinate charts that repeatedly rolled up into the tube shape. Avoid such predicaments.

14. BRING YOUR TOOLS

Review the checklist in principle 28 to determine all the accessories you will need when using your visual aid, such as nonpermanent markers, duct and masking tape, binder clips, Post-it Notes, extension cords, an extra floppy disc with your program, and spare lightbulbs for your equipment. And invest in a nifty laser pointer to help you direct the attention of your audience to the details on the visual aid (and to entertain yourself before the program).

And don't forget: Immediately after you are finished using your accessories, set them down. Do not distract your audience by twirling, bouncing, spinning, gnawing, or jamming them in your ear (anxiety causes eccentric behavior—beware).

15. COORDINATE LOGISTICS

Unless you enjoy sweating like a pack mule lugging a cumbersome visual aid around right before you speak, or agonizing whether it will work, plan ahead. You should have your visual aid set up, tested, and ready well before your audience arrives. They will be forming opinions about you before you begin to speak; if you are red-faced, flustered, and scrambling around as they begin to filter into the room, they will conclude that you are rattled and disorganized. That behavior will not generate confidence about you or your talk.

16. FOCUS ON YOUR LISTENERS

Sometimes a speaker (not you, of course) becomes so engrossed with her visual aid that she forgets about her listeners. She turns her back to them, and begins reading her visual aid, engaging in what is, apparently to her, a fascinating monologue with it. She would probably not know if her listeners left the room during the speech.

Always focus on your audience (principle 29), not on the visual aid. Your listeners will get cranky if you ignore them. Don't use the visual aid as a crutch to compensate for your lack of preparation or to avoid looking at your listeners because you are nervous. They can still see you, and they are far more important than the visual aid. You do not need to persuade, inform, or entertain the visual aid—it is indifferent.

17. SUBSTITUTE THE VISUAL AID FOR NOTES

Provided you have prepared (and it is a capital crime if you have not), you can quickly refer to the points on the visual aid to prompt yourself, so that your presentation flows as planned. Substituting the visual aid for notes also provides you the flexibility to move away from the lectern, which results in a more natural, conversational presentation.

But—and this is a really big *but*—the visual aid should *never* become a crutch or an excuse for not practicing. If you are unprepared and you read to your audience from your visual aid, you will hold their attention for one minute, maybe two if they like you. They can read, so they don't want you to read to them. It dredges up unsavory memories of their boring ancient history teacher from high school.

18. STAND TO THE LEFT

Face your audience, and stand on the left side of the visual aid (your audience's left), and point or gesture toward it with your left hand, because this is how the audience reads text.

Do not position yourself or point to the visual aid in any way that causes you to turn your back on your audience (never a good idea, and probably a really bad idea with a hostile group) or to gesture across your body (such as standing on the right side of the visual aid and pointing with your left arm). You will look like a contortionist.

19. ALLOW THEM TIME TO STUDY YOUR VISUAL AID

Observe the audience members before you remove the visual aid or move to your next point. Are they still studying it or taking notes? Is the material depicted on the visual aid so complex that it requires extra time?

Remember, a topic that you are very familiar with because of your detailed preparation may be new and confusing to members of your audience. Let them study and absorb the information on the visual aid. Be sure they have digested the current point before you move to the next one. Pace yourself, and adjust your rate of delivery as necessary. That increases the likelihood that your message will stick.

20. ADD VARIETY

If you darken the room for long periods while using a visual aid, your audience's attention will drift away. Worse, your audience may become drowsy, and snoring distracts everyone.

Keep your audience alert and engaged by adding variety to your delivery: Periodically switch on the lights, ask questions, solicit their ideas, and vary the pacing.

When you are finished referring to a visual aid, remove it from view: Turn off the projector, darken the screen, or flip the chart to a blank page. Otherwise, many listeners will stay focused in a zombielike trance on the visual aid rather than on listening to you, especially if the visual aid is vibrant (or your presentation is wearisome). Listeners are easily distracted and amused, especially when they are bored.

Stay alert, because visual aids can ruin your presentation in a flash, and they seem to enjoy doing that. Never trust them. But if you plan and practice carefully, a great visual aid can convert an ordinary presentation into an extraordinary one. And always remember: Plug the hole in your clay pot.

PRINCIPLE 38

CREATE MULTIMEDIA
MAGIC

*Technology . . . is a queer thing. It brings you gifts with
one hand, and it stabs you in the back with the other.*

—C. P. SNOW

LEARN TO MASTER THE POWER OF POWERPOINT, the tempting flyer promised. The program guaranteed that attendees would discover how to harness PowerPoint's potential to their advantage, how to mesmerize listeners, and how to blend words and images in a stunning visual package. How could any speaker resist? I couldn't, and I didn't, but I wish I had.

The speakers on the program intended to dazzle the audience with their multimedia presentations. Instead, they fizzled. Their embarrassing gaffes ran the gamut from simple glitches to inexcusable oversights: Their computers were incompatible with the facility's equipment, resulting in awkward and lengthy delays. Their glitzy software programs froze repeatedly. The lettering, graphics, and images were cluttered, confusing, and virtually impossible to decipher. And the speakers were ill prepared; they fumbled along until they ultimately resorted to simply reading what was projected on the screen.

In the ample spare time I had while the speakers floundered, I wondered if they could have planned a worse demonstration. Most of the attendees quickly lost patience; instead of listening, they chose to read newspapers, send text messages, make cell phone calls, or vote with their feet and leave. Rather than convincing the audience members to embrace PowerPoint in their programs, the speakers inspired a renewed appreciation for the simplicity and reliability of the flip chart.

Unfortunately, the speakers' bungling was a disservice to the potential of multimedia. Multimedia can seize your audience's attention, add sparkle to your presentation, and enhance your credibility, expertise, and professional image. High-tech presentations are increasingly becoming the standard in the industry. The graphics can be stunning. Such software as Adobe Persuasion, Corel Presentations, Lotus Freelance Graphics, and Microsoft PowerPoint all heighten the enormous impact of visual aids by offering the following significant advantages:

- You can incorporate graphs, slides, photographs, animation, video clips, and sound to help your audience visualize your message.

- You can scan material from books or magazines and incorporate it into your presentation (but be wary of the dreaded Copyright Police).

- You can download thousands of documents from the Internet to include in your presentation.

- You can quickly add, delete, or modify material, which is difficult with many visual aids.

- You can produce handouts from the slides in your presentation to reinforce the message.

- You can preset your program so that specific material will appear at a predetermined time during the presentation, or you can control the timing with a wireless remote.

Now, for the bad news: Although multimedia presentations can amaze, they can just as easily flop. The more complex the technology, the greater the likelihood that it will eventually fail. And here is the cruel reality: By some twist of fate, these calamities typically occur in a room packed with clients, prospects, competitors, and of course, your boss. And they occur at the most inopportune moments in your presentation:

as you attempt to close the sale, offer recommendations, or share an epiphany.

When they occur—and they will—logic and reason vanish into thin air, and a Herculean struggle between man and machine begins. At these moments, the evil twins—Mr. Hardware and Mr. Software—will do exactly what they want to do, and no amount of cajoling, nudging, swearing, or desperate banging will persuade them to do otherwise. They mulishly refuse to work. The machinery prevails all too often in these epic battles.

Even when they do work as planned, multimedia presentations are not always a blessing. Often they are neither memorable nor helpful if they are not carefully designed. Mastering the tools and software necessary to create powerful multimedia presentations poses special challenges, including all of the following:

- Listeners overwhelmed by a staggering presentation often succumb to sensory overload and miss much of your intended message.

- A multimedia presentation that will not confuse and frustrate your listeners requires meticulous planning and attention to detail.

- You must master the basics of setting up and operating the equipment for each multimedia presentation, adding to your overall preparation time.

- As the complexity of the technology increases, so does the likelihood of a snafu or even a total equipment failure.

TWELVE STEPS TO MULTIMEDIA POWER

You are not prepared for the complexity of a multimedia presentation until you have mastered the basics of creating and using a visual aid, so if you skipped principle 37 (and why would you?), retreat and study that principle. The guidelines below supplement principle 37 and specifically address the problems associated with multimedia visual aids. Always follow these steps before unveiling a high-tech show.

1. KNOW THE BASICS

If you are a technological tenderfoot but you are making a multimedia presentation, you had better take a crash tutorial entitled "Surviving Multimedia Meltdown 101." Master the technology *before* attempting to use it standing in front of an audience. Be prepared to handle simple technical difficulties. It is probably not the best time for on-the-job training when your audience is staring, squirming, and snarling.

Keep a handy list of your hardware and software specifications (the brand and model of your laptop, the type and version of your software), so that you can quickly refer to that information if you have a problem. Those details will escape you in the heat of the moment, when your mind is paralyzed and you are jabbering to the technician on the telephone about "the gizmo that flips the whatchamacallit thingie next to the doodad." That enlightening description of the problem will not prove helpful. If you skip this precaution, have the telephone number for the Dial-A-Prayer hotline readily available.

The purpose of a visual aid is to communicate your ideas,
not to display your virtuosity as an artist or wizardry
with computer graphics. Visual aids should be
simple, clear, and to the point.
STEPHEN E. LUCAS

---

2. MAKE IT SIMPLE

Clarity is critical, a concept lost on many speakers. They use text, photographs, cartoons, animation, slides, and video clips in the same presentation. What results is a disjointed smorgasbord of information—hardly what most spectators of such a circus would call clarity. Just because you can use all these options in your multimedia presentation doesn't mean that you should.

If you overload your presentation, your audience will ignore your message and instead become engrossed in the entertainment: "Wow! I have no idea what the speaker said, but what glitzy graphics!" They should never have to guess what your point was. Rather than trying to impress your audience with a grandiose spectacle, create a multimedia presentation that illuminates and supports your message. Make it simple, memorable, and understandable.

3. CHOOSE COLORS CAREFULLY

Use no more than three harmonizing colors per visual, and maintain consistency throughout your visual aid. If you go wild with color, Confusion and his cousin Chaos will overwhelm your presentation. Also, use distinct color contrasts that make the text easy to read. For example, red and green do not read well when combined on a single visual (even at Christmastime), and it can be difficult to distinguish between certain shades of color, such as blue and purple.

4. SELECT SIMPLE FONTS

Make your fonts simple, consistent, and legible. Use no more than two or three font sizes per visual, with the headings, of course, being largest. If you use too many different sizes or styles (**such as this** *example of **excessive** font styles*), you create confusion. Select fonts that are easy to read from every vantage point in the room. Serif fonts (Better to Best) are suitable for blocks of text, and sans-serif fonts (Better to Best) are useful for headings and titles.

Avoid compressed (**Better to Best**), decorative (*Better to Best*), and artistic (Better to Best) fonts, because your audience will become frustrated trying to read them. Find a different way to express your individuality and personality.

Finally, minimize the use of bold lettering and of all-capital letters. **THEY WILL STAND OUT, BUT CAPS AND BOLD** are challenging to read when they appear in large sections of text.

5. TITLE THE VISUALS

Place a title, or header, at the top of each visual, so that your audience can quickly understand what information you are presenting ("**Ten Advantages of Double Rum-Raisin Ice Cream**" or "**Broccoli: The Silent Killer**"). Set the heading in a larger font to distinguish it from the rest of the text in the visual. Review the guidelines for font sizes in principle 37. And once again, for consistency, use the same size and style of fonts for all the headers in the series of visuals.

Every job is a self-portrait of the person who did it.
Autograph your work with excellence.
ANONYMOUS

---

6. USE UNIFORM TRANSITIONS

Don't use a hodgepodge of techniques to introduce new information or to move from one topic or visual to the next. If your text, graphics, and images appear in an unpredictable combination of zooms, wipes, or cross-dissolves, zipping in from every angle with a flourish of noise, they will become a sideshow. Your distracted audience will stop listening to you ("What speaker? On with the show!") and begin focusing on the entertainment. Make your transitions uniform, smooth, and never distracting.

7. CHECK VISIBILITY

Multimedia visual aids pose visibility challenges. If the lights in the room are too bright, if the morning sun causes a glare, if the screen is too small or positioned too low to be visible, or if the lettering or images are minuscule, your audience will be unable to see what you are displaying. They will quickly grow restless and begin to disengage (which is counterproductive), whine (which is contagious), stew (which grows ugly), or repeatedly ask you to explain what is depicted (which will cause you to mumble words that would shock your grandmother).

The rule is simple: Design your multimedia presentation to ensure that it will be visible from every vantage point in the room at any hour of the day. If you cannot do that, select a different visual aid.

8. TEST AND RETEST

This may sound annoyingly repetitive—because it is—but it cannot be overemphasized: Test and retest your equipment, and for good measure, test it again. Hardware and software problems are commonplace with complex multimedia programs. Ask any of the bungling speakers involved in the PowerPoint debacle. Better yet, question the unfortunate souls who were trapped in the audience during that calamity. Never be Pollyannaish or indifferent about your electronic gizmos, because you will eventually be sorry that you were.

Weeks before you speak, confirm that your equipment is compatible with the equipment you will use at the location where you will speak; frequently it is not. Arrive early on the day of the speech (or even the prior day for that really critical presentation), set up, and test your equipment. Allow enough time before the curtain rises to remedy any problems you discover.

9. ADOPT A FRIEND

The sage advice to adopt an AV friend when you are testing your sound system (principle 35) also applies here. If the facility has an on-site AV specialist, make him your bosom buddy. This expert can help you avoid and quickly resolve any multimedia technical problems. He is also typically familiar with the vagaries in the facility's equipment.

Ask him to be present when you test the equipment. Emphasize his importance to a successful presentation (plead shamelessly if necessary). To recruit his help, entice him with a reward (a generous gratuity for an important program, a BMW 7 Series for that monumental presentation). Assured that he can rescue you from the great visual-aid abyss, you will be able to breathe much easier; indeed, his mere presence will greatly reduce your anxiety.

10. CHOREOGRAPH YOUR PRESENTATION

Speaking while making a multimedia presentation adds an extra layer of complication, because the timing is crucial. The process should appear effortless to your audience, but this appearance will not just magically happen; it takes forethought and practice. A speaker who instructs her assistant just to "throw a few slides into a PowerPoint presentation for me," and then presents without practicing or even reviewing the program (boasting, "Piece of cake! I could do this in my sleep.") is walking a speaking tightrope without a net.

Bill Gates, the CEO of Microsoft, was making a presentation extolling the virtues of his company's latest technology. When he began to demonstrate the product for thousands of technical experts, businesspeople, and members of the news media, it failed. Kaput. Nothing. Shortly thereafter, according to informed sources, Microsoft transferred all the technicians involved in that debacle to its Antarctica office.

The lesson is clear: If one of the world's richest men, with unlimited resources and thousands of the finest technological geniuses at his command, cannot guarantee that his high-tech wizardry will work for him, can you guarantee that it will work for you? Practice.

Success . . . is not often gained by direct effort as by
careful, systematic, thorough preparation for duty.
GEORGE S. BOUTWELL

---

11. SECURE BACKUPS

Always carry a backup disc with your entire program saved on it, in the event that your computer fails and you need to load the program onto a second computer. If feasible, bring a second laptop with the entire program saved on it, or at least know where you can secure another computer in an emergency. You will be thankful that you can quickly switch to Plan B.

12. CREATE A CONTINGENCY PLAN

Sometimes, despite your best efforts, the technology fails, and all your sulking will not fix the problem. Like a Ringling Bros. and Barnum & Bailey Circus, the show must always go on. So, know what you will do, other than hide under the head table or bang the equipment and mumble invectives like a drunken sailor. Devise an alternative plan in the event of a total equipment malfunction.

Be prepared to rely on a more basic visual aid (a flip chart or an overhead projector) if it is appropriate for the size of your audience. Or you may need to quickly add or delete material from your presentation, and, in dire circumstances, proceed without any visual aid.

Does that place a greater burden on you? Certainly. But canceling your presentation is never an option—ever—and forcing your audience to suffer through a lengthy delay while you grapple with the technology is an imprudent decision. Like the hankie or tissues your mother always insisted you carry, always have a backup plan in your hip pocket.

Check out the recommended resource listed at the end of the book as well as the following excellent Web sites, which provide a wealth of information on electronic visual aids:

- Acadia University's PowerPoint Resource Center (http://aitt.acadiau .ca/resources/ppt) has links to sound, video, and graphics for novice PowerPoint users.
- Berkeley Digital Library SunSITE Image Finder (http://sunsite .berkeley.edu/ImageFinder) has images, including photographs and art, covering such topics as people, history, technology, science, space, and nature.

Mastering all the challenges and nuances necessary to create and use a multimedia presentation skillfully requires extraordinary patience and an exacting eye for detail. But these tools are enthroned at the pinnacle of the visual aid hierarchy in the speaking world. They can mesmerize, delight, and inspire your audience. And the return on your investment of time and effort is enormous. Your presentations will shine—and who knows: Bill Gates just might call you for advice.

PART VIII

CONFRONT SPECIAL CHALLENGES

YOUR BOSS HAS JUST LEANED OVER and whispered the five dreaded words you had hoped never to hear: "*Just say a few words.*" You glance at the room of over five hundred people, and you feel like a trapped animal: Your mind is whirring, your heart is thumping, and the room temperature is suddenly soaring. You quickly survey the room for the nearest exit, and you plan your hasty retreat.

He said little, but to the purpose.
LORD BYRON

The bad news: At some point in your professional or personal life, you will have to speak on the spur of the moment. You may need to spontaneously comment at a client or company meeting or propose a toast at your wayward cousin Rosco's sixth wedding. The good news: If you opt not to barrel out the emergency exit, you can excel in this setting by logically organizing and sharing your thoughts. Read on to learn the secrets.

In a perfect world, your presentations would be flawless, every program would run with absolute precision, and you would encounter nary a snag. It may calm you to envision that speaking utopia, but you had better plan for a few challenges when you speak.

Part VIII is your safety net (or security blanket if that is more sooth-ing). It contains battle-tested secrets for speaking spontaneously, and rules that will guide you through the minefield of common obstacles that beset speakers.

PRINCIPLE 39

SPEAK SPONTANEOUSLY

If no thought
your mind does visit,
make your speech
not too explicit.

—PIET HEIN

L aw schools use the Socratic method of teaching. It is an experience that most law students (except those with deviant personalities) loathe. It works like this: The professor (the predator) poses a hypothetical question about some obscure legal issue and then randomly selects from the class a cowering law student (the prey) to respond. The professor relentlessly challenges, probes, and refutes all responses. From the outset, the student is doomed, because every answer, even the right one, is wrong. Professors relish this game because it provides a socially acceptable outlet for their sadistic tendencies. Understandably, students, as they are reduced to quivering masses of gelatin, do not share their professor's glee.

This exercise is designed to train law students to closely listen, to quickly analyze what has been said, and to immediately formulate a coherent response. Soon, the students are thinking and speaking like lawyers (and they are then prepared to enter society and wreak havoc by making simple matters hopelessly complex and confusing).

Although these memories still haunt me, I recognize that the Socratic method was excellent training for speaking spontaneously. Most people never receive similar training. Speaking impromptu nearly immo-bilizes them. When I conduct a presentation skills workshop and solicit participation from the attendees, their reactions are predictable: One attendee immerses herself in her suddenly fascinating handout to avoid all eye contact. Another begins feverishly scribbling something, signaling, "I am busy, so back off!" Still another attendee looks truly pathetic or ter-rified, and I can almost hear him muttering my own refrain from law school: "Please, please, *please,* dear Lord, don't let him call on me!"

Only talk when it improves the silence.
CHRISTOPHER MATTHEWS

The anxiety improvised speaking causes virtually immobilizes some of you. For many, it is far worse than the typical angst that most speak-ers experience when giving a prepared speech. Ironically, you speak spon-taneously every day in one-on-one conversations (telephone banter, exchanges in the hallway), and you do so effortlessly. You listen, respond, gesture, and interact, expressing yourself clearly and logically. But when you are asked to speak in a more formal setting, with people staring at you, your brain is likely to go blank, your body is likely to tense, and mental shutdown is likely to commence.

ELEVEN KEYS TO SPECTACULAR SPONTANEOUS SPEAKING

To avoid the prospect of spontaneous speaking, you can skip only so many meetings or hide under your desk only so many times before peo-ple begin to talk. So what can you do? Try these eleven techniques:

1. FORGET PERFECTION

First, let's demystify the experience of spontaneous speaking. There are probably four people in the world who speak off the cuff flawlessly every time, so the chances that you are one of them are mighty slim. If you have learned that you always have to be perfect when you speak spontaneously, unlearn it now. No one expects you to be a paragon when you speak impromptu, so don't place irrational expectations on yourself.

Unlike a prepared presentation, where you have ample time to methodically select your words and incessantly polish your delivery, you have very little time, or perhaps no time, to formulate an impromptu response. You do not have to say everything you know about your subject, and you may even forget something, but that's fine. Just aim to convey a few thoughts with vigor, in a concise and logical manner.

2. ANTICIPATE PARTICIPATION

Before any meeting or gathering, know the terrain and the players. Determine who will be speaking, the nature of the message, and the typical interaction with the audience. Ask yourself: "Is the speaker's topic likely to generate discussion?" "Are these events generally informal, open discussions?" "Does the speaker encourage audience feedback?" "Is the person facilitating the meeting renowned for terrorizing meeting attendees by randomly calling on them?" (Perhaps she is a frustrated former law school professor.)

Be prepared. Anticipate ways in which you may be asked—or compelled—to contribute. Plan what you might say when you participate. Do this, and you will sound more confident and organized when you speak. That will amaze your friends and disarm your opposition.

If you would hit the mark, you
must aim a little above it.
HENRY WADSWORTH LONGFELLOW

---

3. PRACTICE

I know what you're thinking: "Hello, Einstein! Impromptu speaking, by definition, is done on the spur of the moment. How can I practice?"

Although you cannot practice responses to *exact* questions, of course, you can polish and refine your impromptu speaking skills with specific exercises.

Try this: Ask someone to select a topic and designate a position that you have to advocate. Which topic is not important, provided it is not entirely tasteless. Role-play, and address it just as you would at a meeting. Take the impromptu training a step further, and use the Q & A exercises described in principle 34. This is an excellent way to become comfortable thinking on your feet.

Videotape and critique your responses, using the guidelines outlined in principle 21. Then select another topic, and repeat the practice. Over time you will become more comfortable and, as a result, more convincing. Of course, if you want the ultimate impromptu challenge—and you are slightly masochistic—enroll in law school.

4. FORMULATE RESPONSES

Be an engaged listener, not a detached meeting or program attendee, mindlessly daydreaming, drumming your fingers, and staring at the clock. Focus on what is being said, and contemplate how you will respond if questions arise. Ask yourself questions as you listen: "Does that make sense, or is it pure rubbish?" "Do I agree?" "Is the speaker's reasoning persuasive or specious?" "Has the speaker ignored pertinent information?" "Are there viable alternatives?"

This mental activity will better prepare you to anticipate questions and formulate responses *before* you are asked to participate. Trust me: Even a few seconds of forethought provides a distinct advantage. And here's another plus: It minimizes your risk of babbling.

5. JOT DOWN THOUGHTS

Jot down important points and key words that are mentioned as others speak, to help you recall what has been said. Include your own commentary. For example, note the speaker's key ideas. Then next to them capture your own thoughts by making such simple notations as

"Really?" "Why? " or "No way, Numbskull!" (Don't let your neighbor see that last one.)

If time permits, create a brief outline to provide some structure to your notes. Identify three points you would make. Doing this will help you organize your thoughts in case either you are called upon or you decide on your own to participate. If you just start yammering when you are tapped to speak, without some framework, you are likely to become tangled up beyond salvation.

6. BUILD CREDIBILITY

When you are asked to make an impromptu comment, don't undermine your credibility or handicap yourself with unnecessary apologies ("Gosh, I am sorry, but I really don't know too much about widgets or gadgets . . ."), excuses ("I haven't had my fifth mug of coffee, so I am not thinking clearly yet . . ."), or defensiveness ("Why are you asking me? Why don't you ask Bernice? She *always* has an opinion . . .").

Approach these speaking opportunities with gusto, and do the very best you can under the circumstances.

If I am to speak for ten minutes, I need a week for
preparation . . . if an hour, I am ready now.
WOODROW WILSON

---

7. ACT CONFIDENT

Your listeners read and react both to what you say and how you say it. They study your facial expressions and body language, listen to the conviction in your voice, and evaluate what they see and hear. So whenever you speak, whether you are delivering a prepared or an impromptu presentation, you should convey unshakable confidence (principle 30).

If you wince, whine, stammer, roll your eyes, pout, or stomp your feet when you are asked to "say a few words," you will undermine your credibility and effectiveness. Instead, stand tall, breathe deeply, smile, and—for dramatic impact—pause before you begin. That behavior sends an unmistakable message to your listeners: "I am knowledgeable and self-assured, and I welcome this opportunity." (You can melt into a puddle after you sit down.)

8. DELIVER AN ACTUAL SPEECH

Even when speaking spontaneously, you are more likely to be clear and convincing if you structure your comments as you would for a pre-pared speech (principle 10): a simple opening, two or three points, and a brief summation. Succinct, crisp, structured presentations beat wordy, rambling ones any day.

For example, suppose that Lloyd, the company health nut, has just advocated eliminating all the vending machines in the employee lounge, because, he contends, they "distribute poison that erodes our brains." You could structure your response to his drivel as follows: First, state your position ("Lloyd is a crackpot, and his suggestion is preposterous . . ."). Second, explain your position ("Although Twinkies and Ding Dongs may create a sugar frenzy, this drastic step will crush employee morale and deprive us of one of life's simple pleasures . . ."). Finally, summarize ("In sum, although cutting out KooKoos might eliminate sugar buzzes and increase the company's productivity, we need to first consider less dras-tic alternatives, such as firing Lloyd . . ."). This structure will help you quickly and clearly make your points (and rally the junk food addicts).

9. USE SIGNALS

Just as with a prepared presentation, your impromptu talk should be organized to help your listeners follow along. An excellent way to do that is by providing signposts at key junctures, to let your listeners know where you are going, and when you are moving from point to point: "There are *three* reasons why the proposal should die a swift death. *First,* it is ridiculously expensive. *Second,* those of us who will pay for this are ridiculously poor. And *third,* we can afford this luxury only if we forgo eating, since we will have no money left for food, which is disheartening."

After stating your three points in the opening, you give another signal as you reach each of the points: *"Third,* eating trumps luxury . . . ." These signposts focus your comments. Today's impatient audiences will not spend much time struggling to understand a jumbled message, so make it clear and concise.

10. SLOW DOWN

Sometimes your speaking anxiety will cause you to jabber, and the jabbering accelerates when you have had virtually no time to prepare. When that happens, you look skittish, and you sound scattered. You are also likely to overlook critical points, or you will state them so rapidly that they will zip right past your listeners.

Consciously fight this tendency. Pause for a few seconds before you begin speaking, and slow down as you are speaking.

He does not say a word more than necessary.
CHARLES DE GAULLE

---

11. BE BRIEF

Typically your impromptu presentation should be short. Sometimes a speaker will ramble on and on . . . *and on,* with no end in sight on the speaking horizon. Perhaps she is hoping for a lucid moment, when she might stumble across a clear thought as she struggles to make a point—*any point.* Another speaker mistakenly believes that more words are more convincing. Wrong.

When you are asked to speak off the cuff, it is never an open invitation to blather. In the little time you have, strive to make two or three memorable points, but no more. Have mercy on your audience. Say it succinctly, and take your seat.

If you want to enhance your impromptu speaking skills in a cost-effective manner, join Toastmasters International (www.toastmasters.org).

This exceptional international speaking organization has thousands of clubs throughout the world that meet regularly. It was established to provide individuals the opportunity to practice speaking and to improve their communication skills. Best of all, you can hone your skills in a non-threatening forum (translation: no boss, no clients, no hecklers).

Use the blueprint provided with this principle to refine your impromptu speaking skills. It will prepare you not only to *just say a few words*," but also to say them with enthusiasm and conviction. You can enhance your image as an expert, score points with your clients and superiors, and maybe even persuade a few people along the way, so plunge in!

PRINCIPLE 40

OVERCOME THE
OBSTACLES

Calamity is man's true touchstone.

—FRANCIS BEAUMONT AND JOHN FLETCHER

Imagine a perfect presentation: You would exude confidence as you eloquently delivered your message, exactly as you had planned, while holding your audience's rapt attention from beginning to end. Your thinking would be clear and precise, your logic brilliant, and your ideas compelling and fresh. At the conclusion, your audience would leap from their seats applauding in a near frenzy of excitement and showering you with accolades. You would decide that you were a fabulous speaker and that speaking was really very cushy. It would be a euphoric feeling.

Now, sober up, because here is the more likely scenario: You will occasionally forget portions of your presentation, audience members will distract you, and your audiovisual equipment will betray you. There is a high probability that you will say something that is inaccurate ("When President Kerry signed this legislation . . ."), confusing ("What did they say he said about what she said?"), or foolish ("That was a very *perspiring* message . . ."). You may be stumped by a question, sabotaged by your introducer, or befuddled by logistical problems. Welcome to the *real* speaking world!

Many events occur that can fluster you in the best case, or ruin your speech in the worst. I remember well the morning that one company's

pinstriped Top Dog interrupted my speech, because he needed to immediately see Chester, the sluggard employee, who was busy twiddling his
thumbs in the back of the room, to fire him. As a rule, a midspeech firing dampens the spirit of any presentation.

It is risky to cross your fingers and hope that the Goddess of Good
Fortune will always smile upon you, blessing all your speaking endeav-
ors, and protecting you from every challenge. She is just not that reliable. Eventually she will test you, and usually at the worst time. The
critical question is: Will you be ready?

When I think over what I have said, I envy dumb people.
LUCIUS ANNEAUS SENECA

FIVE SOLUTIONS TO SETBACKS

You can avoid many problems with careful (bordering on obsessive) planning and preparation. But some challenges, like the five listed below, may
be unavoidable despite your best efforts. Here is a game plan for emerging
unscathed. Flexibility is the key, and praying is not a bad idea in desperate
moments. Your goal: Adapt to the situation rather than becoming unglued.

1. EQUIPMENT MELTDOWN

Here is the first unavoidable law of speaking: Your equipment will
fail. That's "will fail," not "may fail." Take the precautionary steps outlined in Part VII, so you can prevent many equipment pitfalls. But sometimes nothing helps, and your double-crossing equipment will just not
work. Sulking or cursing seldom remedies the situation, so here are a few
presentation savers:

- Unless you are positive you can solve the snafu very quickly, take a
  break. Don't make your audience members wait while you struggle
  to resolve the problem. And here is a dirty little speaking secret: No
  audience, in the entire history of speaking (which covers more than

a trillion speeches), has ever objected to a break. It is doubtful that yours will be the first. In fact, an extra break will probably enhance their opinion of your presentation.

- If you cannot get the equipment cart out of the ditch, resort to Plan B (you have one, right?), which might involve quickly replacing the malfunctioning equipment or using a different visual aid.

- If Plan B flops, implement Plan C: Proceed without using any visual aid. Packing up and heading home is never an option.

- After the presentation, proceed to Plan D: Invest in new equipment.

Public calamity is a mighty leveller.
EDMUND BURKE

---

2. CELL PHONE DISTRACTIONS

If you do not have a cell phone surgically attached to your hip or ear, on behalf of all speakers worldwide, thank you. The second sure law of speaking: One or more cell phones will ring while you are speaking, even though before you began, you pleaded with your audience to turn them off. Some people would apparently disconnect their own life support system before they would turn off their cell phones and actually be *inaccessible* for several minutes. That would be much too traumatic.

Sometimes a bozo will even answer the call during your presentation and then carry on a conversation; violence seems appealing in those moments. Another putz will look around stupidly as his phone rings, shrug his shoulders, and then simply let it continue to ring; apparently he is hoping that everyone is deaf and will not notice. How should you deal with this distraction?

- Grit your teeth, smile, and politely ask the sinner to leave the room (or the country), to avoid distracting other audience members.

- Play with the problem, by implementing a rule that if another cell phone rings during the program, the transgressor will have to sing a rap song or demonstrate how to use a hula hoop before the crowd (that can get ugly, so use that threat sparingly).

- Pause and wait until the cell phone stops ringing. Everyone hears it, so ignoring it is futile; if you continue talking, very few will focus on what you are saying. Pausing also heightens the peer pressure on the culprit, since everyone in the audience is being inconvenienced by the delay. The audience members may even band together and toss the cell phone (and, if you are lucky, the offender) out the window. Problem solved.

3. AUDIENCE UNRULINESS

Most audiences have a few disruptive members. One person is antsy by nature, unable to focus or sit still for more than thirty seconds, especially late in the day. Another is rude, surreptitiously whispering, passing notes, or even loudly talking to fellow audience members while you speak. Still another is opinionated; she assumes that it is her inalienable right to loudly critique your presentation as you are speaking: "What?" "Get real!" "That will happen when pigs fly!"

Yield not thy neck
To fortune's yoke, but let thy dauntless mind
Still ride triumph over all mischance.
WILLIAM SHAKESPEARE

Once during one of my speeches, an audience member began snoring. That does not boost your confidence. His honking and snorting were amusing but distracting. I fiendishly considered asking everyone to leave the room, allowing Rip Van Winkle to awaken alone, in a darkened room. Instead, I simply moved closer to him and continued talking. My voice disturbed his slumber, and he awoke, somewhat surprised. He later professed that he *really* enjoyed my talk. Some speaking days are better than others.

Here are several ways to deal with audience distractions:

- Pause, conjure up your most sinister evil eye (such as the one your dad gave you when you backed the family station wagon over his golf clubs), and glare at the offenders. Do this until they finish talking. It will become clear that a few boors are interrupting the program, and audience pressure can be a powerful deterrent.

- Move closer to the distraction. The audience's attention will follow you to the disruption, which often corrects the problem.

- In a nonantagonistic manner (hard to muster when you are seething, I know), smile, and ask the distracting parties if they have a question or maybe an observation they would like to share with the group. Allow them to speak briefly if they choose to do so, address the comments, and then move on with your presentation.

- Politely suggest that it is difficult for everyone to hear if several people are talking at once, and ask them to hold their comments until after the program. If that does not work, and you are feeling feisty, simply muzzle them, and toss them into a closet for the remainder of your presentation (most audience members will gladly help you).

4. HUMOR THAT FLOPS

I have occasionally used humor in my speeches that was simply remarkable. Unfortunately, it was remarkably bad. Sometimes your scintillating wit fizzles. Your colossal punch line may be greeted with deafening silence, and your listeners may stare blankly with cocked heads, raised eyebrows, and baffled expressions adorning their faces. It is so quiet you can hear your heart beat. A few compassionate listeners may nervously titter to break the tension, but don't count on it.

Maybe it was just bad timing, maybe your audience was jammed with humorless stuffed shirts, maybe the planets were misaligned, or maybe—just maybe—it wasn't funny (yes, I know that is unlikely, but at least consider the remote possibility). When you bomb, you will be gripped by fear. Your face will burn, your palms will sweat, and you will desperately pray that—Poof!—you vanish. Since it is unlikely that you will become invisible, you had better have another plan to bounce back. Here are a few ideas:

- Ignore your audience's reaction, and carry on as if what you said was not intended to be funny.
- Handle it the way professional comedians do when their jokes bomb: Poke fun at yourself: "Well, my mom liked it!" "Just a little joke I threw in. Guess it should have been thrown out." Or "Don't worry. Some of these are just for me!"[1]
- Tell yourself that you are okay, but your audience is the problem (delusional behavior is allowed in these moments of distress).

5. THE DREADED BLANK SLATE

We speakers have one recurring nightmare: going blank while speaking. It terrifies us, because we are alone on stage and our misfortune is as public as possible. Occasionally, you will lose your way while speaking, forgetting what you have said, what you were just saying, or what you intended to say next. In the worst case, you will forget where you are and why you are there—wherever it is.

The timid man sees dangers that do not exist.
PUBLIUS SYRUS

You may momentarily stumble during your speech for a variety of reasons: your insufficient preparation (for shame!), your spontaneous decision to deviate from your prepared comments, your anxiety, a question that baffles you, or your functioning on two hours of sleep after a wild night on the town. Whatever the reason, going blank can be slightly embarrassing.

Here are several ways to regain your bearings gracefully:

- Pause and refer to your notes or to the visual aid currently on display.
- Sip water, adjust your visual aid, or move about the room, to stall for time and collect your thoughts.

- Ask for questions from your audience regarding what you have already said in your speech. Address the questions; then simply ask, "Okay, now, where was I?" and hope that some Good Samaritan will clue you in.

- Take a short break to recover (audiences love breaks), if it seems like a logical point to break. Of course, this is not a viable solution if you have gone blank just twelve seconds into your speech.

- Suggest an exercise that will allow you time to recall where you stopped talking. For example, "Pair up with someone sitting close to you, and discuss all the ways you can market this tasty new shrimp ice cream." Or, "Take a moment to list the three most valuable lessons you have learned so far today." (But remember the twelve-second rule from above.)

- Playfully tell your audience that you are lost: "Well, it appears that my tongue has gotten ahead of my mind, and it is going to take a moment for my mind to catch up. Where was I, anyway?" Most audience members are eager to pipe up and help, and this disarming admission humanizes you.

Whatever happens, look as if it were intended.
FIRST RULE OF ACTING

The only sure way never to confront a speaking challenge is never to speak. Some people artfully duck every speaking opportunity—a safe but cowardly solution. Be brave. Sure, there are inherent risks, but don't let that discourage you from speaking. If you plan for the unexpected, you can convert a challenge into a golden opportunity to demonstrate your poise and confidence. And who knows? That triumph alone may be enough to generate that coveted standing ovation.

CONCLUSION

Nothing in the world can take the place of persistence. Talent will not; nothing is more common than unsuccessful individuals with talent. Genius will not; unrewarded genius is almost a proverb. Education will not; the world is full of educated derelicts. Persistence and determination alone are omnipotent.

—CALVIN COOLIDGE

WELL, THERE YOU HAVE IT: How to speak for extraordinary results every time. If it sounds like hard work, it is, but it is well worth your effort. Learning the craft of speaking can be challenging at times, frustrating at others, but also immensely gratifying. Along the way, you will experience euphoric highs and maybe a few disappointing lows. But the personal and professional rewards trump any risks—by a wide margin. When you see a light—or, if you are fortunate, many lights—spark in the eyes of your listeners, you realize that through your words, you have made a difference. That feeling is priceless. My hope is that I have kindled your desire to become a much better speaker than you now are; indeed, a desire for you to become your *very best* every time you speak.

Don't settle for mediocrity. Distinguish yourself from the thousands of speakers every day, in every conceivable forum, who blandly deliver insipid speeches. Challenge yourself. Follow the blueprint in this book, and become a speaker who literally makes listeners sit upright and spellbound. Prepare for that moment, so that when it is showtime, you will own the stage. If there was hope for Jell-O Boy, anything is possible. Let your journey begin!

NOTES

Principle 1: Channel Your Stage Fright

1. Roper Starch, "How Americans Communicate," National Communication Association, www.natcom.org/research/Poll/how_americans _communicate.htm.
2. David Wallechinsky, Irving Wallace, and Amy Wallace, *The Book of Lists* (New York: Morrow, 1977), quoted in George L. Grice and John F. Skinner, *Mastering Public Speaking,* 4th ed. (Boston: Allyn & Bacon, 2001), 44.
3. Stephen E. Lucas, *The Art of Public Speaking,* 7th ed. (New York: McGraw-Hill, 2001), 8.
4. Ibid.
5. Garrison Keillor, "Monologue," *A Prairie Home Companion,* February 13, 1999, Minnesota Public Radio, quoted in Grice and Skinner, *Mastering Public Speaking,* 44.
6. Carol Burnett, "Ask Them Yourself," *Family Weekly,* January 28, 1979, quoted in Grice and Skinner, *Mastering Public Speaking,* 44.
7. Meryl Streep, interview, *Interview,* December 1988, quoted in Grice and Skinner, *Mastering Public Speaking,* 44.

Principle 2: Visualize Speaking Success

1. Vicki Huber, quoted in Lucas, *Art of Public Speaking,* 11.
2. Dr. Wayne W. Dyer, interview by author, Michael Jeffreys, *Success Secrets of the Motivational Superstars: America's Greatest Speakers Reveal Their Secrets* (Roseville, CA: Prima Publishing, 1996), 62.
3. Lucas, *Art of Public Speaking,* 10.
4. Lilly Walters, *What to Say . . . When You're Dying on the Platform* (New York: McGraw-Hill, 1995), xxiii–xxiv.

Principle 3: Park Your Ego at the Door

1. Anthony Robbins, interview by author, Jeffreys, *Success Secrets,* 24.
2. Les Brown, interview by author, Jeffreys, *Success Secrets,* 161, 183.

Principle 7: Use These Tools to Know Your Audience

1. Lucas, *Art of Public Speaking,* 101.

Principle 8: Adopt from the Best Speakers

1. Brian Tracy, interview by author, Jeffreys, *Success Secrets,* 122.
2. Dr. Martin Luther King, Jr., "I Have a Dream," quoted in Lucas, *Art of Public Speaking,* app. B, B7–B10.

Principle 9: State Your Purpose

1. John R. Trimble, *Writing with Style: Conversations on the Art of Writing,* 2nd ed. (Upper Saddle River, NJ: Prentice-Hall, 2000), 56–57.

Principle 10: Organize for Coherence

1. Patricia T. O'Conner, *Words Fail Me: What Everyone Who Speaks Should Know About Speaking* (New York: Harcourt, 1999), 180.

Principle 11: Open with a Hook

1. Trimble, *Writing with Style,* 26.
2. William K. Zinsser, *On Writing Well,* 6th ed. (New York: HarperCollins, 2001), 57.

Principle 12: Revise, Revise, Revise

1. William Strunk, Jr., and E. B. White, *The Elements of Style,* 4th ed. (Boston: Allyn & Bacon, 2000), 72.
2. Ibid., 23.
3. Ibid., 21.
4. Ronald Reagan, "Address to the Nation," January 28, 1986, quoted in Richard L. Johannesen, R. R. Allen, Wil A. Linkugel, and Ferald J. Bryan, eds. *Contemporary American Speeches,* 8th ed. (Dubuque, IA: Kendall/Hunt, 1997), 407–8.

Principle 13: Harness the Power of Stories

1. Gene Griessman, *Abraham Lincoln on Communication*, DVD, www
.presidentlincoln.com (1992).

Principle 16: Close with a Bang

1. General Douglas MacArthur, "Farewell to the Cadets," May 12, 1962,
quoted in Johannesen et al., *Contemporary American Speeches*, 403–4.

Principle 23: Capitalize on Potent Pauses

1. Isaac Stern, quoted in Grice and Skinner, *Mastering Public Speaking*, 299.

Principle 28: Check Your Checklist

1. Lilly Walters, *Secrets of Successful Speakers: How You Can Motivate, Captivate and Persuade* (New York: McGraw-Hill, 1993), 170–71.

Principle 29: Focus on Your Audience

1. Joel Weldon, interview by author, Jeffreys, *Success Secrets*, 330.

Principle 31: Persuade with Passion

1. Anthony Robbins, interview by author, Jeffreys, *Success Secrets*, 23.
2. Dr. Wayne W. Dyer, interview by author, Jeffreys, *Success Secrets*, 61, 63.
3. Mark Victor Hansen, interview by author, Jeffreys, *Success Secrets*, 221.

Principle 36: Capitalize on Visual Aids

1. Michael E. Patterson, Donald Danscreau, and Dianna Newbern, "Effects of
Communication Aids on Cooperative Teaching," *Journal of Educational
Psychology* 84 (1992): 453–61.

Principle 40: Overcome the Obstacles

1. Walters, *What to Say . . . When You're Dying on the Platform*, 3–4.

BIBLIOGRAPHY

Cook, John, ed. *The Book of Positive Quotations*. New York: Gramercy Books, 1999.

Daintith, John, Hazel Egerton, Rosalind Fergusson, Anne Stibbs, and Edmund Wright, eds. *The Macmillan Dictionary of Quotations*. 7th ed. Edison, NJ: Chartwell Books, 2000.

DeVito, Joseph A. *The Essential Elements of Public Speaking*. New York: Pearson, Allyn & Bacon, 2002.

Ehrlich, Eugene, and Marshall DeBruhl, eds. *The International Thesaurus of Quotations*. 2nd ed. New York: Harper Perennial, 1996.

Fletcher, Leon. *How to Design & Deliver Speeches*. 7th ed. Boston: Longman, 2001.

Frank, Leonard Roy, ed. *Random House Webster's Quotationary*. New York: Random House, 1999.

Gianna, Dominic J. *Power Passion & Persuasion: Advocacy Inside & Out*. Minnetonka, MN: The Professional Education Group, 2000.

Grice, George L., and John F. Skinner. *Mastering Public Speaking*. 4th ed. Boston: Allyn & Bacon, 2001.

Griessman, Gene. *Abraham Lincoln on Communication*. DVD, www.president lincoln.com, 1992.

Jeffreys, Michael. *Success Secrets of the Motivational Superstars: America's Greatest Speakers Reveal Their Secrets*. Roseville, CA: Prima Publishing, 1996.

Johannesen, Richard L., R. R. Allen, Wil A. Linkugel, and Ferald J. Bryan, eds. *Contemporary American Speeches*. 8th ed. Dubuque, IA: Kendall/Hunt, 1997.

Kaplan, Justin, ed. *Bartlett's Familiar Quotations*. 17th ed. Boston: Little, Brown, 2003.

Keillor, Garrison. *A Prairie Home Companion,* February 13, 1999, Minnesota
    Public Radio. Quoted in Grice and Skinner, *Mastering Public Speaking.*

Knowles, Elizabeth, ed. *Oxford Dictionary of Quotations.* 5th ed. New York:
    Oxford University Press, 1999.

Lucas, Stephen E. *The Art of Public Speaking.* 7th ed. New York: McGraw-Hill,
    2001.

Metcalfe, Sheldon. *Building a Speech.* 5th ed. Toronto: Thomson Wadsworth,
    2004.

Strunk, William, Jr., and E. B. White. *The Elements of Style.* 4th ed. Boston:
    Allyn & Bacon, 2000.

Torricelli, Robert G., ed. *Quotations for Public Speakers: A Historical, Literary,
    and Political Anthology.* New Brunswick, NJ: Rutgers University Press,
    2001.

Trimble, John R. *Writing with Style: Conversations on the Art of Writing.*
    2nd ed. Upper Saddle River, NJ: Prentice-Hall, 2000.

Walters, Lilly. *Secrets of Successful Speakers: How You Can Motivate, Captivate
    and Persuade.* New York: McGraw-Hill, 1993.

———. *Secrets of Superstar Speakers: Wisdom from the Greatest Motivators of Our
    Time.* New York: McGraw-Hill, 2000.

———. *What to Say . . . When You're Dying on the Platform.* New York: McGraw-
    Hill, 1995.

Weissman, Jerry. *Presenting to Win: The Art of Telling Your Story.* Upper Saddle
    River, NJ: Financial Times Prentice-Hall, 2003.

Zinsser, William K. *On Writing Well.* 6th ed. New York: HarperCollins, 2001.

RECOMMENDED RESOURCES

Principle 1: Channel Your Stage Fright

Desberg, Peter. *No More Butterflies: Overcoming Stage Fright, Shyness, Interview Anxiety, and Fear of Public Speaking.* Oakland, CA: New Harbinger, 1996.

Grice, George L., and John F. Skinner. *Mastering Public Speaking.* 4th ed. Boston: Allyn & Bacon, 2001.

Jeffreys, Michael. *Success Secrets of the Motivational Superstars: America's Greatest Speakers Reveal Their Secrets.* Roseville, CA: Prima Publishing, 1996.

Lucas, Stephen E. *The Art of Public Speaking.* 7th ed. New York: McGraw-Hill, 2001.

Motley, Michael T. *Overcome Your Fear of Public Speaking: A Proven Method.* New York: McGraw-Hill, 1995.

Richmond, Virginia P., and James C. McCrosky. *Communication: Apprehension, Avoidance & Effectiveness.* 5th ed. Boston: Allyn & Bacon, 1998.

Web Site

Starch, Roper. "How Americans Communicate," National Communication Association (www.natcom.org/research/Poll/how_americans_communicate.htm).

Principle 12: Revise, Revise, Revise

Barzun, Jacques. *Simple & Direct.* Chicago: University of Chicago Press, 1994.

Garner, Bryan A. *Garner's Modern American Usage.* New York: Oxford University Press, 2003.

Graves, Robert, and Alan Hodge. *The Reader Over Your Shoulder.* 2nd ed. New York: Random House, 1979.

Johannesen, Richard L., et al., eds. *Contemporary American Speeches.* 8th ed. Dubuque, IA: Kendall/Hunt, 1997.

Merriam-Webster's Manual for Writers & Editors. Springfield, MA: Merriam-Webster, 1997.

Strunk, William, Jr., and E. B. White. *The Elements of Style.* 4th ed. Boston: Allyn & Bacon, 2000.

Trimble, John R. *Writing with Style: Conversations on the Art of Writing.* 2nd ed. Upper Saddle, NJ: Prentice-Hall, 2000.

Venolia, Jan. *Write Right!* 3rd ed. Berkeley, CA: Ten Speed Press, 1995.

Zinsser, William K. *On Writing Well.* 6th ed. New York: HarperCollins, 2001.

Principle 13: Harness the Power of Stories

Davis, Donald D. *Telling Your Own Stories.* Little Rock, AR: August House, 1993.

Lipman, Doug. *Improving Your Storytelling.* Little Rock, AR: August House, 1999.

Maguire, Jack. *The Power of Personal Storytelling.* New York: Putnam, 1998.

Storytelling magazine. Published by National Storytelling Network (www .storynet.org/).

Principle 14: Make 'Em Laugh

Carter, Judy. *The Comedy Bible.* New York: Simon & Schuster, 2001.

Robertson, Jeanne. *Don't Let the Funny Stuff Get Away.* Houston: Rich Publishing, 1998.

Principle 15: Quote for Credibility

Baron, Joseph L. *A Treasury of Jewish Quotations.* New York: Jason Aronson, 1997.

Bisbort, Alan. *Famous Last Words.* Rohnert Park, CA: Pomegranate Communications, 2001.

Ehrlich, Eugene, and Marshall DeBruhl, eds. *The International Thesaurus of Quotations.* 2nd ed. New York: Harper Perennial, 1996.

Frank, Leonard Roy, ed. *Random House Webster's Quotationary.* New York: Random House, 1999.

Harper Book of American Quotations. New York: Random House Value, 1991.

Hemphill, Charles F. *Famous Phrases from History.* Jefferson, NC: McFarland, 1982.

James, Simon, ed. *A Dictionary of Economic Quotations.* London: Croom Helm, 1981.

Knowles, Elizabeth, ed. *Oxford Dictionary of Quotations*. 5th ed. New York: Oxford University Press, 1999.

Partnow, Elaine, ed. *The New Quotable Woman*. New York: Facts on File, 1993.

Peter, Lawrence J. *Peter's Quotations*. New York: William Morrow, 1982.

Riley, Dorothy Winbush, and D. Winbush Riley. *My Soul Looks Back, 'Less I Forget: A Collection of Quotations by People of Color*. New York: Harper-Collins, 1995.

Web Sites

Bartleby.com: Great Books Online (www.bartleby.com).

Galaxy Search Engine & Directory (www.galaxy.com/b/q?k=quotations).

The Quotations Page (www.quotationspage.com).

Quoteland.com (www.quoteland.com).

Principle 22: Project Vocal Power

Hahner, Jeffrey C. *Speaking Clearly: Improving Voice and Diction*. 6th ed. New York: McGraw-Hill, 2001.

Love, Roger. *Set Your Voice Free*. Boston: Little, Brown, 1999.

Principle 25: Gesture with Conviction

Guerrero, Laura K., Joseph A. Devito, and Michael L. Hecht, eds. *The Nonverbal Communication Reader: Classic and Contemporary Readings*. 2nd ed. Prospect Heights, IL: Waveland Press, 1999.

Knapp, Mark L., and Judith A. Hall. *Nonverbal Communication in Human Interaction*. 4th ed. Fort Worth, TX: Harcourt Brace College Publishers, 1997.

Principle 31: Persuade with Passion

Brembeck, Winston, and William S. Howell. *Persuasion: A Means of Social Influence*. 2nd ed. Englewood Cliffs, NJ: Prentice-Hall, 1976.

McCrosky, James C. *An Introduction to Rhetorical Communication*. 7th ed. Boston: Allyn & Bacon, 1997.

Perloff, Richard M. *The Dynamics of Persuasion*. Hillsdale, NJ: Lawrence Erlbaum, 1993.

Walters, Lilly. *Secrets of Superstar Speakers: Wisdom from the Greatest Motivators of Our Time*. New York: McGraw-Hill, 2000.

Principle 34: Take Command of "Q&A"

Mira, Thomas K. *Speak Smart.* New York: Random House, 1997.

Wilder, Claudyne. *The Presentations Kit: 10 Steps for Selling Your Ideas.* 2nd ed. New York: Wiley, 1994.

Woodall, Marian. *Thinking on Your Feet: How to Communicate Under Pressure.* Lake Oswego, OR: Professional Business Communications, 1996.

Principle 36: Capitalize on Visual Aids

Robbins, Jo. *High Impact Presentations: A Multimedia Approach.* New York: Wiley, 1997.

Web Sites

Acadia University's PowerPoint Resource Center (http://aitt.acadiau.ca/resources/ppt/).

PresentationPro: The PowerPoint Experts (www.presentationpro.com).

Principle 38: Create Multimedia Magic

Brown, Alan L. *Power Pitches: How to Produce Winning Presentations Using Charts, Slides, Video and Multimedia.* Chicago: Irwin, 1997.

Principle 39: Speak Spontaneously

Web Sites

National Speakers Association (www.nsaspeaker.org).

Toastmasters International (www.toastmasters.org).

Principle 40: Overcome the Obstacles

Walters, Lilly. *What to Say . . . When You're Dying on the Platform.* New York: McGraw-Hill, 1995.

INDEX

ABOUT THE AUTHOR

There is no finish line.

—NIKE SLOGAN

DAVID J. DEMPSEY, JD, is the President and CEO of Neon Zebra, LLC, a presentation skills training company based in Atlanta, Georgia. Neon Zebra is dedicated to teaching people how to communicate with power, passion, and persuasion every time they speak. David has spent more than twenty-five years in the speaking arena as a university professor teaching public speaking, a professional speaker, an author, and a presentation skills trainer. His straightforward blend of expert advice, hands-on teaching techniques, and real-world experience enable the busy professionals he coaches to immediately become more effective in front of any audience. Neon Zebra is passionate about its mission and uncompromisingly pursues excellence in all the services it provides.

David grew up in a small town in western Nebraska. He began his career as a trial lawyer in Atlanta in 1980. He is a veteran of the courtroom, having tried many cases at both the state and federal levels. It is there that he developed an enthusiasm for speaking and presenting. In 1986, while practicing law, David also began teaching beginning and advanced public speaking as an adjunct professor at Oglethorpe University in Atlanta. His classes are consistently among the highest-rated at the university. One university dean described him as "an amazing resource and an instructor who awakens a skill in people that they did not know they had."

David has honed his own speaking talents in the competitive speaking arena. He is a Distinguished Toastmaster, the highest distinction conferred upon a small fraction of the approximately one million members of Toastmasters International. He has twice been named Georgia state champion of the Toastmasters International World Championship of Public Speaking (1987 and 2000). David was also the 2004-2005 President of the Georgia Chapter of the National Speakers Association, an organization made up of the best professional speakers in the country.

He is also the author of *Legally Speaking: 40 Powerful Presentation Principles Lawyers Need to Know* (Miranda Publishing, 2002), a book that shares insights, tips, and proven principles David learned in his years as a successful trial attorney. This critically acclaimed book has been endorsed by Senator Bob Dole, Senator Saxby Chambliss, Governor Carl Sanders, former U.S. Attorney General Griffin Bell, and former Association of Trial Lawyers of America President Mary Alexander, among others.

David is convinced that everyone can speak with confidence and conviction, and it has become his mission to show them how. To learn more about Neon Zebra, LLC, visit the Web site www.neon-zebra.com. For a schedule of workshops and seminars, to book David to speak at your next meeting or conference, or to schedule a presentation skills assessment, please contact him at Neon Zebra, LLC, 1-800-729-2791 or 770-481-3050, or by e-mail at info@neon-zebra.com.

ORDER FORM

❑ Please send me _____ copies of *Better to Best: How to Speak for Extraordinary Results . . . Every Time!* at $24.95 each, plus $5.00 for shipping and handling per book. Allow 15 days for delivery, and be sure to add sales tax (8%) for products shipped to a Georgia address. Special discounts are available on quantity purchases by corporations, associations, and others. For details, contact the "Special Sales Department" at the address below.

❑ My check or money order for $ _____ is enclosed.

❑ Please charge my ❑ American Express ❑ MasterCard
    ❑ Discover ❑ Visa

Card # _____

Exp. date _____

Signature _____

Name on card _____

Organization _____

Name _____
PLEASE PRINT

Mailing address _____

City _____ State _____ Zip _____

Telephone _____ Fax _____

E-mail _____

MIRANDA PUBLISHING, LLC
Two Ravinia Drive, Suite 1255
Atlanta, Georgia 30346
TOLL-FREE: 1-800-359-5731   PHONE: 770-901-5852
FAX: 770-481-3250
E-MAIL: info@mirandapub.com